BOOTLEGGER'S
200 PROOF
BLACKJACK

MIKE "BOOTLEGGER" TURNER

SQUAREONE
GAMING GUIDES

This book, which contains the ideas and opinions of its author, is both educational and recreational in nature. It offers accurate and appropriate information regarding casino gambling; however, neither the publisher nor the author guarantee specific gaming outcomes. As a recreational pursuit, legalized casino gambling can be a source of great enjoyment. If, however, it becomes compulsive or addictive, don't hesitate to seek counseling. Help is available:

National Council on Problem Gambling, Inc.
24-Hour Confidential National Hotline: 1-800-522-4700
Website: www.ncpgambling.org/

Gamblers Anonymous
Website: www.gamblersanonymous.org/

Cover Designer: Jacqueline Michelus
Interior Graphics and Typesetting: Gary A. Rosenberg
Editor: Carol Rosenberg

Square One Publishers
115 Herricks Road
Garden City Park, NY 11040
877-900-BOOK
www.squareonepublishers.com

Library of Congress Cataloging-in-Publication Data

Turner, Mike (R. Michael)
   Bootlegger's 200-proof blackjack / Mike "Bootlegger" Turner.
     p. cm.
   Includes bibliographical references and index.
   ISBN 0-7570-0048-7
  1. Blackjack (Game) 2. Gambling systems. I. Title: 200-proof blackjack.
II. Title: Bootlegger's two hundred-proof blackjack. III. Title.

GV1295.B55T87   2005
795.4'23—dc22

                         2005002875

Printed in the United States of America

10   9   8   7   6   5   4   3   2   1

CONTENTS

To my wife,
who is known as "Bootie"
in the blackjack community.
She is the best advantage play I ever made.

INTRODUCTION

I'd never thought of myself as a gambler. I had no interest in join-ing my buddies' Friday-night poker games, I never bet on sporting events, and I avoided the lottery. On rare occasions, I'd go to the horse races when invited and place a two-dollar bet just to be social. Gambling simply wasn't in my blood. So, when I learned that I had to attend a work-related convention in Las Vegas many years ago, I vehe-mently complained about it. I told anyone who would listen that I'd gladly go anywhere but there. But the job said I had to go, and so I went.

My wife joined me for a weeklong stay at one of the finest casino hotels on the Vegas strip. As we made our way through the casino to our room that first day, we found the place very uninviting. A cacoph-ony of assorted bells, buzzers, and beeps came at us from all directions. We witnessed the antics of a slot-machine jackpot winner and were assaulted by shouts from the rollers at the craps tables. Deeper into the casino, we sidled past a group of semicircular tables surrounded on one side by folk in deep concentration.

Although some of the casino patrons looked like they were having a good time, far too many others wore gloomy expressions. My wife and I were not tempted to join what seemed like a group of unpre-dictable inmates on a day trip from the nearest asylum.

However, as the week progressed, I made the trip through the casino many times and had sort of become accustomed to the sounds. Like Alice in Wonderland, I was becoming "curiouser and curiouser." I noticed that people were actually winning money at the slot machines and that some of the folk at those semicircular tables had impressive stacks of chips in front of them. What I found most curious, though, were the money-laden electric carts, flanked by straight-faced security personnel, that would make their way from the tables and slots to the cashier's booth periodically throughout the day.

Obviously, there was a huge amount of money going into the casinos, and I wanted to know if there was a way to get some of the money out. Although my wife and I didn't gamble much on that trip (we played the nickel slots before we left just so we could say we did it), I felt something stirring inside me. When I got home, I began my quest to "beat the house."

I read every book I could find on the subject of casinos and casino gambling. It was a difficult task to separate the wheat from the chaff, especially for a person who wasn't particularly well schooled in the mathematics of gambling. After many false starts and some embarrassing and sometimes financially painful moments, I finally started to understand what was going on in the casinos and how to take advantage of it.

For reasons I'll share later in this book, blackjack became my game of choice, and I attacked it with a vengeance. I learned what I could from the many excellent books available and had to unlearn a few things from the bad ones. I surfed the Internet, looking for more. I met with other blackjack players and learned as much as I could from them and their experiences. I even met up with several professional players whose advice was invaluable in my quest to become the best blackjack player I could be.

Over the years, I discovered that there are four types of blackjack players. The first is the clueless player. This player sits down at the table, puts the money in the betting square, takes the cards dealt, and then doesn't have any notion of what to do next. To this player, each hand is a mystery. He would probably be far more comfortable at the slot machines and most likely spends a lot of time there.

Then there is the so-called experienced player. Although this player has been around for a while, he plays with only a semblance of basic strategy. He knows from experience what some of the correct plays are, but he doesn't know enough of them. For example, he knows to stand on a 13 when the dealer is showing a 6, and he knows he should hit on a 15 when the dealer is showing a 9. He also knows that he should split certain hands. But he doesn't know *why* he should do those things. While he isn't exactly clueless, he is an ignorant player. The so-called experienced player is the player the house depends on. He thinks he knows enough to come out ahead and keeps coming back for more.

Next is the basic strategy player. This player has learned the proper strategy for each hand. He knows how to handle double-down opportunities and what to do with hands that should be split. He knows the rules and which ones will work to his advantage. He can play the house just about even. And, if he finds the right game, he can even play ahead of the house. But as good as the basic strategy player is, he is not the player feared by the house. In the long run, the house still makes money from this player.

The advantage player is the player the house fears. This player is a skilled card counter and knows the game inside and out. He has the advantage from the moment play starts. If he is playing for high stakes and it's discovered that he's a counter, a casino will stop him from playing in its house. However, there are many advantage players out there who manage to avoid being discovered and actually make a nice secondary income from playing blackjack.

What kind of player do you want to be? If you are willing to spend some time reading this book and using the methods explained here, you can become an accomplished blackjack player. You might be satisfied with being a basic strategy player. A good basic strategy player is welcome in most casinos and will be treated well. If such a player knows how to minimize his losses while maximizing his comps (casino "freebies"), he can do very well in the battle against the house.

Even if you have never stepped into a casino, this book can teach you to be a strong basic strategy player. It will demonstrate how to play the game properly, how to pick the right game conditions, how to figure out the proper betting levels for your bankroll (the money you have to spend on gambling), how to avoid going broke, and how to make the most out of a casino's comping system.

Perhaps you want to be an advantage player. If that is your desire, this book will teach you the most basic advantage skill—card counting.

It explains the most popular card-counting system in use today and how to use it in the casino environment. After reading this book and applying its concepts, you should know which blackjack games to play, how to play them, and how to manage your bankroll. You should know how to increase your longevity, what to do if you are barred from play, and how to keep coming back for more. Even an experienced card counter might pick up a trick or two from this book and perhaps discover a new way to approach the game.

This book is written in two parts. Part One is for the player who knows little or nothing about casinos or the game of blackjack. It is for the person who would like to be a strong basic strategy player. Part Two is for the person who wants to be an advantage player. For that person, this book should be considered a starting point. A true advantage player is always looking for ways to improve his game and sharpen his skills. The Resources section at the back of the book is useful for that purpose.

In short, *Bootlegger's 200-Proof Blackjack* is for people who are as clueless as I was back when I started out on my quest to beat the casinos, as well as for players with some experience who need to know more. My goal was to produce a book like the one I wish I had when I started out. If, after reading this book, you can walk out of a casino with a smile on your face, this book will have accomplished its purpose.

PART ONE

THE BASIC STRATEGY
PLAYER

THE GAME OF BLACKJACK

Walk into any modern casino, and you'll see a wide variety of gambling opportunities—baccarat, Big Six Wheel, blackjack, Caribbean Stud Poker, craps, keno, roulette, slot machines, video poker, Pai Gow poker, three-card poker, and even that old child's card game War. Many casinos offer poker rooms, where flesh-and-blood opponents can play against one another. And, if the casino offers sports-related betting, you can bet on just about any event that's happening in the sports world. On top of that, casinos are always trying out new games at the tables and on the machines.

With so many different games out there, why choose blackjack? Simply because blackjack offers the best chance to the average player who wants to get in on the comps (casino "freebies"), who wants to play the house as close to even as possible, and who might even want to make a little money in the process. The game of blackjack is easy to learn and fun to play, and just about any casino that offers table games offers blackjack.

Most important, blackjack is a good choice because it's also a game of skill. If early casinos had known that players had an advantage, they probably never would have offered the game to their patrons. But by the time a good computer analysis of the game could be performed, blackjack was already a casino fixture. Then, with the introduction of card counting in Edward O. Thorp's landmark book *Beat the Dealer*, blackjack quickly became America's most popular table game.

In this chapter, you'll learn the meaning of terms such as *house advantage* (or *house edge*), *odds*, and *probabilities*, and how this understanding can be used to make an informed decision about what sort of games you wish to play. This chapter also covers the basic rules of casino blackjack, as well as an outline of basic table etiquette in a casino setting. You will see phrases throughout this chapter (and this book) such as "almost always" or "usually." It is as sure as the fact that this book is printed on paper that you will encounter a casino blackjack rule or custom that either isn't covered here or is different from what you're about to read.

UNDERSTANDING HOUSE ADVANTAGE

Casino games are designed with a built-in *house advantage*, also called a *house edge*—a casino's advantage over a player on any given bet.

Stanford Wong, a renowned gambling authority, once told me that casinos believe that as soon as you walk through the door, all the money you have on you belongs to them. It is just a matter of time before you make the transfer from your pocket to their vaults. All of the games casinos offer are designed to do just that—separate you from your money. In the process, the casinos wine and dine you, fawn over you, and make you feel like you are just about the most important person in the world. You will swear they love you. Depending on your level of betting, you will be showered with gifts, free meals, free rooms, free show tickets, and even free airfare to return for your next round of gambling. If you are a high-stakes bettor, you might even get tickets to the Super Bowl or a week's vacation in Aruba.

Do these people really love you? Not for a millisecond. They love your money and that's as far as it goes. That's why casino games are designed with a built-in *house advantage*, also called a *house edge*—a casino's advantage over a player on any given bet. Unless some method of advantage play is employed, the game of blackjack carries a house advantage. But even for the non-advantage player, this game offers the best overall odds in the house.

Odds and Probabilities

Odds is an expression of the likelihood that a certain event will occur out of all the possibilities that exist compared to the likelihood of that same event not occurring. Let's look at a coin toss as an example. When you toss a coin, it can land on either heads or tails. The odds of getting either heads or tails are expressed as the ratio 1:1, which is stated verbally as "one to one." If you add them together, you get "two," which is the total number of possible outcomes. There is one chance of getting heads, and one chance of getting tails. We can also say that there is one chance in two of getting heads, which can be expressed as the ratio 1:2. This ratio represents the *probability*—the likelihood that a certain event will occur—of the coin's landing on either heads or tails. This probability ratio can be converted to a percentage. In this case, the probability of getting heads would be 50 percent. Although probability can be expressed as a ratio, to avoid confusing it with the odds, it will be expressed as a percentage throughout this book.

So, let's suppose that you wagered $1 that the coin will land on heads. If you were betting with a friend, you would lose your dollar bet if the coin landed on tails. If the coin landed on heads, you would come away with $2—your original $1 bet and your friend's $1 bet. This type of payoff is known as *even money*. You won the same amount that you wagered. Neither you nor your friend had a house advantage on that bet.

If a casino were to offer coin tossing as a game, it would want a built-in house advantage on the game. One way to get a house advantage would be to offer less of a payoff than the true odds would dictate if the player wins, but continue to collect the full wager made by the bettor if he loses. The casino might pay ninety cents on the dollar, so that if the player won, he would get ninety cents in winnings. If a player made 100 bets, he could expect to lose fifty bets and win fifty bets. He would wager $100, but he would end up with only $95 if the results followed the 50 percent probability. He would lose $50 on the times the coin landed on the opposite side, and his winnings would only amount to $45—that is, ninety cents times fifty. In this case, the house advantage would be 5 percent of all the money wagered. At first blush, this doesn't seem fair. The casino really isn't offering the true payoff based on the odds of the game. However, casinos don't like to gamble. They save that for their patrons. After all, they are running a business. The house advantage is the price of admission. If there were no built-in house advantage, casinos wouldn't exist, and this book would have no purpose.

In any honest blackjack game, the probability of winning a hand is about 44 percent, the probability of losing a hand is about 47 percent, and the probability of getting a push is about 9 percent. These percentages vary slightly depending on the specific rules and the basic strategy for a given game, but not by any significant amount.

On the other hand, gamblers are hoping that on any given night, the odds will turn out to be in their favor. If they were tossing coins, they hope that lightning will strike and they will win more than 50 percent of the coin tosses. The fact is, there are thousands of gamblers in the casinos who do beat the odds for that moment every day. If that didn't happen, the casinos would quickly go out of business, because no one would play if they didn't have some kind of reasonable chance of beating the odds occasionally. The house is relying on the fact that it plays thousands and even millions of hands, and that in the long run, the true odds will tell, and the casino will come out ahead. Mathematicians call this *the law of large numbers.*

The law of large numbers dictates that with thousands or millions of trials, the games offered by casinos will be close enough to their true odds to allow the casino to make a profit with its artificially induced house advantage. It also means that the more times a player returns to play, the less likely he is to be ahead overall.

The House Advantage in Blackjack

The house advantage in blackjack is difficult to compute. This is because there are thousands of combinations of cards that can occur in blackjack, and players make individual playing decisions—right or wrong. Also, not all winning bets pay the same. For example, a blackjack, or a natural, which is an Ace and a 10-valued card, pays 3:2 in most casinos, which means it pays $3 for every $2 bet, for a total return of $5

Expected Value

The expected value (EV), or expectation, of a game is the percentage of the total amount bet that a player can expect to win or lose over the long run for a particular set of game conditions. For example, if a player is playing basic strategy in a game with an expected value of –0.15 percent, he can expect to lose 0.15 percent of the total money he bets in the game. If he were playing a game at the rate of 100 hands per hour, betting $10 per hand, his expectation would be minus $1.50. The more hands a person plays, the more likely he is to be at or near the expectation for the game.

on a $2 bet, counting the original wager. Some blackjack games, however, pay less than 3:2 on a blackjack. (These games will be discussed in detail later. For now, it's enough to know that such games should be avoided.)

When you cut through all the math of the game, the basic reason the house has an advantage in blackjack is because it immediately wins the bet when a player *busts*—that is, goes over a card total of 21. It doesn't matter if the dealer subsequently busts herself when completing her hand for any players remaining in the game.

Setting aside blackjack clones, such as Spanish 21 or Super-Fun 21, and double-exposure blackjack, the advantage in blackjack games found in North America runs from about 0.63 percent advantage for the house to 0.13 percent advantage for the player. To give you some idea how this compares to other common casino games, Table 1.1 below lists the house advantage for various games you may encounter when you venture into a casino.

Game	House Advantage
Baccarat (8 deck) player bet	1.24 percent
Baccarat (8 deck) bank bet	1.06 percent
Baccarat (8 deck) tie bet	14.36 percent
Big Six Wheel	11.11 to 24.07 percent
Caribbean Stud	5.24 percent
Casino War (common rules)	2.88 percent
Chuck-a-Luck	7.87 to 25 percent
Double-Down Stud	2.67 percent
Keno	20 to 35 percent
Let It Ride Poker	3.51 percent
Roulette, American (Double Zero)	5.26 percent
Roulette, European (En Prison, Single Zero)	1.35 percent
Spanish 21	0.76 percent
Super-Fun 21	0.77 percent
Three-Card Poker	2.32 to 7.27 percent

Table 1.1
The House Advantage in Common Casino Games

THE BASICS OF CASINO BLACKJACK

Casino blackjack, also called *twenty-one*, is a card game that is played with one or more decks of regulation playing cards. Most casinos feature blackjack games with one, two, four, six, or eight decks. (Some continuous-shuffling machine games feature three- or five-deck games. These games are discussed more later. For now, it's enough to know that these games should be avoided.)

Blackjack is played at a semicircular table with up to seven playing spots. The dealer faces the players from the flat side of the table. Figure 1.1 shows the basic blackjack table layout.

In casino blackjack, the play is against the dealer, not against the other players at the table. The object of the game is to get a card total as close to, but not over, 21. If a player's hand is closer to 21 than the dealer's hand, the player wins. If the player *busts*—that is, goes over 21—he loses his wager, or *bet* as it is referred to throughout this book. If the dealer busts and the player's hand is still in play, the player wins the hand. If both the player and the dealer have the same card total, the hand is a tie, or a *push,* and no money changes hands. (There are some

Figure 1.1
The basic blackjack
table layout.

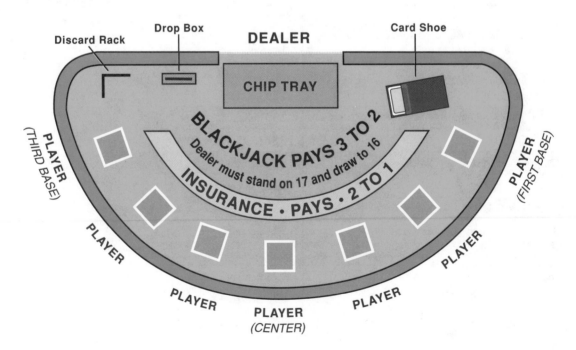

varieties of blackjack, particularly charity versions of the game, in which a player loses on a push. Don't play a game with this variation unless you want to donate your money to charity. The house advantage is horrendous.)

Card Values and Totals

The cards 2 through 10 are valued at their numerical value, while face cards have a value of 10. Aces have a value of either 1 or 11. For example, if a player has an Ace-7, the card total could be either 8 or 18. When an Ace can be counted as 11 without going over 21, the hand is called a *soft hand*. When an Ace can only be counted as a 1, the hand is called a *hard hand*. If a player chooses to hit the Ace-7, or *soft* 18, and he receives a 10-valued card, he now has a *hard* 18. Any hand that does not include an 11-valued Ace is considered a hard hand.

The total of an Ace and any 10-valued card is 21. This is called a *blackjack* or a *natural*. No other hand with a value of 21, such as 5-5-Ace, is considered a blackjack. In other words, a player who hits to a card total of 21 does not receive the blackjack payoff. By the same token, if the dealer hits her original hand to a multicard total of 21, it has no effect on a player's blackjack, which is still a winning hand for the player.

The values of the cards in a hand that doesn't include an Ace are simply added together to get the final hand total. For example, a Jack-9 would have a value of 19 and a 6-7-6 would have a value of 19. (Except for rare casino promotions, the suit of the cards has no value or bearing on the hand.)

Minimum/Maximum Bets

When you *buy in*, or purchase chips from the dealer, the denomination of the chips she'll give you depends on the table minimum and, of course, on the amount you purchase. There's usually a sign (but not always) on the left side of the table that clearly states the minimum and maximum bets permitted at that table. Table minimums and maximums can be different at each casino and even at different tables in the same casino. Table minimums may be as low as fifty cents and as high as $500 (sometimes they can even be higher if a player requests it). Table

Aces have a value of either 1 or 11. When an Ace can be counted as 11 without going over 21, the hand is called a *soft hand*. When the Ace can only be counted as 1, the hand is called a *hard hand*. Any hand that does not include an Ace that can take the value of 11 is considered a hard hand.

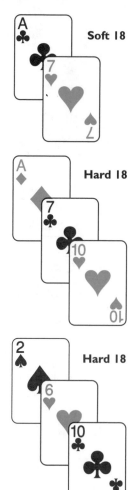

Soft 18

Hard 18

Hard 18

The total of an Ace and any 10-valued card is 21. This is called a *blackjack* or a *natural*.

Examples of Blackjack

Chip Values

In American casinos, the color of the chips, sometimes called *checks*, represents their value. The denominations of the most common chip colors are listed below. But remember, as in most things about blackjack, there are always exceptions to the rule.

White chips = $1*   Green chips = $25

Pink chips = $2.50   Black chips = $100

Red chips = $5   Purple chips = $500

*Some casinos use slot-machine tokens to represent a dollar.

The color of chips with higher denominations varies more from casino to casino. Orange chips, often called *pumpkins*, are usually worth $1,000, and gray chips are sometimes worth $5,000. Chips with higher denominations are usually slightly larger than chips of $100 or less.

maximums can range from as low as $10 to as much as $10,000 or higher. Before joining a game, be sure you are clear on the minimum and maximum bets permitted at that table to avoid a potentially embarrassing situation.

The Play

Before the cards are dealt, the players place their bets on the marked playing squares (or circles, as the case may be) directly in front of them on the table. Then, the dealer deals the cards, starting with the player to her left. On the initial deal, each player is dealt two cards, one at a time. Depending on whether the game being played is a shoe game or hand-held game, the players' cards are dealt either face up or face down. (There's more on this later.) In both shoe games and hand-held games, the dealer deals herself one face-down card, known as the *hole card*, and one face-up card, known as the *upcard*.

If the dealer's upcard is an Ace, she'll offer the players *insurance*—the opportunity to make a side bet. (See page 47 for an explanation of insurance and its pitfalls.) In most American casinos, if the dealer has a 10-valued card showing, she'll check her hole card to see if she has blackjack but will not offer the players insurance. If the dealer has blackjack, the round is over and the dealer collects all bets or declares a push for players who also have blackjack.

Basic Plays

Hit. Receive an additional card from the dealer.

Stand. Refuse an additional card from the dealer.

If the dealer does not have blackjack, play on the round continues and each player can choose to *stand* on his hand (refuse an additional card) or he can choose to *hit* his hand (receive an additional card) until he is satisfied with the total he receives or until he busts. There are other possible plays, such as doubling down and splitting pairs, which will be discussed later.

At this point, the dealer collects the bets on busted hands and pays off the bets on any blackjacks. Blackjacks are traditionally paid off at a rate of 3:2, or one and a half times the player's bet. The 3:2 payoff is in addition to the player's original bet. In other words, if a player's bet was $5.00 and that player got blackjack, he would receive $7.50 from the dealer, for a total of $12.50 in his betting square. (Beware of games in which the payoff for blackjack is 6:5. We'll take a closer look at the negative effects of this variation later.)

After collecting the bets on busted hands and paying off blackjacks, the dealer reveals her hole card. In most casinos, the dealer reveals her hole card even if there are no active hands left in play. Assuming there are players with active hands remaining in the round, the dealer continues play on her hand until it is complete. (The dealer is bound by specific rules regarding hitting and standing, as explained under "Rules and Rule Variations" on page 17.)

If the dealer busts, she pays off all the active hands in the round. Even though the dealer has busted, players who also went over 21 still lose their bets (and, indeed, the dealer had already collected their bets by this time). If the dealer doesn't bust, players whose hands total more than the dealer's win their bets and are paid at this time. Winning hands that are not blackjacks are paid *even money*. In other words, the player receives a payoff equal to his original bet. A $5 bet would be paid $5, which is placed next to the player's original bet in the betting square, giving the player a total of $10 in his betting square. Players whose hands total less than the dealer's lose their bets, which are then collected by the dealer. Players whose hands total the same as the dealer's "push the hand" and no bet is paid or collected.

Once again, the players place their bets, and the next hand is dealt and played.

Blackjacks are traditionally paid off at a rate of 3:2, or one and a half times the player's bet. Winning hands that are not blackjacks are paid *even money*. In other words, the player receives a payoff equal to his original bet.

SHOE GAMES VERSUS HAND-HELD GAMES

Casinos offer a variety of blackjack games that may be dealt either from a *card shoe* (a rectangular box that holds multiple decks of cards) or by a dealer who holds the cards in her hands. In days of old, casinos offered nothing but hand-held single-deck games. While plenty of casinos still offer hand-held games and many offer a variety of both, shoe games are the most common games you'll encounter in American casinos.

Shoe Games

In a shoe game, the dealer pulls the cards from the card shoe and slides the cards across the table felt to the players' positions. The cards are almost always dealt face up. In face-up games, players are not permitted to touch the cards. Even if a player wants to split a pair, he cannot touch them. He simply places his additional bet in or next to the betting square and the dealer splits them for him.

All of the shoe games I have ever encountered were multiple-deck games, usually with four decks or more. There are some very rare instances of double-deck games being dealt from shoes, but these are exceptions to the rule.

Beware of Continuous-Shuffling Machines

You may encounter blackjack games that are dealt from continuous-shuffling machines, or *CSMs* as they are often called. These machines may hold three, four, five, or more decks. After one or two rounds are played, the dealer returns the cards to the machine and shuffles them into the unused cards. In other words, the players are always being dealt a game as if it were from a fresh shoe.

Obviously, this makes it impossible to count the cards, so card counters avoid these games like the plague. While they don't hurt basic strategy players much, they do increase the number of hands played per hour, which means that the basic strategist will lose more money per hour. (There's more to come on how the speed of the game affects a player's expectation.)

Don't confuse continuous-shuffling machines with ordinary shuffling machines. In some cases, shuffling machines are simply used to shuffle a deck, pack, or shoe of cards after the cards have been played.

Hand-held Games

Hand-held games are commonly referred to as *pitch* games, since the dealer *pitches* the cards to each player as she deals. In the vast majority of hand-held games, the cards are dealt face down. Players can reveal their cards if they wish, since there is no need to hide the cards as one would in a poker game.

In hand-held games, players may hold the cards only in *one* hand. The logic here is that if both hands are used to hold the cards, it may be easier for players to mark the cards, add cards to the deck with a little sleight-of-hand, or other such underhanded things.

Hand-held games are *almost* always single- or double-deck games. I say "almost" because a few casinos try to pull a fast one on their players. Multiple decks are placed in a shuffling machine, and the dealer removes one or two decks' worth of cards and pitches them to the players as if it were a one- or two-deck game. Casinos may advertise these games as hand-held games, hoping players won't realize that they are just shoe games in disguise. A player might think he is playing a single- or double-deck game when in reality he may be playing a four-, five-, or six-deck game (or even more, depending on the casino).

Table 1.2 on page 18 sets forth the various protocols that should be followed in both shoe (or face-up) games and hand-held (or face-down) games when executing the various plays described under "Rules and Rule Variations" in the following section.

As the number of decks in a blackjack game increases, so does the house advantage.

RULES AND RULE VARIATIONS

Different casinos often have different blackjack rules and sometimes offer promotions with special payoffs on certain hands. It would be virtually impossible to cover all of the rule variations and practices, because—except in New Jersey, where the rules of the game are defined by the Gaming Commission—the house can make just about any set of rules it wants and call the game "blackjack." Therefore, it's very likely that someday you will encounter a variation not mentioned here. However, the most common rules and rule variations are discussed below.

Included are abbreviations for each rule variation. To avoid wordy phrasing, these abbreviations are used throughout this book. For the most part, these abbreviations have been borrowed from Stanford Wong's *Current Blackjack News* magazine, and have become part of the

Table 1.2   Movements and Phrases to Indicate Your Next Play

In Shoe and/or Face-Up Games	In Hand-Held and/or Face-Down Games	Dealer's Response
Hit		
Tap or scratch the table next to your betting square with your fingers.	Scratch the cards on the tabletop toward yourself.	The dealer gives you another card.
Stand		
Wave your hand over your cards.	Tuck the cards under your bet.	The dealer moves on to the next player.
Double Down		
Place your additional bet next to the original bet in the betting square.	Place your additional bet next to the original bet and place your cards face up above the betting square.	The dealer gives you one additional card, either face up or face down, depending on the casino.
Split		
Place your additional bet next to the original bet in the betting square. If re-splits are permitted, place any subsequent bets next to the bets already placed.	Place your additional bet next to the original bet in the betting square. Place your cards side by side face up above the betting square. If re-splits are permitted, place any subsequent bets next to the bets already placed. (At this point, the dealer will usually handle the cards.)	If it isn't clear, the dealer will ask you if you are doubling or splitting. She will then deal another card to one of the split cards and wait for your response for hitting, standing, or doubling (if permitted) and then repeat for the next split card. Re-splits are handled in the same fashion.
Surrender		
Say, "Surrender."	Say, "Surrender."	The dealer will take half your bet after checking for a blackjack, if appropriate. In some casinos, a small marker is placed next to your bet, and half the bet is collected when play on the entire round is complete.
Insurance		
Place your insurance bet in the area marked insurance pays 2:1 on the table above the betting squares when the dealer offers it.	Place your insurance bet in the area marked insurance pays 2:1 on the table above the betting squares when the dealer offers it.	The dealer checks for blackjack. If she has it, she pays off the insurance bet by placing the chips next to the bet. If she doesn't have it, she collects the insurance bet.
Even Money		
Say, "Even money."	Say, "Even money."	The dealer pays you even money and places your hand in the discard tray.

lingua franca, or trade language, of blackjack players. It will serve you well to know them. (Once you've read the various discussions, check out "Quick Reference Guide to Rule Abbreviations" on page 20.)

Most casinos don't post a list of rules for players to refer to for a particular game, but some rules, such as standing on 17s, may be printed on the table felt. Even if a casino does place a rule card on the table, these cards rarely list all of the rules for that game. Moreover, the rules can vary from table to table depending on the number of decks and other factors. The best listing of rules for American casinos can be found in *Current Blackjack News*, which is updated on a monthly basis. Casinos can change rules without notice, however, so if you are uncertain about the rules, it is best to ask the dealer.

Dealer Stands on All 17s (S17)

The dealer must stand on a hand that totals 17, whether or not it is hard or soft—that is, whether or not the hand contains an Ace. In a game with this rule, a dealer stands on a 10-7, a 9-8, and an Ace-6. This rule is favorable to players.

Dealer Must Hit Soft 17s (H17)

The dealer must stand on a hard 17 but must hit a soft 17. In a game with this rule, the dealer would hit an Ace-6 or an Ace-2-4. Compared with the S17 rule, this rule increases the house advantage.

Double Down on the First Two Cards (D2)

Just about all casinos allow for the opportunity to *double down* after receiving the first two cards. This rule allows a player to increase his bet on a favorable hand. The player "doubles" his original bet by placing additional chips in the betting square and takes only one hit card from the dealer to complete his hand. A player can often double down for less than, but not more than, his original bet. While doubling for less is not uncommon, this play is not recommended for the basic strategy player. The double-down plays expressed in the basic strategy tables in this book are designed to get the greatest return by using a full bet.

If it turns out that the dealer has blackjack, the additional bet is returned to the player and only the original bet is collected.

Quick Reference Guide to Rule Abbreviations

D2. Double down is permitted on the first two cards.

D3. Double down is permitted on hands made up of three cards.

D4. Double down is permitted on hands made up of four cards.

D8. Double down is permitted only on two-card hand totals of 8, 9, 10, or 11.

D9. Double down is permitted only on two-card hand totals of 9, 10, or 11.

D10. Double down is permitted only on two-card hand totals of 10 or 11.

DAS. Double down is permitted after splitting pairs.

ENHC. The dealer does not take a hole card until players' hands are complete.

ES. The early surrender option is available.

H17. The dealer is required to hit soft 17s.

LS. The late surrender option is available.

RSA. Re-splitting Aces is permitted.

S17. The dealer is required to stand on hard and soft 17s.

Double Down Only on Certain Hand Totals (D8, D9, and D10)

Some casinos permit players to double down only on certain hand totals. Single-deck games originating in northern Nevada tend to allow doubling only on two-card hand totals of 10 and 11 (D10). Some casinos allow doubling only on two-card hand totals of 9, 10, and 11 (D9), and others allow doubling only on two-card hand totals of 8, 9, 10, and 11 (D8). When compared with allowing double downs on any two-card hand total, these restrictions are not in the player's favor. (Although still in the minority, rule variations such as these have found their way out of northern Nevada and are now found in casinos throughout the United States.)

Double Down on Three or More Card Hand Totals (D3 and D4)

Some casinos allow players to double down on three-card hands (D3), some allow it on four-card hands (D4), and some allow doubling down on any number of cards in a player's hand. This rule variation, which is favorable to the players, is rarely employed.

Double Down After Splits (DAS)

This rule allows a player to double down after he has split a pair (see "Splitting Pairs" below). When DAS is permitted, the same rules for doubling down on the original hand are applied. If re-splits are allowed, the player can double down on any re-split hand as well. This rule is quite common and is very favorable to the players.

Splitting Pairs

This very common rule allows a player to split *any* pair in his original two-card hand into two separate hands. The player must then make an additional bet equal to the original bet. Once the pair is split, the player is dealt one additional card to each split card. Then each two-card hand is played separately. He can take one or more hit cards, just as he would for any other hand—unless he has split a pair of Aces. In the case of split Aces, most casinos allow the player to receive only one additional card on each Ace. If the player is dealt a 10 on his Ace, the hand is not considered a blackjack and is only paid even money if the player wins the hand.

The fact that an Ace-10 hand is not a blackjack on a split hand is purely arbitrary. If players received the blackjack payoff on split hands that result in an Ace-10, the house advantage would disappear. The house isn't going to let this happen. So, the split Ace-10 is just another 21, and it can be pushed by a dealer's 21.

Generally speaking, pairs can be re-split after the first split if another equally valued card is dealt to one of the original cards. Again, Aces are a common exception. Although not completely unusual, most casinos do not allow re-splitting a second pair of Aces. When Aces can be re-split, the rule variation is referred to as RSA (re-split Aces). This rule variation is favorable to players.

Casinos sometimes limit the number of times a pair may be split. The most common rule allows up to four re-splits. If a player is faced with the opportunity to split more than four times, he should ask the dealer if further re-splits are acceptable.

By the way, any two-card combination of 10-valued cards—10s, Jacks, Queens, and Kings—are counted as pairs. However, as you will later learn, splitting 10-valued cards is not recommended for the basic strategy player.

It's Not Natural

A split hand that results in a new hand made up of an Ace and a 10-valued card does not receive the blackjack bonus. Moreover, it can be pushed by a dealer's multicard total of 21.

A blackjack hand that has a value of 12 through 16 is referred to as a *stiff hand*.

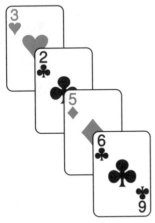

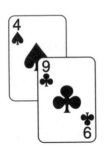

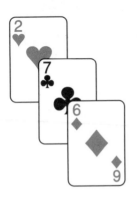

Typical Stiff Hands

As in doubling down, if the dealer has blackjack, she collects only the original bet—not the additional bet made when the cards were split.

Late Surrender (LS)

The late surrender option allows a player to withdraw from the hand and forfeit only half of his bet after the first two cards have been dealt. If the dealer has blackjack, however, the player does not have this option. (Compare this to "early surrender," discussed below.)

This rule is favorable to the player, but the few players who use it often misplay it. Many of them tend to surrender any hand that is *stiff* (that is, a hand that has a value of 12 through 16) against a dealer's 9, 10, or Ace. If you follow the basic strategies for late surrender set forth later in the book, you don't have to worry about misplaying this valuable option.

Early Surrender (ES)

As opposed to late surrender described above, the early surrender option allows a player to surrender his hand and forfeit half of his bet *before* the dealer checks her hand for blackjack.

This rule is more valuable to the player than late surrender, but it is very rare. It is offered in some blackjack machines, but not in any live casinos that I'm aware of. Given the constant changes that take place in the competitive world of casino blackjack, one never knows if some casino somewhere will decide to offer this rule at some point in the future. It is a rule that is valuable enough to mention here.

Insurance and Even Money

When the dealer's upcard is an Ace, she'll offer the players *insurance* before checking her hole card for blackjack. Insurance is simply a side bet—usually an amount equal to half the original bet—made by the players that the dealer has blackjack. (Be aware that the odds are relatively good that the dealer will *not* be hiding a 10 under that Ace.) Casinos call this *insurance* because they want to make it seem like they're giving the players an opportunity to protect their hands against a dealer's blackjack. This is nonsense, of course. When a player takes insurance, he is making an entirely separate bet.

If a player makes this bet and the dealer has blackjack, he is paid off at a rate of 2:1. This means that if he bet $5 on insurance, he'll receive $10. However, he'll lose his initial $10 bet. If the dealer does not have blackjack (the more likely scenario), she'll collect the insurance bet and the play on the round will continue. In this case, the player is down $5 at the start of the hand.

If a player has blackjack when the dealer offers insurance, he can tell the dealer he wants to take *even money*, which is just another term for insurance. This means that he will receive an amount equal to his bet whether or not the dealer has blackjack. In essence, he's giving up his chance to receive the 3:2 payoff.

For more detailed information about these two plays, see "Never Take Insurance or Even Money" in Chapter 4 on page 47.

6:5 Payoff for a Player's Blackjack

This variation isn't discussed in most older blackjack books. It was simply an accepted fact that the normal payoff for a blackjack was 3:2. Occasionally, one might run across special, favorable situations where blackjacks pay 2:1, or sometimes even 3:1, but those are limited exceptions to the rule and are usually instituted for a limited time to advertise or promote a casino.

Times have changed. Several casinos now offer "blackjack" games that pay only 6:5 for a player's blackjack. In this version of the game, a $5 bettor would only get a payoff of $6 for a blackjack, instead of the normal $7.50 he would get in a 3:2 game. Worse yet, there are some blackjack games that offer only even money for a player's blackjack.

A good rule of thumb is to avoid any blackjack variation that offers a payoff that's less than the standard rate of 3:2. Such games are strictly for suckers.

Don't Settle for Less
Avoid any blackjack variation that offers a payoff on a player's blackjack that's less than the standard rate of 3:2.

European No-Hole Card (ENHC)

As the name suggests, ENHC is a rule that is commonly found in European casinos, but it can also be found on some cruise ships and Caribbean venues, as well as in some Canadian casinos. And from time to time, it even pops up in American casinos.

In this version of blackjack, the dealer does not take a hole card until all the players complete the plays on their hands. At that point, the dealer draws another card to complete her two-card hand and then proceeds from there.

The primary difference between the ENHC rule and games without this rule is that if a player has doubled or split his hand, he loses the additional amount bet on those plays if the dealer has blackjack. As explained earlier, in American-style blackjack, those extra bets are returned to the player if the dealer has blackjack. Obviously, this rule can be a costly one for the players.

NUMBER OF DECKS IN PLAY AND RULE VALUES

The number of decks in play has a significant impact on the value of the game being played. Nearly all the games you will find in North America will be one-, two-, four-, six-, or eight-deck games. Generally speaking, the fewer the decks in play, the lower the house advantage.

In a single-deck game with S17, D2, re-splits permitted on non-Ace pairs, and a 3:2 payoff on blackjacks, the player's advantage is .04 percent. As the number of decks and rules change, the advantage changes as well.

You can use Tables 1.3 and 1.4 to compute the house advantage (or in rare cases, the player's advantage) for a particular set of rules and number of decks in play. Beginning with a slight advantage for the player—that is, a base figure of 0.4—you can add or subtract the value of the rule or number of decks, expressed in the tables as a percentage. Naturally, negative numbers are meant to be subtracted and positive numbers are meant to be added to the base figure. Rules with negative numbers are favorable to the house, while rules with positive numbers are favorable to the player.

Suppose you know a casino has a six-deck game with S17, DAS, and LS. To figure out the advantage for that particular game, here is what your calculations will look like:

1. Start with the base figure: .040

2. Plug in the figure for six decks (see Table 1.3):   −.542

3. Plug in the figure for DAS for six-deck games
   (see Table 1.4):   +.142

4. Plug in the figure for LS (S17) for six-deck games
   (see Table 1.4):   +.075

5. Add or subtract the figures to arrive at your total: −.285

    The advantage in this game is −.285 percent. In other words, the house has a .285 percent advantage over the player.

Number of Decks	Number of Cards	Advantage
One deck	52	.040%
Two decks	104	−.320%
Four decks	208	−.489%
Six decks	312	−.542%
Eight decks	416	−.569%

Table 1.3
Percent Advantage of Decks in Play

Rule	One Deck	Two Decks	Four Decks	Six Decks	Eight Decks
H17	−.190%	−.205%	−.213%	−.215%	−.216%
DAS	+.140%	+.143%	+.143%	+.142%	+.142%
D10	−.263%	−.211%	−.185%	−.176%	−.172%
D9	−.131%	−.107%	−.095%	−.091%	−.089%
RSA	+.032%	+.053%	+.065%	+.069%	+.072%
LS (S17)	+.022%	+.053%	+.069%	+.075%	+.077%
LS (H17)	+.036%	+.071%	+.089%	+.095%	+.098%
ES (S17)	+.620%	+.625%	+.628%	+.628%	+.629%
ES (H17)	+.700%	+.710%	+.715%	+.717%	+.718%
ENHC	−.110%	−.110%	−.110%	−.110%	−.110%
2:1 blackjack payout	+2.320%	+2.285%	+2.267%	+2.262%	+2.260%
6:5 blackjack payout	−1.390%	−1.377%	−1.370%	−1.368%	−1.366%

Table 1.4
Percent Advantage of Rule per Decks in Play

Adapted from *The Theory of Blackjack*, Sixth Edition, by Peter A. Griffin, Huntington Press, 1999.

TABLE ETIQUETTE

When you approach a blackjack table for the first time, it's not necessary to act like a know-it-all. Don't be afraid to ask questions. If you tell the dealer that you are new to the game, she will probably be quite willing to explain what is expected of you. Meanwhile, the discussions below should help prepare you.

Buying In

The first thing you do when you sit down at a casino blackjack table is *buy in*. You place the amount of money you want to start with on the table above the betting squares (or circles, as the case may be). Do not hand the money directly to the dealer. She can't take it. It must be placed on the table. The dealer will understand that you wish to purchase chips. Do not place your money *inside* the betting square; if you do, the dealer may assume that you are playing the entire amount on the next hand. Many casinos permit *money plays*—that is, they allow cash money to be used instead of chips. The dealer may ask you if money plays. Unless that is what you intend to do, make sure she knows you are only buying in.

Money Plays
When a bet is made in cash rather than with casino chips.

The dealer counts your money on the table, in clear view of the surveillance cameras. She will tell the pit boss—the dealer's supervisor—how much she is cashing by calling out the amount of the buy in. Once the pit boss acknowledges her, she places the money in the drop box attached to the table on the dealer's right and gives you an equivalent amount of casino chips or *checks,* as they are called by casino personnel.

You can keep your chips in your pocket or purse or somewhere else off the table, but it is customary for players to keep them in a stack or pile on the table in front of them. Some casinos provide a set of wooden trays around the rim of the table for players to keep their chips in, but even when those trays are provided, most players wind up stacking their chips on the table as if the trays weren't there at all.

Placing the Bet

After the buy in, the player places his bet in the betting square marked on the table in front of him *before* the hand is dealt. Then play commences as described earlier. A player may choose to play more than one hand per round if there are open seats at the table. If he is playing two or more hands, each bet is placed in a separate betting square.

In general, a player must bet at least twice the table minimum on each hand to play two hands and sometimes more to play three or more hands. This is not a universal rule, so it is always a good idea to ask the dealer what the minimum bet is for more than one hand.

If your bet includes more than one denomination of chip, you should place the largest denomination chip on the bottom and the smallest denomination chip on top of your bet in a single stack of chips.

During Play

Be sure to use the hand motions and gestures that are appropriate for the type of game you are playing. Review Table 1.2 on page 18 once more to become familiar with the proper protocol. As you may recall, in shoe games, the cards are usually dealt face up and players may not touch them. In hand-held games, the cards are usually dealt face down and players may hold them in one hand.

During play, you will often encounter players who either give advice or seek advice. Once you become familiar with basic strategy play, you will find that many players don't know the correct play for many of the hands they see. I suggest that you ignore the advice you are given, even if it comes from dealers or other casino personnel, and that you be very careful about dispensing advice to others. Even if you are correct, there is always a strong chance the player will lose and subsequently blame you for his loss. There is nothing wrong with discussing the hands in play with other players. In fact, I give some advice in the next chapter about using such tactics to slow the game down. However, when the discussion is said and done and someone asks you how to play his hand, the best response is to say, in a polite and friendly way, "Sir [or Madame], it's your money. You should play your hand anyway you wish."

Conclusion of the Round

When a hand is over and the round is concluded, the dealer will pay off winning hands and collect the bets for the losing hands that were left in play at the end of the round. She will pay a winning hand by placing the chips won in the betting square next to the player's original bet. The player can collect his winnings at that point, change the size of his bet if he wishes, or choose not to play the next hand and place no bet in the square.

Make sure your bet is in the betting square before the dealer starts to deal the next round. Once the dealer has begun dealing, it's too late to place a bet.

Know Before You Go

By the time I sat down for my first hand of casino blackjack, I'd already memorized basic strategy and had played thousands of hands at home. I thought I was prepared to play the game—if not like an expert, then at least like a knowledgeable player. I was wrong. There were many things the books hadn't told me.

The casino was in the Upper Peninsula of Michigan. At the time, it was little more than a bar with some blackjack tables and slot machines. It had a four-deck game that was dealt out of a card shoe. I walked into the place, not quite sure what to do, but confident that I knew four-deck strategy. I spied a cage marked CASHIER, and walked over to it. I placed my money on the counter and asked for some chips.

"You can't buy chips here," the lady in the cage said incredulously.

"Why not? You're the cashier and I need some chips for my money," I said confidently, having complete ignorance on my side.

"Well, sir," she replied with her best straight face, "In this casino, you get your chips at the table."

"Why didn't you say so? I guess you do things differently up here in the U.P.," I said, compounding my ignorance with blather, and I sauntered away.

"The lady in the cage tells me I have to buy my chips here," I said as I approached the table. "I'll take twenty dollars worth."

The guy at third base snickered, but the dealer just smiled and said, "Give me your money."

I handed him twenty bucks and he gave me a stack of white chips, each worth a dollar. He dropped my cash into the drop box, and I wondered how he would retrieve the money through that thin slot when I wanted to cash out.

I took my seat and waited for something to happen. The dealer looked at me quizzically. "Are you going to place your bet, sir?" he asked.

"I bet two bucks," I replied, eager to get the game started.

The guy at third base let out a loud guffaw, and I began to feel a little uneasy and not so confident.

"Then please put two chips in the square in front of you," the dealer politely intoned.

I looked around and noticed the chips sitting

If you remove your chips from the square and do not put another bet in the square quickly, the dealer may assume you are sitting out a hand and deal around you. Make sure your bet is in the square before the dealer starts to deal the next round. Once the dealer has begun dealing for the next round, it's too late to place a bet.

When and How to Tip

Dealers and cocktail waitresses depend on tips for much of their income. You are under no obligation to tip anyone, but an occasional *toke* (casino slang for *tip*) for good service is not a bad thing to do. If you on everyone else's betting square, and sheepishly placed my bet.

The dealer distributed the cards face up to each player. When I received my cards, I picked them up to look them over. At this point, the guy at third base was coughing up his drink between peels of laughter. The dealer glared at me. If he'd had a ruler with him, he surely would have smacked my hands.

"Sir," he said with something less than infinite patience, "You can't touch the cards. Please put them back down on the table."

"Oops," I said, with a sheepish grin on my face.

Play resumed and each player indicated that he wanted to stand or take a hit card by either waving his hand over the cards to indicate that he was standing or tapping the table with his finger to indicate a hit. The play came to me and I said confidently, "Hit me!" Just then, the guy at third base fell off his chair.

The dealer shook his head. "Sir, you have to indicate what you want to do with a hand motion."

"Boy, you guys sure do things differently up here in the U.P.," I said.

And so it went, into the night, with the dealer patiently explaining to me each nuance of play. By the time I was finished playing, I had actually doubled my original buy in, and had won some respect from the third basemen. I gave the dealer my chips and told him I wanted to cash out. He took my forty white chips and gave me one green chip and three red chips.

"I'd rather have cash," I told him, and promptly lost what little respect I'd gained.

"Cash your chips in at the cashier's cage," the dealer told me curtly, quite finished being patient.

"OK," I said. As I walked away, I shook my head and mumbled, "They sure do things differently up here in the U.P."

Of course, they don't do things differently in the Upper Peninsula of Michigan—at least not when it comes to the normal table protocol. Although the books I'd read prepared me for the proper plays to make, the authors assumed I already knew something about what happens at the tables. As you can see, I was woefully unprepared. Take a lesson from me and prepare yourself for the casino environment.

wish to tip the dealer, one very common way to do it is to place an additional bet on the edge of the betting square, apart from your bet. The dealer will understand that this is intended to be a tip and that if the hand is won by the player, she will share in his good fortune. You can also simply give the dealer a tip by placing a chip or chips in the area above the insurance line on the table before or after a round is dealt and telling the dealer it is a tip.

You can tip a cocktail waitress simply by giving her the tip as you are served. You can give her cash money, slot tokens, or chips. Just drop the tip in her hand or on her serving tray. I have found that a small tip goes a long way with cocktail waitresses.

This is just a short description of how to tip. There is a discussion about the pitfalls of tipping too much in Chapter 4.

CONCLUSION

This chapter has taught you some of the basics of how to play blackjack. You should have a good idea of what happens when you sit down at a blackjack table and what is expected of you as a player. So far, the rules and the common variations of those rules have been covered. This chapter included advice about how to buy in at a table, how to make and collect a bet, and how to complete the physical actions of playing the game. This doesn't mean a novice player is now ready to go to a casino and put his money in the betting square. There is still a lot to learn. The next chapter goes into detail about the proper strategies you need to know to make the best play for any possible hand.

BASIC STRATEGY

The first modern basic strategy for blackjack was developed by four scientists who worked at the Aberdeen Proving Ground in Maryland: Roger R. Baldwin, Wilbert E. Cantey, Herbert Maisel, and James P. McDermott. They published their findings in the September 1956 issue of the *Journal of the American Statistical Association*. Since that time, revisions to basic strategy have been made based on more sophisticated computer studies. As a result, casinos have made changes to the conditions of the game, particularly by adding more decks.

In this chapter, you'll find basic strategy tables for different numbers of decks and sets of rules, along with an explanation of why certain plays are made. You'll also find advice on how to memorize the basic strategy for the game you expect to play most often. This chapter also examines some of the common misconceptions about proper playing strategy that you will inevitably hear from players and dealers at the tables. A good grounding in basic strategy, knowing the reasons for it, and exposure to some of the erroneous "advice" you are likely to get are important for a novice player who wants to get a proper start.

HAVE FAITH IN BASIC STRATEGY

Be assured that the basic strategy tables in this chapter present the best plays in any given situation based on the player's hand total and the dealer's upcard. These tables have been painstakingly developed over the years by great minds and accurate computers. If you play according to basic strategy, you will be playing the best game you can, short of card counting or some other method of advantage play. Don't let anyone tell you otherwise.

When you become adept at basic strategy, you'll surely encounter players and even dealers who will disagree with your style of play. But don't let these blackjack know-it-alls or discouraging dealers deter you from using basic strategy.

Here's an example of what you may be up against: One night, I was playing center between two players at a $5 table in a single-deck game with no surrender. The older gentleman to my left was playing perfect basic strategy. The player to my right was betting strictly black chips—$100 a pop. Every play the older fellow made drew sharp comments from the black chipper.

When the fellow split a pair of 8s against the dealer's 10, the black chipper shouted, "That's idiotic! Any fool knows better than to split eights against a dealer's ten. You just took one lousy hand and turned it into two lousy hands."

"He made the right play," I interjected.

The split 8s resulted in one losing hand and one winning hand, for an overall tie. My hand was a pat 17, so I didn't take a hit. As it happens, I wound up losing my hand.

The bad-mannered know-it-all became further incensed, and cried, "If you guys want to see how an idiot plays, I'll show you!" He then placed an additional $400 in the betting square to double down on the hard 14 the dealer had dealt him. He promptly busted and lost his $800.

He stalked away from the table, mumbling something about having to play with simpletons and fools. He was right about one thing: He had certainly shown us how an idiot plays.

The amount of money another player bets is absolutely no indication of his knowledge of the game. Don't think that because someone places a large bet he knows something you don't. Oftentimes, dealers don't know any more about basic strategy than the players do, so it is best to ignore their advice, too. You will hear all sorts of folk wisdom about the best way to play. Some people will tell you not to split 8s against a dealer's 9, 10, or Ace. Some will tell you that you should take insurance if you have a total of 19 or 20. Others will tell you that you should always take even money for your blackjack against a dealer's Ace.

If you play at third base—that is, if you're the last player on the dealer's right—some players may chastise you if the dealer wins. This is because the third baseman is the last player to make a decision before the dealer reveals her hole card. If the dealer wins, some players may accuse you of having done something wrong that "caused the whole table to lose." If the dealer has a stiff hand (a 12 through 16) and you take a hit card, they will say you took the dealer's bust card. If you don't take a hit card and the dealer hits to a winning hand, they will say you should have taken a hit card so the dealer would bust. None of this makes sense. Every card dealt or not dealt affects the outcome of the hand. In the long run, it doesn't matter what the third baseman does. Sometimes, taking a card or not taking one will result in a dealer's win and sometimes it will result in a player's win. You cannot predict the outcome, and you shouldn't worry about what happened in a specific play.

Sometimes, your gut may tell you that you shouldn't make a certain basic strategy play. If you give in to that feeling, sometimes you'll be right, but more often you'll be wrong and your bankroll will suffer. Stick to the proper basic strategy plays set forth in this chapter and be confident that you are making the best plays you can make.

The position at the blackjack table closest to the dealer's right is often called *third base*. The third baseman is the last player to make a play decision before the dealer completes her hand. He'll often get slack from other players for having done something "wrong" if the dealer ends up hitting to a winning hand.

BASIC STRATEGY TABLES

The basic strategy tables in this section are adapted from several sources, including Ken Smith's website www.blackjackinfo.com. There are many sources available on the Internet and in various books, but given the same set of rules and the same number of decks, there shouldn't be any variations from one source to another. Any set of basic strategy plays should be based upon the plays that will result in the player's winning the most or losing the least for a particular set of circumstances.

Tables 2.1 and 2.2 show the proper basic strategy for shoe games of four, six, and eight decks, S17 and H17, respectively. (For a reminder of the various rule abbreviations, see "Rules and Rule Variations" on page 17.) Tables 2.3 (S17) and 2.4 (H17) are for single-deck games, and Tables 2.5 (S17) and 2.6 (H17) are for double-deck games.

If you are not sure which games you will be playing, Table 2.1 is the one to learn. It is as close to a one-size-fits-all type of strategy as you will find. If, on a rare occasion, you happen to run across a three-, five-, or seven-deck game, use the strategy for four or more decks. Of course, if you know which game you will be playing most often, be sure to memorize that table first. If you are going to a casino or a vacation spot where you will likely play a variety of games, bring this book with you and take the time to study the tables before heading down to the casino floor.

Let's assume that you are playing a game commonly found in American casinos—a six-deck game with S17 and DAS. Using Table 2.1, determine the proper play for a hard 16 against a dealer's upcard of 10. Find the section of the table labeled "Hard Hand Totals," and look for "16" in the row for "Player's Hand." Follow the row across until you are under the column labeled "10" representing the dealer's upcard. You will see the letter H, which means you should hit your hand. (A legend is included below every table.)

In some cases, you will see two choices. For instance, look at Table 2.3, and you will see "D/H" for certain plays. This means double down if you can; otherwise, hit the hand. Using a player's hand total of 9 as an example, you will see that the table instructs you to either double or hit if the dealer's upcard is 2, 3, 4, 5, or 6. However, if you are playing in a game that is D10—that is, a game that allows a player to double only on a two-card total of 10 or 11—then the doubling option is not available, so you would hit. You would also have to hit a card total of 9 if your hand consisted of more than two cards (except in the rare cases when doubling on three cards is permitted). So, when the table offers more than one choice, take the first choice if permitted; if not, go with the second choice.

With the exceptions above duly noted, the plays in these tables are for any number of cards that a player has in his hand. For example, still referring to Table 2.1, suppose you have an initial two-card total of 8 and the dealer's upcard is 9. The table would have you hit your 8. Suppose you hit it and draw a 5, for a new hand total of 13. The table would still have you hit the hand. Now, you take another hit and receive a 3, for a total of 16 in your hand. According to the table, you still need to hit the hand.

These tables may look formidable, but they can be memorized with practice and time. There are some suggested methods of learning these strategies later in this chapter.

When Player's Hand Is	When Dealer's Upcard Is									
	2	3	4	5	6	7	8	9	10	Ace
Hard Hand Totals										
8	H	H	H	H	H	H	H	H	H	H
9	H	D	D	D	D	H	H	H	H	H
10	D	D	D	D	D	D	D	D	H	H
11	D	D	D	D	D	D	D	D	D	H
12	H	H	S	S	S	H	H	H	H	H
13	S	S	S	S	S	H	H	H	H	H
14	S	S	S	S	S	H	H	H	H	H
15	S	S	S	S	S	H	H	H	H	H
16	S	S	S	S	S	H	H	H	H	H
17	S	S	S	S	S	S	S	S	S	S
Soft Hand Totals										
A-2	H	H	H	D/H	D/H	H	H	H	H	H
A-3	H	H	H	D/H	D/H	H	H	H	H	H
A-4	H	H	D/H	D/H	D/H	H	H	H	H	H
A-5	H	H	D/H	D/H	D/H	H	H	H	H	H
A-6	H	D/H	D/H	D/H	D/H	H	H	H	H	H
A-7	S	D/S	D/S	D/S	D/S	S	S	H	H	H
A-8	S	S	S	S	S	S	S	S	S	S
A-9	S	S	S	S	S	S	S	S	S	S
Pairs										
2-2	SP/H	SP/H	SP	SP	SP	SP	H	H	H	H
3-3	SP/H	SP/H	SP	SP	SP	SP	H	H	H	H
4-4	H	H	H	SP/H	SP/H	H	H	H	H	H
5-5	D	D	D	D	D	D	D	D	H	H
6-6	SP/H	SP	SP	SP	SP	H	H	H	H	H
7-7	SP	SP	SP	SP	SP	SP	H	H	H	H
8-8	SP	SP	SP	SP	SP	SP	SP	SP	SP	SP
9-9	SP	SP	SP	SP	SP	S	SP	SP	S	S
10-10	S	S	S	S	S	S	S	S	S	S
A-A	SP	SP	SP	SP	SP	SP	SP	SP	SP	SP

Table 2.1
Basic Strategy for Shoe Games, S17 (4, 6, and 8 decks)

H – Hit.   **S** – Stand.   **D/H** – Double down if permitted; otherwise, hit.   **SP** – Split.
D/S – Double down if permitted; otherwise, stand.   **SP/H** – Split if DAS; otherwise, hit.

Table 2.2
**Basic Strategy for
Shoe Games, H17
(4, 6, and 8 decks)**

When Player's Hand Is	When Dealer's Upcard Is									
	2	3	4	5	6	7	8	9	10	Ace
Hard Hand Totals										
8	H	H	H	H	H	H	H	H	H	H
9	H	D	D	D	D	H	H	H	H	H
10	D	D	D	D	D	D	D	D	H	H
11	D	D	D	D	D	D	D	D	D	D
12	H	H	S	S	S	H	H	H	H	H
13	S	S	S	S	S	H	H	H	H	H
14	S	S	S	S	S	H	H	H	H	H
15	S	S	S	S	S	H	H	H	H	H
16	S	S	S	S	S	H	H	H	H	H
17	S	S	S	S	S	S	S	S	S	S
Soft Hand Totals										
A-2	H	H	H	D/H	D/H	H	H	H	H	H
A-3	H	H	H	D/H	D/H	H	H	H	H	H
A-4	H	H	D/H	D/H	D/H	H	H	H	H	H
A-5	H	H	D/H	D/H	D/H	H	H	H	H	H
A-6	H	D/H	D/H	D/H	D/H	H	H	H	H	H
A-7	D/S	D/S	D/S	D/S	D/S	S	S	H	H	H
A-8	S	S	S	S	D/S	S	S	S	S	S
A-9	S	S	S	S	S	S	S	S	S	S
Pairs										
2-2	SP/H	SP/H	SP	SP	SP	SP	H	H	H	H
3-3	SP/H	SP/H	SP	SP	SP	SP	H	H	H	H
4-4	H	H	H	SP/H	SP/H	H	H	H	H	H
5-5	D	D	D	D	D	D	D	D	H	H
6-6	SP/H	SP	SP	SP	SP	H	H	H	H	H
7-7	SP	SP	SP	SP	SP	SP	H	H	H	H
8-8	SP	SP	SP	SP	SP	SP	SP	SP	SP	SP
9-9	SP	SP	SP	SP	SP	S	SP	SP	S	S
10-10	S	S	S	S	S	S	S	S	S	S
A-A	SP	SP	SP	SP	SP	SP	SP	SP	SP	SP

H – Hit.   **S** – Stand.   **D/H** – Double down if permitted; otherwise, hit.   **SP** – Split.
D/S – Double down if permitted; otherwise, stand.   **SP/H** – Split if DAS; otherwise, hit.

When Player's Hand Is	When Dealer's Upcard Is									
	2	3	4	5	6	7	8	9	10	Ace
Hard Hand Totals										
8	H	H	H	D/H	D/H	H	H	H	H	H
9	D/H	D/H	D/H	D/H	D/H	H	H	H	H	H
10	D/H	D/H	D/H	D/H	D/H	D/H	D/H	D/H	H	H
11	D/H	D/H	D/H	D/H	D/H	D/H	D/H	D/H	D/H	D/H
12	H	H	S	S	S	H	H	H	H	H
13	S	S	S	S	S	H	H	H	H	H
14	S	S	S	S	S	H	H	H	H	H
15	S	S	S	S	S	H	H	H	H	H
16	S	S	S	S	S	H	H	H	H	H
17	S	S	S	S	S	S	S	S	S	S
Soft Hand Totals										
A-2	H	H	D/H	D/H	D/H	H	H	H	H	H
A-3	H	H	D/H	D/H	D/H	H	H	H	H	H
A-4	H	H	D/H	D/H	D/H	H	H	H	H	H
A-5	H	H	D/H	D/H	D/H	H	H	H	H	H
A-6	D/H	D/H	D/H	D/H	D/H	H	H	H	H	H
A-7	S	D/S	D/S	D/S	D/S	S	S	H	H	S
A-8	S	S	S	S	D/S	S	S	S	S	S
A-9	S	S	S	S	S	S	S	S	S	S
Pairs										
2-2	SP/H	SP	SP	SP	SP	SP	H	H	H	H
3-3	SP/H	SP/H	SP	SP	SP	SP	SP/H	H	H	H
4-4	H	H	SP/H	SP/D	SP/D	H	H	H	H	H
5-5	D	D	D	D	D	D	D	D	H	H
6-6	SP	SP	SP	SP	SP	SP/H	H	H	H	H
7-7	SP	SP	SP	SP	SP	SP	SP/H	H	S	H
8-8	SP	SP	SP	SP	SP	SP	SP	SP	SP	SP
9-9	SP	SP	SP	SP	SP	S	SP	SP	S	S
10-10	S	S	S	S	S	S	S	S	S	S
A-A	SP	SP	SP	SP	SP	SP	SP	SP	SP	SP

Table 2.3
Basic Strategy for Single-Deck Games, S17

H – Hit.   **S** – Stand.   **D/H** – Double down if permitted; otherwise, hit.   **SP** – Split.
D/S – Double down if permitted; otherwise, stand.   **SP/H** – Split if DAS; otherwise, hit.

Table 2.4
Basic Strategy for Single-Deck Games, H17

When Player's Hand Is	When Dealer's Upcard Is									
	2	3	4	5	6	7	8	9	10	Ace
Hard Hand Totals										
8	H	H	H	D/H	D/H	H	H	H	H	H
9	D/H	D/H	D/H	D/H	D/H	H	H	H	H	H
10	D/H	D/H	D/H	D/H	D/H	D/H	D/H	D/H	H	H
11	D/H	D/H	D/H	D/H	D/H	D/H	D/H	D/H	D/H	D/H
12	H	H	S	S	S	H	H	H	H	H
13	S	S	S	S	S	H	H	H	H	H
14	S	S	S	S	S	H	H	H	H	H
15	S	S	S	S	S	H	H	H	H	H
16	S	S	S	S	S	H	H	H	H	H
17	S	S	S	S	S	S	S	S	S	S
Soft Hand Totals										
A-2	H	H	D/H	D/H	D/H	H	H	H	H	H
A-3	H	H	D/H	D/H	D/H	H	H	H	H	H
A-4	H	H	D/H	D/H	D/H	H	H	H	H	H
A-5	H	H	D/H	D/H	D/H	H	H	H	H	H
A-6	D/H	D/H	D/H	D/H	D/H	H	H	H	H	H
A-7	S	D/S	D/S	D/S	D/S	S	S	H	H	H
A-8	S	S	S	S	D/S	S	S	S	S	S
A-9	S	S	S	S	S	S	S	S	S	S
Pairs										
2-2	SP/H	SP	SP	SP	SP	SP	H	H	H	H
3-3	SP/H	SP/H	SP	SP	SP	SP	SP/H	H	H	H
4-4	H	H	SP/H	SP/D	SP/D	H	H	H	H	H
5-5	D	D	D	D	D	D	D	D	H	H
6-6	SP	SP	SP	SP	SP	SP/H	H	H	H	H
7-7	SP	SP	SP	SP	SP	SP	SP/H	H	S	H
8-8	SP	SP	SP	SP	SP	SP	SP	SP	SP	SP
9-9	SP	SP	SP	SP	SP	S	SP	SP	S	S
10-10	S	S	S	S	S	S	S	S	S	S
A-A	SP	SP	SP	SP	SP	SP	SP	SP	SP	SP

H – Hit.   **S** – Stand.   **D/H** – Double down if permitted; otherwise, hit.   **SP** – Split.
D/S – Double down if permitted; otherwise, stand.   **SP/H** – Split if DAS; otherwise, hit.

When Player's Hand Is	When Dealer's Upcard Is									
	2	3	4	5	6	7	8	9	10	Ace
Hard Hand Totals										
8	H	H	H	H	H	H	H	H	H	H
9	D/H	D/H	D/H	D/H	D/H	H	H	H	H	H
10	D/H	D/H	D/H	D/H	D/H	D/H	D/H	D/H	H	H
11	D/H	D/H	D/H	D/H	D/H	D/H	D/H	D/H	D/H	D/H
12	H	H	S	S	S	H	H	H	H	H
13	S	S	S	S	S	H	H	H	H	H
14	S	S	S	S	S	H	H	H	H	H
15	S	S	S	S	S	H	H	H	H	H
16	S	S	S	S	S	H	H	H	H	H
17	S	S	S	S	S	S	S	S	S	S
Soft Hand Totals										
A-2	H	H	H	D/H	D/H	H	H	H	H	H
A-3	H	H	H	D/H	D/H	H	H	H	H	H
A-4	H	H	D/H	D/H	D/H	H	H	H	H	H
A-5	H	H	D/H	D/H	D/H	H	H	H	H	H
A-6	H	D/H	D/H	D/H	D/H	H	H	H	H	H
A-7	S	D/S	D/S	D/S	D/S	S	S	H	H	H
A-8	S	S	S	S	S	S	S	S	S	S
A-9	S	S	S	S	S	S	S	S	S	S
Pairs										
2-2	SP/H	SP/H	SP	SP	SP	SP	H	H	H	H
3-3	SP/H	SP/H	SP	SP	SP	SP	H	H	H	H
4-4	H	H	H	SP/H	SP/H	H	H	H	H	H
5-5	D	D	D	D	D	D	D	D	H	H
6-6	SP	SP	SP	SP	SP	SP/H	H	H	H	H
7-7	SP	SP	SP	SP	SP	SP	SP/H	H	S	H
8-8	SP	SP	SP	SP	SP	SP	SP	SP	SP	SP
9-9	SP	SP	SP	SP	SP	S	SP	SP	S	S
10-10	S	S	S	S	S	S	S	S	S	S
A-A	SP	SP	SP	SP	SP	SP	SP	SP	SP	SP

Table 2.5
Basic Strategy for Double-Deck Games, S17

H – Hit.   **S** – Stand.   **D/H** – Double down if permitted; otherwise, hit.   **SP** – Split.
D/S – Double down if permitted; otherwise, stand.   **SP/H** – Split if DAS; otherwise, hit.

Table 2.6
**Basic Strategy
for Double-Deck
Games, H17**

When Player's Hand Is	When Dealer's Upcard Is									
	2	3	4	5	6	7	8	9	10	Ace
Hard Hand Totals										
8	H	H	H	H	H	H	H	H	H	H
9	D/H	D/H	D/H	D/H	D/H	H	H	H	H	H
10	D/H	D/H	D/H	D/H	D/H	D/H	D/H	D/H	H	H
11	D/H	D/H	D/H	D/H	D/H	D/H	D/H	D/H	D/H	D/H
12	H	H	S	S	S	H	H	H	H	H
13	S	S	S	S	S	H	H	H	H	H
14	S	S	S	S	S	H	H	H	H	H
15	S	S	S	S	S	H	H	H	H	H
16	S	S	S	S	S	H	H	H	H	H
17	S	S	S	S	S	S	S	S	S	S
Soft Hand Totals										
A-2	H	H	H	D/H	D/H	H	H	H	H	H
A-3	H	H	D/H	D/H	D/H	H	H	H	H	H
A-4	H	H	D/H	D/H	D/H	H	H	H	H	H
A-5	H	H	D/H	D/H	D/H	H	H	H	H	H
A-6	H	D/H	D/H	D/H	D/H	H	H	H	H	H
A-7	D/S	D/S	D/S	D/S	D/S	S	S	H	H	H
A-8	S	S	S	S	D/S	S	S	S	S	S
A-9	S	S	S	S	S	S	S	S	S	S
Pairs										
2-2	SP/H	SP/H	SP	SP	SP	SP	H	H	H	H
3-3	SP/H	SP/H	SP	SP	SP	SP	H	H	H	H
4-4	H	H	H	SP/H	SP/H	H	H	H	H	H
5-5	D	D	D	D	D	D	D	D	H	H
6-6	SP	SP	SP	SP	SP	SP/H	H	H	H	H
7-7	SP	SP	SP	SP	SP	SP	SP/H	H	S	H
8-8	SP	SP	SP	SP	SP	SP	SP	SP	SP	SP
9-9	SP	SP	SP	SP	SP	S	SP	SP	S	S
10-10	S	S	S	S	S	S	S	S	S	S
A-A	SP	SP	SP	SP	SP	SP	SP	SP	SP	SP

H – Hit.   **S** – Stand.   **D/H** – Double down if permitted; otherwise, hit.   **SP** – Split.
D/S – Double down if permitted; otherwise, stand.   **SP/H** – Split if DAS; otherwise, hit.

BASIC STRATEGY FOR EARLY OR LATE SURRENDER

Tables 2.7 and 2.8 show the basic strategy for early surrender and late surrender, respectively. (See "Rules and Rule Variations" on page 17 for a discussion on surrender.) As mentioned earlier, the option for early surrender is almost nonexistent. It's included here simply because it's available in some blackjack machines and because there's a chance it could be offered as a special promotion. However, for practical purposes, concentrate on learning the strategy for late surrender.

Surrender when...	
Player's Hand Is	and Dealer's Upcard Is
Hard 17	Ace
Hard 16	9, 10, or Ace
Hard 14, 15	10 or Ace
Hard 12, 13	Ace
Pair of 8s*	10 or Ace

**Table 2.7
Early
Surrender
Strategy**

*If the game includes DAS, surrender the 8s if three or more decks are used; otherwise, split the 8s.

Surrender when...	
Player's Hand Is	and Dealer's Upcard Is
7-7	10 (in any single-deck game)
	Ace (in a single-deck game with H17)
8-7	10 (in an eight-deck game)
	Ace (in a four-deck game or more with H17)
9-6 or 10-5	10 (in any game)
	Ace (in any game with H17)
8-8	Ace (in any game with H17 and *no* DAS of two or more decks)
9-7	9 (in any game of three or more decks)
	10 (in any game)
	Ace (in any H17 game)
	Ace (in any S17 game of two or more decks)
10-6	9 (in any game of four or more decks)
	10 or Ace (in any game)
9-8	Ace (in any H17 game of two or more decks)
10-7	Ace (in any H17 game)

**Table 2.8
Late
Surrender
Strategy**

Basic Strategy Variations for European No-Hole Card (ENHC)

In the ENHC version of blackjack, discussed on page 23, the dealer wins all additional bets when she has blackjack. For this reason, take heed of the following:

- Do not double down on any hand if the dealer's upcard is a 10 or Ace.
- Do not split Aces if the dealer's upcard is an Ace.
- Do not split 8s if the dealer's upcard is a 10 or Ace.
- If you can surrender, surrender a pair of 8s to a dealer's 10 or Ace.

INSIGHT INTO SOME BASIC STRATEGY PLAYS

Much of basic strategy is self-intuitive: It makes sense to hit hands totaling less than 12 and to stand on hands totaling 18 or more. However, many basic strategy plays don't make immediate sense. The following discussions will help fortify your newly gained knowledge and keep you confident that you're making the best plays despite the sneers of so-called table experts. Any percentages noted in the following sections are based on a single-deck game, but the strategy holds true for any number of decks or set of rules mentioned in this book, unless otherwise specified. All of the plays described below are listed in the tables, so there's no need to memorize any of this information.

Stand on All Hard 17s or Greater

Using a single-deck game as our example, and assuming the player has a 10-7, a dealer showing a 10 has a 59.2 percent chance that she will have a 17 or better. She is going to beat your hand outright 53 percent of the time. Why doesn't it make sense to hit that 17 instead of standing on it? Because hitting that hand will automatically bust you 67.3 percent of the time, and it won't matter what the dealer's hole card is. If you have a three- or four-card total of 17 (which would be made up of many low cards), the dealer's odds of beating you have improved. This is because your chances of receiving another low card have decreased due to the presence of many low cards. A total of 17 is a lousy hand and that is why you will often hear it referred to (with apologies) as the "mother-in-law" hand. You want to hit it, but you can't.

Stand on Stiffs Against a Dealer's 4, 5, or 6

Any hard hand total of 12 through 16 is referred to as a *stiff hand*. It is a hand that is likely to bust if it is hit. If the dealer's upcard is a 4, 5, or 6, there's an excellent chance she's holding a stiff hand. If the dealer's upcard is 4 and no 10s are showing, the dealer will have a stiff nearly 49 percent of the time. With an upcard of 5 or a 6, she will be stiff more than 50 percent of the time. It is better to let the dealer bust and stand even on a hard 12 than to take the same chance of busting yourself. Note, however, that if the dealer's upcard is a 2 or a 3, hit your 12 (see "Hit a 12 Against a Dealer's 2 or 3" below).

If the dealer's upcard is a 4, 5, or 6, there's an excellent chance she's holding a stiff hand.

Hit a 12 Against a Dealer's 2 or 3

The standard litany heard at the tables that "a deuce is the dealer's ace" often seems true. The dealer's upcard is a 2 and she somehow manages to pull a miracle 21 out of the deck by getting a 10-9 or some combination of low cards totaling 21. Since the dealer must hit to a total of 17 or greater, this is a relatively common occurrence. Sometimes, it occurs so often that it seems like some hanky-panky's going on. There isn't. It's just the odds. In a single-deck game in which the dealer's upcard is a 2 and her hole card is a 10, there are four 9s that will give her 21 and four 8s that will give her 20. If her hole card isn't a 10, there are twelve possible hole cards (7s, 8s, and 9s) that will give her a hand total of 9, 10, or 11, which are all excellent hands to hit. The same logic works for a dealer's upcard of 3. Therefore, standing on that 12 of yours will only increase the dealer's chances of winning, so hit it.

Always Split 8s

Many players and dealers swear that it is foolhardy to split 8s against a dealer's 9, 10, or Ace. Their thinking is *why turn one lousy hand into two lousy hands*? The short answer is that you will lose less money. A card total of 16 is the worst hand to have to hit, but hitting an 8 is tolerable. If you can win one hand and lose one hand after the split, winding up with a push, you are ahead of the game. And if you pull an Ace, 2, or 3 on the split 8s, you can turn a very bad hand into two very good hands. There are rare exceptions to this in games with the surrender option, as noted in Tables 2.7 and 2.8 on page 41.

Hit Soft 17s

This is a hand you should take advantage of whenever you can. Some folks treat a soft 17 (Ace-6) just like a hard 17 (10-7) and stand on it. However, if the dealer's upcard is a 2, 3, 4, 5, or 6, a player should take advantage of the favorable doubling opportunity it presents because of the increased probability that the dealer will bust. In a single-deck game, there are fifteen cards that will improve the hand and sixteen 10s that will make it no worse. So hit that baby . . . hard.

What to Do With Soft 20s, 19s, and 18s

A soft 20 (Ace-9) is a good hand to stand on. There's no reason to hit it in any game. In a single-deck game and a double-deck H17 game, double down on a soft 19 (Ace-8) against a dealer's 6 to increase your win, since the dealer is more likely to bust with an upcard of a 6 than with any other upcard. However, stand on a soft 19 in shoe games, since the dealer's chances of busting decrease with more decks in play. You won't miss much if you choose not to double down on a soft 19 in any game.

Don't double down on a soft 18 (Ace-7) against a dealer's 2, because the dealer has many chances to improve her hand. Doubling down on that soft 18 rather than just hitting your hand against a dealer's 3, 4, 5, or 6 will slightly improve the expected value of that hand.

Don't Split 9s Against a Dealer's 7

According to basic strategy, you should split 9s against a dealer's 2, 3, 4, 5, 6, 8, or 9, but not against a dealer's 7. The reason for this is quite simple. There is an excellent chance that the dealer has a 17 or a stiff hand (12 through 16) and your pair of 9s (18) will stand up quite well against either.

The reason for splitting 9s against a dealer's 9 is that your 18 is not a strong hand against a dealer's 9. By splitting and hitting each hand, you have a shot at getting a 19 or a soft 20 on one or both hands.

Don't Split 5s or 10s

When it comes to a pair of 5s or 10s, the table litany that asks why break up a winning hand finally applies. Clearly a pair of 10s (20) is a very strong hand and a pair of 5s (10) is a very good beginning.

You will still encounter players who split 10s, but as the familiar saying goes, "only idiots and card counters split 10s." Idiots do it because they don't know any better, and card counters do it because they have identified a situation in which splitting 10s gives them the advantage. If you aren't counting cards, don't do it.

Not splitting 5s should be a no-brainer, but there is at least one so-called gambling expert who recommends splitting 5s against a dealer's 5 or 6. If you take this advice, you will be passing up a good opportunity to double down on a strong hand. Moreover, you'll be exchanging your 10 for two hands that are very likely to result in a pair of stiff hands when hit. Also, many of the cards you would need for another good opportunity to double down on one or both of those split hands—that is 5s and 6s—are already in play.

When to Split 4s

Whether or not to split 4s requires special consideration. In a game without DAS, 4s should not be split. If you cannot double after splits, a starting hand of 8 is better than two starting hands of 4. This is because the player has as high as a 57 percent chance (depending on the dealer's upcard) of receiving a card that will give him a stiff hand. If the dealer has a 7 or greater showing, he will have to hit again, possibly resulting in a busted hand.

In a game with DAS, however, *do* split a pair of 4s against a dealer's 4, 5, or 6—the dealer's weakest upcards. If your hit card on either or both of those hands is an Ace, 5, 6, or 7, you have a good opportunity to double down against the dealer's weak upcard.

When to Splits Other Pairs

In a game with DAS, 2s and 3s are split against a dealer's upcard of 2 through 7. The reason is threefold: first, when you hit 2s or 3s, you have a good chance of getting a hit card that will provide you with the

Why Break Up a Winning Pair?

If you aren't counting cards, *never* split 5s or 10s.

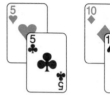

opportunity to double down; second, with an upcard of 2 through 7, there's a greater chance the dealer will get a stiff hand; and third, a pair of 2s or a pair of 3s makes a poor starting hand. Splitting 6s and 7s against a dealer's potential stiff follows the same logic.

You may wonder why it is okay to split 6s but not 5s. As explained earlier, a pair of 5s gives you a good starting hand of 10, while a pair of 6s gives you a terrible starting hand of 12. It is better to give yourself another shot at getting a better hand, especially against a dealer's likely stiff.

Double-Down Hands

One reason blackjack is such a close game against the house is because it provides a player with opportunities to increase his bet when he has the advantage.

When doubling down, there are slight differences between single-deck games and multiple-deck games. For instance, in a single-deck game, you would double down on a 9 against a dealer's 2, but you would not do this in a multiple-deck game. Since your card total of 9 would naturally be made up of low cards (2-7; 3-6; or 5-4), you would have a good chance of receiving a higher-valued hit card such as an 8, 9, 10, or Ace and a smaller chance of getting another low card, which would result in a stiff hand. By the same token, the dealer would have a greater chance of having a 10 as a hole card, for a stiff-hand total of 12, which she will have to hit again. The effects of removing these low cards from the deck are much greater in a single-deck game than in a multiple-deck game, because the more cards there are in play, the more diluted these effects become.

Also, in a single-deck game, you would double down on an 11 against a dealer's upcard of an Ace since your chance of receiving a 10-valued card as a hit card is significantly greater than it would be in a multiple-deck game. In this case, you would already know that the dealer doesn't have a 10-valued card as a hole card since she checks her hand for blackjack when her upcard is an Ace. Again, these chances are greatly diluted in multiple-deck games.

The same reasoning holds true in the case of a card total of 8 against a dealer's upcard of 5 or 6 in a single-deck game. The effects of removal of the cards that make up a player's hand of 8 (2-6; 3-5; 4-4), along with the 5 or 6 in the dealer's hand are enough to make this the proper play in single-deck games, but not enough to justify doubling in multiple-deck games.

Never Take Insurance or Even Money

No matter what advice you hear, basic strategy players should *never* take insurance, which is offered by the dealer when her upcard is an Ace. (Like splitting 10s, this is a play that card counters make because they have been keeping track of all the cards played.) The bet has nothing to do with "insuring" your hand against a dealer's possible blackjack. If you take insurance, you are simply making a side bet that the dealer has a 10 under her Ace. The dealer will have a 10-valued card under her Ace 31.37 percent of the time *off the top*—that is, in the first round of play. If your hand or the hands of other players include 10-valued cards, then the chances of the dealer's having a 10-valued card as a hole card are even lower. By making this bet, all you're doing is setting yourself up for less of a payoff and therefore a greater loss.

Dealer's Hand

"Insurance?"

"No, thank you!"

As explained earlier, even money is the same thing as insurance. It's simply a shortcut that avoids having to go through the motions of making the insurance bet. Still, many players take even money, and many dealers advise players to take it. It's a bad bet. You are not only giving the house superior odds on the bet, but you are also giving up the likely 3:2 payoff on your own blackjack.

To clarify this, let's assume a player who has blackjack has $10 in the betting square, and the dealer's upcard is an Ace. If he were to go through the motions of taking insurance, he would place $5 in the insurance area on the table. Then, the dealer would check for blackjack. If she had it, she would pay the player $10 for his insurance bet and would declare a push on the hand. If she doesn't have it, however, the player would lose the $5 insurance bet and would win the hand at a 3:2 payoff for the blackjack. (Either way, he comes out ahead by only $10.) To cut out all these steps, a player with blackjack simply tells the dealer he wants even money. He'll receive that same $10 profit whether or not the dealer has blackjack. And if she doesn't, he has lost out on the favorable 3:2 payoff.

When to Surrender

Late or early surrender gives you an opportunity to lose less money on lousy hands. When you use it, dealers and players alike will often chastise you. Don't let them deter you from making the right play. I have heard comments like "I came here to gamble, not to surrender."

Late or early surrender gives you an opportunity to lose less money on lousy hands. Not opting to surrender at the proper times when it is offered is a form of surrender in and of itself.

Or "The casino wouldn't offer that bet if it didn't have the advantage." While you may well have come to the table to gamble, you didn't come to give up more money than you should. Not taking surrender at the proper times when it is offered is a form of surrender in and of itself. You are surrendering more money to the casino. While it is true that casinos want to take as much of your cash as they can, it is also true that they are in a very competitive business. They offer this advantageous rule as an incentive for you to play at their house rather than at the one across the street. You should exploit it if you can.

Of course, it is also true that the casino will make more money from players who use the surrender option when it isn't the optimal play. The strategy for surrender shown in Tables 2.7 and 2.8 on page 41 has been computed to give players the best return on their bets. In the case of this rule, it is obviously a negative return, but it is less so than playing out the hand.

Basic Strategy Misconceptions

Let's clear up some misconceptions about basic strategy. First of all, many people think basic strategy is based on the assumption that the dealer's hole card is a 10. Many of the basic strategy plays certainly seem like that assumption is being made, but if that were the underlying reason, it would make sense to hit a hard 17 if the dealer's upcard were an 8 or higher. It wouldn't make sense to double down on an 11 against a dealer's 10, and it wouldn't make sense to split 8s against a dealer's 9 or 10. In all of these examples, assuming the dealer's hole card is a 10-valued card, the dealer's hand would be too strong for the recommended basic strategy plays.

There are also many who believe that a player can gain an advantage over the house with the use of basic strategy alone. This is not usually the case. This would be true in a single-deck game with S17 and DAS, but such a game is virtually nonexistent. With proper game selection and the exploitation of comps, as explained in the next chapter, a player can gain an overall advantage. Unfortunately, he cannot do it just by playing perfect basic strategy.

There are even some people who think that basic strategy is merely an invention used to sell books and software. Nothing could be further from the truth. From the beginning, basic strategy has been the product of rigid mathematical analysis, developed by serious mathematicians and scientists with the use of computers. Basic strategy tells us the very best way to play any given hand. If it is a strong hand for the player, basic strategy will allow the player to make the maximum amount of money on the hand. If the player is saddled with a weak hand, the use of proper basic strategy will allow the player to lose the least amount of money on the hand.

LEARNING TO MAKE THE CORRECT
BASIC STRATEGY PLAYS

There are quite a few good computer programs available to help you remember all the basic strategy plays. Most of them offer a wide variety of game conditions and rules. These programs generally include various exercises on the proper use of basic strategy and often prompt the player on which play to make or inform the player if he has made a mistake. Playing virtual blackjack is a great way to practice the game before you play at a casino. If you'd like to learn on your computer, I highly recommend the program Casino Vérité Blackjack. But I learned basic strategy without the use of computers, and you can too.

Simply get a deck of cards and practice the game on your kitchen table. You will be dealing for both the dealer and yourself. It's not necessary to practice with more than one deck even if you're trying to memorize the strategy for multiple-deck games. The idea here is to learn the strategy for the hand you deal yourself against the dealer's upcard by referring to the table you wish to memorize.

I concentrated on learning basic strategy on hard-hand totals first, then on pairs, and finally on soft-hand totals. If you find learning what to do with a specific hand troublesome, deal yourself that hand. Keep that hand in front of you and turn up a card for the dealer's upcard. Then, refer to the table you wish to memorize to determine the proper play. Then, keeping that same hand in front of you, turn up a new card for the dealer. Refer to the table once again. Continue turning up a new card for the dealer until you've exhausted the deck. Once you've done this a few times, you should find that the proper play for that hand is seared in your memory.

If you know which game you will be playing most often, learn that strategy first. If you are unsure, begin with the strategy in Table 2.1 on page 35. Even if you encounter other games, this strategy is widely accepted as a "generic" strategy and will work well for most games. While it is true that you will give up a slight amount by using a generic strategy over a specific strategy, the amount you lose is negligible. You will find that once you have the generic strategy down cold, learning the changes for specific games usually isn't too difficult.

Some people learn basic strategy plays by using flash cards. Although this is not my preferred method of learning, it might be

> If you know which game you will be playing most often, learn that strategy first. If you are unsure, begin with the strategy in Table 2.1.

yours. Make a set of flash cards by using index cards with the player's hand and dealer's upcard on one side and the proper play on the other.

I used to carry around the basic strategy charts and would study them whenever the opportunity presented itself. Even now, many years after memorizing basic strategy plays, I take a notebook with me that contains the proper strategy for just about any game that exists. I usually take a few moments to review these strategies before I visit a casino that might have rule variations I'm not as familiar with.

At the end of this book, you'll find a perforated generic basic strategy card that you can tear out of the book and slip into your pocket for quick reference. You'll recognize this card as Table 2.1 on page 35, which will work well in a pinch if you don't know the specific strategy for a particular game.

CONCLUSION

Once you have thoroughly reviewed and learned the material in this chapter, you should be a good basic strategy player. You will be well grounded in the proper way to play the game of blackjack as it is offered in the casinos. By using the strategies included here, you will be able to extract the maximum value of the game that can be had, short of using more advanced methods such as card counting. You will not come out ahead, however. The next chapter shows you how to play basic strategy and take advantage of the casino freebies. This is what can put you ahead of the game.

COMPS, GAME SELECTION, AND MONEY MANAGEMENT

Getting the most out of your casino experience requires knowledge and planning. A player should know how comps (casino "freebies") are calculated and what he needs to do to get them. He should know what level of betting and amount of playing time are required to get the comps he wants and who in the casino can give him what he wants. He should then develop a plan that will maximize his level of comps and minimize his level of losses. Such a plan includes proper casino and game selection and good money management. This chapter provides the basic strategy player with everything he needs to know to make his experience enjoyable and profitable—or at least not such a drain on his bankroll.

PLAYING THE COMP GAME

Basic strategy alone is not enough to beat the casinos in terms of cold, hard cash. In the long run, a basic strategy player will generally lose a little more than he wins. The best way to make up for that loss is by learning to play the "comp game" with the casinos.

Most casinos offer their players *comps*, short for *complimentary gifts*, in return for time spent gambling in their houses. Comps can run the gamut from free drinks, meals, rooms, gifts, and show tickets to cash rebates or coupons to reimburse airfare and even trips to the Super Bowl or to an exotic resort. It all depends on how much you bet and how long you play.

If you register at the players club, the casino will keep track of your play. The pit boss will record the amount of your buy in, your betting level, and how long you play. This information will be used to evaluate your value to the casino as a player, and you can take advantage of it to gain valuable comps from the casino. Generally speaking, the comps you earn are kept in an "account" for you, and you can use them during a future visit if you don't use them up in a single stay at a casino.

How Comps Are Calculated

Most casinos offer their players *comps*, short for *complimentary gifts*, in return for time spent gambling in their houses. Comps can run the gamut from free drinks, meals, rooms, gifts, and show tickets to cash rebates on airfare and even trips to an exotic resort.

The level of comps a player can get depends primarily on the player's average bet and how much time he spends at the tables. Many casinos assume that they have a 2 percent advantage over the average blackjack player and return about 40 percent of their expected win over a player in the form of comps. Many of them also assume that the average blackjack game consists of about 60 hands per hour per player. Although some studies have shown that the average is actually about 100 hands per hour, the 60-hands-per-hour assumption gives the casinos an edge in computing comps. Many casinos use the following formula to figure a player's comps: *Hours played × 60 × average bet × 2 percent × 40 percent.*

Using this formula, a player who puts in four hours at the tables with an average bet of $10 will get about $19.20 worth of comps—that is, 4 (hours played) × 60 (hands per hour) × $10 (average bet) × 2% (house advantage) × 40% = $19.20. If that player is playing a game with a 0.5 percent house advantage at the more accurate average of 100 hands per hour, he is trading $20 in losses (that is, 4 hours played × 100 × $10 × 0.5 percent) for $19.20 in comps. That translates into a loss of a mere eighty cents. You'll learn how a wise player can earn more in comps than he loses at the tables.

It is difficult for a table games player to accurately track his comp credits. Although the above formula is widely used, there is usually no way to know if the casino actually uses this formula or if it uses some variation of it. Most casinos will not come right out and tell you how they calculate comps. The casino will not prepare a handy statement that tells you how much you have coming to you in comps. The best way to find out what kind of comps you have coming to you is to ask a table games host.

Comps and the Players Club

Virtually every casino in the United States has some sort of players club. Although these clubs can go by a variety of names, they serve the same general purpose—to entice players to frequent their casinos by offering rewards and promotions. Sometimes, they are called *slot clubs* or they may go by a theme name such as *Champions Club* or *Emperors Club*.

If you are visiting a casino for the first time or if you are not a member of the players club at your regular casino, stop by the players club booth to see what promotions are taking place. Usually, the players club will be in a prominent location on or near the casino floor. If you are not sure where it is located, ask any casino employee, who will direct you to its location.

It's almost always worthwhile to join the club wherever you play. You might get free meals, free show tickets, or even free money just for joining the club. You will also be placed on the casino's mailing list. Once you have established yourself as a player, you are likely to receive valuable offers through the mail, including free rooms and cash coupons in addition to other comps.

Your player's card might look something like this.

As a member of the club, you will receive a card that resembles a credit card. Some casinos use separate cards for table players and slot-machine players. Check with the pit boss or the players club to find out if a special table player's card is required.

When you sit down to play and are ready to buy in, present your card to the pit boss if she is standing near your table or comes over to your table as you settle in. She'll need to record the amount of your buy in, whether you present the card or not. If the pit boss isn't in the immediate area, you can ask the dealer to give the card to the pit boss or simply put it on the table in clear view. The dealer will place it at the rear edge of the table for the pit boss to see when she comes by.

The pit boss will track your initial buy in and any subsequent buy in and the length of time you play. She'll stop by the table occasionally to record the size of your bets. She'll also take note of the amount of chips you take with you when you leave the table. This information is often recorded on a card kept at the table for each player. Some casinos use a card-scanning device that scans the barcode on your players card and will enter your information into a computer to track your play. Even more sophisticated methods of tracking play and the size of bets are being developed. (See "Advanced Tracking Methods" below.)

Comps and the Table Games Host

A table games host is a casino executive whose primary job is to keep the players happy so they'll come back to the casino to play again and again. The table games host usually makes the final call for comps that go beyond a free meal at the buffet or the coffee shop.

When dealing with the table games host, don't worry about being perceived as pushy or too forward. It is the host's job to cultivate players for the casino, and she will be happy to talk to you.

It is a good idea to ask to speak to a table games host when you join a players club. Introduce yourself to the host and get her business card. Tell her that you're a blackjack player and you would like to know what levels of play are expected to get various comps. This information will be useful to you in determining where you want to play as you develop your long-term gambling plans.

Casinos usually have a number of table games hosts, and there is normally at least one host on duty. Become familiar with the host or hosts who are on duty during the hours you normally play. Although

Advanced Tracking Methods

With electronics shrinking in size, it is now possible to implant scanning devices in playing cards and casino chips. Some casinos are already experimenting with chips fitted with radio-frequency identification (RFID) tags. Not only is the use of these chips useful for weeding out counterfeit chips and catching those who use them, but they can also be used to record the size of players' bets. Use of these chips should not negatively affect the players.

However, a new technology called MindPlay has been added to the casinos' arsenal. Mind-Play uses special blackjack tables that can read the denomination of the chips being bet and can also read specially marked cards and tell the dealer what cards have been dealt and which cards remain. In fact, they can specifically identify the next card waiting to come out of the shoe. The potential for casino cheating with the use of this device is very high, and it is surprising that the Gaming Control Board in Nevada has permitted its use at all. With the information gained, the dealer could prematurely shuffle anytime it appears that the remaining cards are favorable to the players. It removes the randomness from the game and should not be allowed. I strongly recommend that you avoid MindPlay tables.

you can cultivate a relationship with more than one host, it's generally best to deal with one. Developing a relationship with a specific host may make the difference in getting a comp if you are on the cusp. Once you get to know that host, you can decide for yourself if that host is doing all she can for you. If you don't think she is, find another one.

If you have never dealt with a table games host, you might want to call ahead to several casinos in the location you wish to visit and speak with a host to find out who is offering the best deal. Let the host know when you will be visiting, the length of your visit, what games you expect to play, and your betting level. Sometimes, you may be offered a comp up front with the hope that your play will justify the comp, or perhaps you'll receive a casino rate—a rate below retail—for your room.

The way you will be received by a host is based on what kind of action you plan to give the casino. If you call ahead and tell a host that you are a $10 bettor, it is likely that you will get a polite brushoff, but you still might manage to get a casino rate for your room. If you tell the host you are a $100 bettor, your reception is likely to be much warmer. Either way, you have nothing to lose but your time and the cost of your phone calls. It is likely that you will have put yourself a few lengths ahead of the starting block just by making these calls. If a host has offered you a comp, such as a free meal or show tickets, contact her when you arrive at the casino to let her know you're there.

> The way you will be received by a host is based on what kind of action you plan to give the casino.

Standards for Comps

You will quickly learn that different casinos have vastly different standards for comps. For example, a room, food, and beverage (RFB) comp will be much more difficult to get at an upscale casino on the Vegas strip than at a smaller downtown casino. Getting a comp on a Midwestern riverboat often requires higher levels of play than what would be required at a Mississippi casino.

The value of comps is partly a direct result of the extent of the competition in the area. If the nearest competitor is fifty miles away, it is less likely that you will get the same kind of comps you can get when the nearest competitor is next door or across the street. Therefore, *where* you play can make a big difference in the comps you receive. You might want to stay at a top-of-the-line casino and enjoy the luxurious rooms and the ambiance offered in those places. You might not be so choosy and find a middle-of-the-road casino that will give you a clean room and decent meals. If all you want is a place to flop, then any low-roller's joint might do. You may find that the level of play needed just to get free meals at the Bellagio would get you the full RFB treatment at the Lady Luck in downtown Las Vegas.

When you play is also an important factor. Comp levels are not static. They often depend on the season and the amount of business a casino is getting at any given time. You can usually get better deals Sunday through Thursday than you can get on the weekends, and non-holiday weekends are often better when it comes to earning comps than holiday weekends. If there is a major event going on in the area—a heavyweight championship fight, for example—comps will be more difficult to get, if not impossible, for low-to-medium players. The week between Christmas and New Year's Eve is a tough time for comps, while the weeks between Thanksgiving and Christmas are an excellent time to get good deals. In Las Vegas, the very hot months of July and August are good times to get the most out of comps and take advantage of special promotions.

Making the Most of Your Comp Dollars

The value of the comps you can get often depends on the season and the amount of business a casino is getting at any given time. For example, in Las Vegas, the very hot months of July and August are good times to get the most out of comps and take advantage of special promotions.

The comps a casino has promised you in advance can often be improved upon when you arrive at the casino. Suppose you've booked yourself into a medium-rollers casino on the Las Vegas strip. You like the location and the casino, but the only thing the host offered you was a casino rate for your room. One way to increase your comp dollar is to get meal comps from the pit boss. After you have been playing blackjack for a half hour or so, ask the pit boss for a meal comp when she comes around to your table. She'll usually give you give a free meal or two that may not be deducted from your comp account. This may not sound like much, but when you're on vacation, free meals for two can go a long way toward stretching your vacation budget. In most casino venues, a meal for one person usually costs at least $10. Three meals a day translates into at least $30 per day. If you receive meal comps for two for all three meals, that translates into a savings of at least $60.

Suppose you are putting in four hours of play a day at your host casino, and you want to apply the comps you earn there to your room bill. You can save up your comp dollars at your host casino by putting in some play at nearby casinos that have liberal meal-comping policies. There are many casinos, such as those in Nevada and Mississippi, that will give you a free meal comp for two for a minimal amount of play. At some casinos, it isn't at all hard for a $5 bettor to get a free meal at the buffet or coffee shop. Some casinos will even give you a meal comp when you buy in at the table, but you have to ask.

Another way to save comp dollars is to use any casino coupons you received in the mail or pick up at check-in. These coupons may be for free meals, free rooms, free show tickets, and even cash. Also, ask your players club for a "funbook." Many casinos offer these promotional booklets, which contain all sorts of worthwhile coupons. (See "Coupon-omy" in Chapter 5 for information on the use and value of coupons.)

As a gesture of goodwill, table games hosts will often make concessions for players whose levels of play don't qualify them for a full comp on a room if they are viewed as potential return customers or as players who may give them more valuable play in the future. So, when the end of your stay at the casino nears—the evening before you leave, for example—contact your host to see if she can reduce your room bill. Don't wait until checkout time to make this request, since the host may not be available when you're ready to leave. More often than not you will find that she is willing to do something on your behalf. She may reduce your room rate or discount items or meals you may have purchased and charged to your room.

Surplus Comp Credits

If you find that you have a surplus of comp credits after getting the basics, such as a room and meals, you might want to use the excess credits by making purchases in the casino gift shops. You can pick up items for your own personal use or to be used as gifts. If you have a large excess of comp credits, you might even want to consider making purchases for resale to others. Anything you purchase with comp credits is yours to do with as you please, but any cash you make on resale is something you should mention to your accountant.

CHOOSING THE BEST GAME CONDITIONS

The casino you choose to play at might offer a variety of blackjack

More for Less

How to get comps is just one part of the comping equation. How to get the most comps for the least amount of play is another key to winning the comp game. This strategy involves the games you play and the way you play them.

games, including a single-deck table, a few double-deck tables, some shoe games, and games that use either automatic shufflers or continuous-shuffling machines. The expectation might be different for each one of these games. However, your wisest choice may not be the game with the most favorable expectation. Read on to learn more.

Make Game Speed Your Primary Consideration

The number of hands played per hour is essential to your comp game. If you are a basic strategy player playing for comps, speed is your enemy. You'll want to choose the games with the fewest number of rounds per hour. (As you'll learn in Part Two, card counters will want to choose the quickest games.)

As a basic strategy player, you have a negative expectation for each hand—that is, the chance that you will lose a hand is greater than the chance that you will win a hand. So, the law of large numbers dictates that the more hands you play, the more you will lose. If you reduce the number of hands you play per hour, you'll lose less money. But you'll often receive the same comp credit you would receive if you were playing in a faster game.

In general, games in which the cards are dealt face down and are held by the players are slower than games in which the cards are dealt face up and are handled only by the dealer. Hand-held, hand-shuffled, single-deck games are typically the slowest-moving games. Hand-held, hand-shuffled, double-deck games are a little quicker but are usually slower than games dealt from a shoe. Games that use automatic shufflers are generally faster than shoe games. And games that use continuous-shuffling machines are the fastest. (Avoid tables with continuous-shuffling machines since they will increase your hourly loss rates rather significantly.)

Stanford Wong performed a study of game speed, which he discusses in his book *Professional Blackjack*. He discovered that a single player at a six-deck shoe game averaged 248 rounds per hour. He even found some select dealers who could deal as many as 500 rounds per hour to a single player in a hand-shuffled game. If you factor out the hand shuffling and figure in an automatic shuffler, the number of rounds would increase significantly. Automatic shufflers eliminate shuffle time, which means more rounds per hour. In games that use continuous-shuffling machines, the time it takes to exchange the cards is also eliminated. This translates into even more hands per hour.

On the other end of the spectrum, Wong found that in a six-player single-deck game that deals only one round between shuffles, the average game speed was 48 rounds per hour. However, a single-deck game with only one player with six rounds between shuffles yielded an average of 173 rounds per hour.

The games you play will usually fall somewhere between these extremes. The trick is to find a game closer to the lower end of the scale. With a little observation and scouting—along with your own tactics to slow down a game (discussed later)—you may even beat the speed of 48 rounds per hour.

The difference in the number of hands you play per hour can be dramatic, despite the house advantage. Suppose you have a choice between a heads-up single-deck game—that is, a game between just you and the dealer—that offers the rules H17 and RSA (with an off-the-top house advantage of a mere 0.158 percent) and a six-deck game with the rules S17, DAS, RSA, and LS (with an off-the-top house advantage of 0.309 percent). The six-deck game is crowded, with five players already sitting at the table.

If you are a $10 bettor, you will have an expected loss of $2.63 per hour at the heads-up single-deck game where you play 167 hands per hour. If you play at the crowded six-deck table, with a game speed of 56 hands per hour, you will have an expected loss of $1.73 per hour. That is a 52 percent difference in your rate of loss. In other words, you'll lose less at the crowded game, even though the single-deck game offers a better expectation per hand. Meanwhile, the casino will usually apply the same formula for calculating comps no matter which table you are sitting at.

As you can see, crowded tables are far better than tables with only one or two players. Not only is the game slower because more hands per round are being dealt, the social interaction that occurs at crowded tables also slows down the game. Keep in mind too that the dealer at the table also sets the game pace. (See "The Dealer—Speed Demon or Break-In" on page 60 for some things to be on the lookout for when choosing which table to play at.)

The Dealer—Speed Demon or Break-In?

Dealers operate at different speeds. Stop and observe a dealer for a few moments before choosing to sit down at her table. Avoid dealers who are lightning fast. Choose a table with a dealer who is slow and deliberate in her movements. Chatty dealers are good. Break-in dealers—dealers in training—are best of all. They are usually slow and tend to make mistakes on the outcome of hands or the proper payoff for bets. If you are watchful, you can bring the mistakes in the house's favor to the dealer's attention, and slow down the game even more. You may choose to stay quiet about the mistakes in your favor, however.

If you encounter a speedy dealer and have other reasons to stay at the table, slow her down. Take a couple of extra seconds to make your play decisions. Each time she deals herself an Ace and offers you insurance, act like you are thinking about accepting it. You might even accept it once so that the dealer thinks you might really make this play and will pause a few extra moments when she deals herself an Ace and offers insurance.

Some speedy "know-it-all" dealers might assume they know your next play and not wait for your signals before dealing you another card or not. Don't let a dealer do this. Stop her and remind her that you are playing the cards, not her. It's your money on the table, not the dealer's. The dealer is paid to deal the cards, but it is your game. Take control of the game you are paying to play and don't let the dealer rush you by allowing her to make decisions for you.

Develop Slowing Tactics

Take a few moments to check out the blackjack games in play. Look for crowded tables and slow dealers. If all the tables are crowded, count the hands being dealt and time them. You don't have to do this for more than a few minutes, but it is time well spent.

Once you have chosen a game that seems to be moving at a slow pace, you can slow it down even more. Start by buying in for a relatively small amount of money, say five times your planned bet. In other words, if you're going to be making $10 bets, start with a buy in of $50. The dealer will call out the amount of your buy in and will wait for the pit boss to acknowledge it. The pit boss will make her way to your table and take your player's card. If it takes more than fifteen minutes for the pit boss to get there, make sure you mention that you've been there for a while so you get the maximum credit for your time. Once you are sure you have the pit boss tracking your play, buy in for a larger amount after a few rounds. Use small bills, like fives or tens rather than large ones so that the dealer must spend time separating the bills and counting them out. This may frustrate some of the other players, but they'll get over it.

Strike up a conversation with the dealer or join in on the other players' conversations. If no one is talking, strike up a conversation of your own. For instance, ask the other players about their hometowns, what they do for a living, and if they have any children.

You don't have to be the life of the party at the table if it is not your thing. But you can be a good listener. You can be gracious and friendly with as little as a smile and a nod. Being a good listener can slow down the game just as much as being a good talker. When you do listen to the other player or dealer, stop your own play until the person is finished talking.

Some people recommend doing things like spilling drinks or other obnoxious behaviors to slow down the game. However, if you get too obnoxious or too clumsy, you may drive the other players away from the table and you don't want to do that. As you now know, more players equal a slower game. Being a good table companion—by smiling often, laughing at jokes, and paying rapt attention to your tablemates—can pay off by keeping them at your table or returning to your table during another session. Also, if you have proven yourself to be a friendly person whose presence is welcomed by other players, dealers, and the pit boss, the close decisions when figuring comps are much more likely to go in your favor.

Take your time making playing decisions. Ask the dealer and the other players for advice. Of course, it doesn't matter what they say; you aren't really looking for advice. You just want to slow down the play of the game. Also, be sure to order a drink—a nonalcoholic drink—whenever the cocktail waitress comes by. (Drinks, alcoholic or otherwise, are free at many casinos.)

Another slowing tactic is to take frequent bathroom breaks while the cards are in play. Many people wait until the shuffle break to visit the restrooms. You don't have to do that. Wait until right after the shuffle but before the next round is dealt and then take your break. The dealer will save your spot and watch your chips for you—be sure to mention that you'll be right back. You can drastically reduce the number of hands you play per hour with this simple tactic. One ten-minute break per hour while the cards are in play in a crowded shoe game can

It Pays to Be Friendly

If you've proven yourself to be a friendly person whose presence is welcomed by other players, dealers, and the pit crew, the close decisions when figuring comps are much more likely to go in your favor.

reduce the number of hands you play per hour by about ten. If the cards are in play when you return from your break, wait until the next shuffle before resuming play—tell the dealer you don't want to interrupt the flow of the game by resuming play until then. Most players will actually consider this a courtesy.

You can also determine when it's a good time to take a bathroom break by paying attention to the cards. If you've seen an excess of 10-valued cards and Aces come out in previous rounds, it would be a good time to take that break. After a surplus of high cards has been dealt, it is likely that the house advantage has grown. You don't have to be a card counter to recognize this. By making this simple observation during your play, you can time your breaks to coincide with moments when the casino has a greater than normal advantage. This translates into a smaller loss for you in the long run.

In most casinos, players can sit out hands without leaving the table and then reenter the game when ready. In order to sit out a hand, remove your bet from the betting square. The dealer may ask you if you wish to play the next hand. If she does, just say no. Very few casinos have strict "no-midshoe entry" rules, which do not permit players to reenter a game or join a game until the next shuffle. But even that rule would help slow your game down. It is not recommended that you make a habit of sitting out hands because doing so too often may upset the other players at your table and may even lead the pit boss into suspecting that you are a card counter. Doing it on occasion, however, shouldn't create a problem.

You don't have to be a card counter to recognize that after a surplus of high cards has been dealt, it is likely that the house advantage has grown.

Play Games With Poor Penetration

Look for tables with poor penetration. *Penetration* is how far into the deck, pack, or card shoe the dealer goes before shuffling. Card counters want to play games that are deeply penetrated because they can track more cards and increase their bets in advantage situations. Comp players want just the opposite. Poorly penetrated games reduce the rounds played per hour because there are more frequent breaks for shuffling. Many casinos offer games with poor penetration to discourage card counters. As a comp player, you can take advantage of this.

To determine penetration in shoe games, look for the placement of the *cut card* in the card shoe. The *cut card*, or *shuffle card* as it is sometimes called, is a plastic card the dealer inserts into the stack of cards to indicate when it's time to shuffle. The color of the cut cards can vary from one casino to another, but will usually be a different color from the deck. In some casinos, dealers place the cut card halfway through the card shoe. In a six-deck shoe game, dealers are usually required to place the cut card at about the four-deck level.

Cut cards are often used in double-deck games and in some single-deck games, but this practice varies from one casino to the next. Avoid double-deck and single-deck games that use cut cards for the reason mentioned under "Pitfall 1: The Cut-Card Effect" on page 82 in Chapter 4.

In many double-deck games, the dealer deals the equivalent of one deck before the shuffle. In single-deck games, the most commonly seen penetration is the *rule of six*. According to this rule, one player gets five rounds of play, two players get four rounds, three players get three rounds, and so on. In other words, the number of players plus the number of rounds always adds up to six. If you can find single-deck games that deal to the rule of six or less (and you will), you will have found a game that can be easily exploited for comps.

> **The Rule of Six**
>
> In single-deck games, the most commonly seen penetration is the *rule of six*. According to this rule, the number of players plus the number of rounds always adds up to six.

Avoid Preferential Shuffling

Suppose you sit down at a good double-deck game. The dealer is dealing out about 60 percent of the cards before shuffling. Suddenly, one of the players puts out a larger than usual bet. The dealer then prematurely shuffles before dealing the next round. You are probably witnessing a *preferential shuffle*. The dealer believes the player who suddenly raised his bet is counting cards and assumes that the advantage has shifted from the house to the players. By shuffling the cards, she has taken that advantage away from the players, including you, and brought it back to the casino. If this is done consistently, it means you are playing more often at a greater disadvantage than expected.

Sometimes, dealers count the cards themselves and will prematurely shuffle the cards even if a player hasn't raised a bet. If this is happening, it is very likely that you are playing only in situations in which you have a disadvantage.

If you are at a table where the cards are not shuffled at a consistent point in the pack, leave the table. Preferential shuffling is just a legal form of cheating that casinos use to foil card counters. It not only affects the counters at the table, but also negatively impacts every other player. You will be better off in the long run if you avoid dealers and casinos that engage in this nefarious practice.

Be Aware of Changing Game Conditions

When game conditions change, be willing to switch tables or leave the table for a while. For example, the full table that you began at might lose some of its players, which as you've learned is to your disadvantage. If there are crowded tables in the casino, switch over to one of them. Or maybe the slow and deliberate dealer you've been playing against has been replaced by a speed demon. If the speed demon is a break dealer—that is, she's just substituting while your preferred dealer takes a break—this might be a good time for you to take a break, too. If it looks like she will be at your table for a while, scout out a slower table. If there are no suitable games at the moment, take a break and come back later when it's more crowded. Don't let yourself be lulled into playing when the conditions aren't optimal for your style of play.

Choosing Wisely—A Review

Here's a summary of the important points discussed above:

- Game speed is more important than the off-the-top expectation of a particular game.
- Crowded single- and double-deck games should be your first choice.
- Crowded shoe games are better than empty or nearly empty hand-held games.
- Avoid tables that have automatic shufflers whenever possible, and *never* play at tables with continuous-shuffling machines.
- Buy in with small bills, and do it frequently.
- Play slowly and deliberately. Take your time when making play decisions.
- Join in the conversation at the table or start your own. Take the time to listen to other players.

- Take frequent breaks. Don't take your break at the shuffle, but after play has started. Be observant and take breaks after you have seen an excess of high cards. When you return to the table, wait until the next shuffle before resuming play.

- Take the time to order nonalcoholic drinks from the cocktail waitress.

- Choose games with poor penetration.

- Leave the table if you suspect a preferential shuffle is being used.

- Leave the table when conditions change that speed up the game.

MONEY MANAGEMENT FOR THE BASIC STRATEGY PLAYER

Money management has been a much-abused term in gambling literature over the years. In fact, it has been so abused that I hesitate to use the term in this book. However, for all the misuse and misapplication of the phrase, it is still the best way to describe how to handle a playing bankroll. The advice in this section is intended only for the recreational player who wants to play good basic strategy blackjack and make up his losses in comps. If you plan to give card counting a try, money management should be handled in an entirely different manner (see Chapter 7).

A good money management system helps you get the greatest return on your gambling dollars.

There are scores of books by self-professed experts that go into great detail about some fanciful betting system or other. Some advise players to increase their bets after losing a hand. Some advise them to increase their bets after winning a hand. Some go into long convoluted explanations about series of hands and try to convince their readers that raising or lowering their bets after some combination of wins or losses will result in winning play. There are authors who advise their readers to change tables after a certain series of losses or to look for "winning tables," by observing things like full ashtrays or the stacks of chips in front of the players at the tables. None of that nonsense changes the odds of the game.

In any honest blackjack game, the probability of winning a hand is about 44 percent, the probability of losing a hand is about 47 percent, and the probability of getting a push is about 9 percent. These percentages vary slightly depending on the specific rules and the basic strategy for a given game, but not by any significant amount. Changing the size of a bet, changing tables, or looking for "winning tables" will not and cannot change those numbers. The cards don't know and don't care what happened on the last hand. How much money gets put into the betting square doesn't change the odds. The fullness of the ashtrays has no effect on the game, nor does the size of the chip stack in front of any particular player tell you anything that is useful to know while playing the game.

Good money management does not involve "win goals" or "loss limits." It is not some form of progression or regression betting (see "Progression Betting Exposed" on page 67), and it has nothing to do with what happened on the last hand or series of hands. Good money management involves a plan of action that takes into account a player's *risk of ruin* (the percent chance a player will take of losing his entire bankroll) over a given period of time, what the player's bankroll is, and what the player hopes to achieve with his play.

A real money-management system for a non-counting blackjack player is one that gets the player the most bang for his gambling buck. It tells him how much money he needs to have on hand to sustain a reasonable risk of ruin over a given period of time or number of hands. You don't have to be a math genius to figure this out. With a little advance planning, it's easy to figure out how much money you need to sustain you for any gambling trip.

> Good money management involves a plan of action that takes into account a player's *risk of ruin* (the percent chance a player will take of losing his entire bankroll over a given period of time), what the player's bankroll is, and what the player hopes to achieve with his play.

Figuring Out How Much Money You Need

You are preparing for a trip to Las Vegas. You called ahead and found a casino where you'd like to play. You know what level of betting you'll need to maintain to get the comps you want. Now, you must figure out how much money you'll need and whether you can afford it.

While the expectation for different games is a good measure for determining the inherent value of a game, it is not very useful in determining how much money you may lose over a given number of hands played. As you'll soon learn, expectation alone doesn't tell you very much.

Suppose after some searching you have located a casino that offers a good single-deck game with a small house advantage of 0.19 percent.

Progression Betting Exposed

Some methods of progression betting—increasing the amount wagered in increments until a hand is won—may win a short series of rounds more often than they will lose. This gives the impression that the progression works, but disaster will strike. Players who use this method will eventually be left wondering how their chips suddenly found their way into the dealer's tray.

The Martingale progression is probably the oldest progression. It is quite simple and every gambler will eventually consider a "Martingale" on his own even if he hasn't read about it. It is simply doubling each bet after a loss until a hand is won. When the bettor reaches the winning hand, he will gain back what he has lost plus the amount of the original wager. For example, the player bets and loses $2. Next, he bets and loses $4. Then, he bets and loses $8. Finally, he bets and wins $16. His losses total $14—a difference in his favor of $2 (the original bet). Gambler's logic tells us that every losing streak must end sooner or later, and when it does, we will make a profit using this system.

Discounting pushes, a blackjack player has a 51.65 percent chance of losing a hand and a 48.35 percent chance of winning a hand. In the "endangered" deeply penetrated single-deck game, a series of losing hands will ever so slightly increase a player's expectation. But this is based on the likely composition of losing hands and not on the fact a hand was won or lost. This is due to the fact that players tend to lose hands when a lot of low cards are dealt, leaving more high cards in the deck, which increases the player's advantage. For all practical purposes, the slight gain that comes from a series of losing hands in such a game is irrelevant and the likelihood of winning or losing the next hand remains fairly constant.

With those winning and losing percentages, a losing streak of two hands is likely to occur 26.68 percent of the time. A three-hand losing streak will occur 13.78 percent of the time, and a four-hand losing streak will occur 7.12 percent of the time. If a person were to bet a five-step Martingale—doubling the bet five hands in a row—he would win that series 92.88 percent of the time. At first glance, it looks like the Martingale bettor has found the keys to the cashier's cage. A closer look reveals the weakness of this scheme.

A bettor who started with a $5 bet would win $5 every time he wins a series. If one were to study 100 such series, the player wins 92.88 series and loses 7.12. Rounding off, that is a win rate of 93 and a loss rate of 7. If we discount doubles, splits, and blackjacks, the player would win a total of $465 in 100 attempts of a five-step Martingale. Each series loss would amount to $155, discounting possible losses from splits and doubles. Seven of those losses amounts to $1,085. The player's net loss is $620. The gains from doubles, splits, and blackjacks cannot make up for that loss.

Progression advocates try to deny the basic math of the game. They will accuse those who rely on cold, hard mathematical logic of being unoriginal thinkers who can't think "outside the box." They will say that real-world conditions are not the same as those found in computer simulations and that such things as "winning tables" or "card clumping" (nonrandomized shuffles possibly producing advantageous clumps of cards) really exist and the secret to winning lies in being able to find such conditions. It is like saying that someone who believes 2 + 2 = 4 isn't taking the "real world" into account.

An honest deck has fifty-two cards in it. Those cards have a finite number of combinations that will add up to 21 or less. Cards that are left in play and cards that are taken out of play are what matters. Any system that does not rely on identifying those cards, where they are in the deck, and when the cards left in play swing the advantage over to the player is a bogus system based on false assumptions, no matter how sophisticated or "logical" it might sound.

The absolute truth about betting progressions is that they cannot possibly overcome the house advantage. No kind of betting scheme that is based on winning or losing the last hand or some series of hands can defeat the inherent negative expectation that exists in casino games.

With some very rare exceptions, casino blackjack games offer a negative expectation for even a perfect basic strategy player. In the long run, the player will lose the amount he bets times the percentage of negative expectation for the game. No betting progression ever devised can change that simple fact. If a betting progression requires a bettor to put more money in the betting square than he would if he were simply flat betting, he will lose more money.

You now know that you want to play a slow game and how to identify one. You plan a three-day visit and you will be playing four hours a day. You want to find conditions where you play no more than sixty hands per hour. The casino host you contacted has told you that four hours a day with an average bet of $50 will get you a room comp. You get out your trusty calculator and figure out that your expectation over twelve hours of play is a loss of $68.40 (average bet × hands played per hour × number of hours played × house advantage). A trip bankroll of a few hundred dollars ought to be plenty, right?

Wrong. Blackjack is, after all, a game of chance. Granted, it is a game where the odds favor the casino, but you can win a bundle in twelve hours of play and you can lose a bundle. The more you play, the closer to your expectation you will come, but there is no guarantee that you will play to expectation. In fact, the opposite is far more likely. You may exceed your expectation or you may not meet it.

In any relatively short period of play, chances are you will be far away from the statistical expectation, or expected value, of the game because the law of large numbers has not yet come into play. In reality, you will fall somewhere within the realm of *standard deviation* (SD), a statistical measure of the distribution of possible results. Standard deviation is found by squaring the *variance*—that is, the difference between what is expected and what actually occurs.

In his book *Professional Blackjack,* Stanford Wong writes, "One way to find variance is to subtract the expected value from each possible outcome, square those differences, multiply each square, in turn, by its probability of occurring, and sum. The sum is called the variance, and the square root of the variance is called the standard deviation." Wong's explanation may sound quite involved, but it is simply one way of saying that there is a very specific range of total losses to total wins within which you are likely to fall. Statistically speaking, in the game of blackjack, you have a 68.3 percent chance of falling within one standard deviation, a 95.4 percent chance of falling within two standard deviations, and a 99.7 percent chance of falling within three standard deviations based on a normal distribution curve, more familiarly known as the bell curve.

All casino games have an SD number, figured in the manner described by Wong. The SD number for blackjack is roughly 1.14 per hand.

To find one standard deviation, multiply the SD number by the square root of the total number of hands played. In the example above, you want to play twelve hours of blackjack at no more than sixty hands per hour. To find one SD, determine the square root of 12 × 60 and multiply it by the SD. Anybody who has a calculator with a square-root function can do it.

12 (hours) × 60 (hands played per hour) = 720

The square root of 720 is 26.83

26.83 × 1.14 (SD number for blackjack) = 30.59

You have found the standard deviation for the number of hands you will play: 30.59. Now, take this number and multiply it by the average bet of $50, for a figure of approximately $1,530. That is one SD for this particular set of circumstances. Now factor in the expectation for the game. In the example used, your expectation is a loss of $68.40 (average bet × hands played per hour × number of hours × house advantage). Add the negative expectation of $68.40 to the figure of $1,530 for a total loss of $1,598.40. Then, subtract the $68.40 from the SD figure of $1,530, to get a total win of $1,461.60. Now you know that 68.3

percent of the time, you will fall within the range of being down $1,598.40 to being up $1,461.60.

Keep in mind that there's a chance you will find yourself within the range of two SDs 95.4 percent of the time. To figure out the range for two SDs, add one SD (in this case, $1,530) to both figures and you will find that you may be down as much as $3,128.40 to up as much as $2,991.60. Figured the same way, three SDs will find you in the hole $4,658.40 to being $4,521.60 in the black—and there is a 99.7 percent chance this will occur. It is possible to be outside the range of three SDs, but the probability of that occurring is 0.3 percent.

Using the same formula, let's say you want to stay at a downtown Las Vegas casino for a week. You've been told that a casino rate for your room can be had for four hours of play with an average bet of $10. This casino offers a double-deck game with a casino advantage of 0.525 percent. If you plan to play all seven days, you will put in twenty-eight hours of play to get the good room rate. Using the advice in this book, you play an average of sixty hands per hour. You will play 1,680 hands and give the casino $16,800 worth of action. The expected loss for your game will be $88.20. The square root of 1,680 is 41. Multiply this by the standard deviation per hand of 1.14 and you will get 46.74. Multiply 46.74 by the average bet of $10 and you will get 467.40. Add this to the expected loss of 88.20 and subtract the expected loss from this figure. One SD for a $10 bettor will be minus $555.60 to plus $379.20. Two SDs will be minus $1,023 to plus $846.60. Three SDs will be minus $1,490.40 to plus $1,314.

Risk of Ruin

By now, you may be thinking that this game just takes too high a bankroll. How much of a bankroll it takes depends upon your willingness to take some risks and how much risk is acceptable to you. You have to determine what you consider an acceptable *risk of ruin*—that is, what chance you are willing to take that you will lose your entire bankroll.

In the first scenario above, as a $50 bettor, you would want to bring a bankroll of $4,700 with you in order to play it safe. In the second scenario, as a $10 bettor, you would need a bankroll of $1,500 for the same level of risk. But what if you are willing to accept a 10 percent chance of

Only you can determine what you consider an acceptable *risk of ruin*— the chance you are willing to take that you will lose your entire bankroll.

losing it all? How about a 20 percent chance? If you're a real daredevil, you might even be willing to accept a 50 percent chance!

What are the real chances of loss? Figured with the excellent computer program Blackjack Risk Manager 2002, a $50 bettor who plays twelve hours has a 5 percent chance of losing $3,045, a 10 percent chance of losing $2,555, and a 20 percent chance of losing $2,000. A $10 bettor who plays for twenty-eight hours has a 5 percent chance of losing $990, a 10 percent chance of losing $840, and a 20 percent chance of losing $665.

To figure out how much of a trip bankroll you need based on your willingness to accept a loss, look at Table 3.1 on page 72. The table assumes you will play four hours a day at sixty hands per hour for anywhere from one to seven days. It also assumes that the standard deviation is 1.14 per hand and that the rate of loss is 0.5 percent.

Instead of dollar amounts, the term *unit* is used to represent the player's bet to encompass all levels of betting. To figure out the dollar amount you need, simply multiply the number of units by the bet you intend to make. Suppose during your gambling trip, you will be playing a total of twelve hours, you will be making $10 bets, and you will only accept a 5 percent risk of ruin. Find the total hours you will be playing in the first column, then move across the table to the "5 Percent Risk of Ruin" column, and, at the intersection, you will see 63 units, or $630 (63 units × $10 bets).

Of course, these figures will vary in real games depending on the expectation for the game and the actual number of hands played per hour for the game. These figures are simply a guide for determining the approximate size of a trip bankroll based on an acceptable risk of ruin.

Although Table 3.1 allows for as much as a 50 percent risk of ruin, it is recommended that you play to a lower risk. There is a good chance that you will run out of money halfway through your trip and that could cause a problem with the comps you had planned to earn if you play at a 50 percent risk. If you do lose your bankroll, make sure your host is aware of your loss. Large losses can be the exception to the rule when it comes to calculating comps.

Improving the Numbers

You can improve on the numbers shown in Table 3.1 if you play only

Table 3.1 **Risk of Ruin Calculator for a Trip Bankroll**

Days/Hours Played	5 Percent Risk of Ruin	10 Percent Risk of Ruin	20 Percent Risk of Ruin	30 Percent Risk of Ruin	40 Percent Risk of Ruin	50 Percent Risk of Ruin
1/4	36 units	30 units	26 units	20 units	16 units	13 units
2/8	51 units	44 units	35 units	28 units	23 units	19 units
3/12	63 units	54 units	42 units	34 units	28 units	23 units
4/16	74 units	62 units	49 units	40 units	33 units	27 units
5/20	83 units	70 units	56 units	46 units	37 units	30 units
6/24	91 units	77 units	61 units	50 units	41 units	34 units
7/28	99 units	84 units	67 units	55 units	45 units	37 units

slow games and use the tactics discussed for slowing them down even more. It is possible to play only forty hands per hour with a little fore-thought and advance planning. You can get the same comps at the slower game and lose less money, which requires a smaller bankroll.

Another way to improve the numbers is by playing two hands instead of one. If you play two hands at 75 percent of your normal single-hand bet, you can increase your bet size in the eyes of the pit boss but keep your risk about the same. For example, if you regularly bet $10, you could make two bets of $7.50 each and the pit boss may credit your play the same way she would a $15 bettor. Note, however, that many casinos require a player to play twice the table minimum for each hand if he wishes to play two hands. In such instances, a player would have to play two hands of $20 each at a table with a $10 minimum. This may be more than your bankroll can stand. Make sure that you ask the dealer what the minimum bet is for two-handed play. If you are playing for small amounts, such as $5 or $10 per hand, this method may not be practical. However, if you are betting $25 or more per hand, you may want to find a lower limit table and play two hands using the 75 percent method.

With a bet that is capped with fifty cents (that is, $10.50 instead of $10, for instance), you can sometimes produce an extra gain because most casinos don't pay off bets with quarters. A blackjack with a $7.50 bet should pay $11.25. Chances are, however, you will get an extra twenty-five cents for a total payoff of $11.50 on this bet. True, it isn't much, but when you are playing in a game with a negative expectation, every little bit helps. (Be sure that the figure isn't rounded down to $11. If this is the casino's method, don't cap your bet with that extra fifty cents.) An added benefit of capping your bets with fifty cents is that it slows down the game since it'll take a little more time for the dealer to pay off a winning hand.

CONCLUSION

If you have paid close attention so far, it should be clear to you that playing basic strategy blackjack is no road to riches. In fact, in terms of pure money lost, it is a sure road to ruin. Playing the game as a basic strategy player is not a way to pay the bills and put food on the table. Given the unpredictability of standard deviation, it is entirely possible for a player to play many sessions of winning blackjack—but don't be fooled into thinking this style of play is profitable.

What it can be is a way to spend your entertainment dollars and get a lot of enjoyment in return. It can be a way to have low-cost vacations in world-class resorts that many folks could never afford if they paid retail rates.

The next chapter is designed to alert you to some of the mistakes players make and how to avoid them.

MISTAKES, PITFALLS, AND THE TRUTH ABOUT CASINO CHEATING

Gambling is full of mistakes and pitfalls, and blackjack is no exception. From overplaying your bankroll to ignoring basic strategy to succumbing to the free drinks and other casino traps, it's easy to make the wrong move. A player should have a definite plan before making a trip to a casino, and a wise player sticks to it. The more a player deviates from his chosen path, the more likely it is that he will wind up with no bankroll and nothing to show for it. If he stays with his plan, he can accomplish his goals and sometimes even exceed them.

This chapter explores some common errors players make while gambling, as well as the pitfalls that may await an unwary gambler in a casino. It also discusses the issue of casino cheating, and touches upon ways to recognize that you are being cheated.

COMMON MISTAKES

Even the best and most savvy blackjack players make mistakes, and you will probably be no exception. However, being aware of the following seven common mistakes can reduce your chances of making an error. To know them is to avoid them.

Recognize comps for what they are: a way for casinos to entice you to bet higher and play more just to get the satisfaction that comes from obtaining a "free" room, "free" food, and other "freebies."

Mistake 1. Overplaying Your Bankroll for Comps

Don't overplay your bankroll to get comps. With the information provided in the previous chapter, you can plan a comfortable level of play, what sort of comps you can get for that play, and the best way to maximize those comps. Recognize comps for what they are: a way for casinos to entice you to bet higher and play more just to get the satisfaction that comes from obtaining a "free" room, "free" food, and other "freebies." They are designed to feed the player's ego and make him believe that the casino thinks he's important. Treat comps as a business proposition and don't be fooled by the casino's VIP treatment. Your first concern should be what you can afford to bet. Once you have figured that part out, see what comps you can get for that level of play and take it from there. Don't put the comps in front of your bankroll; put them behind it.

Mistake 2. Betting More After a Sizeable Win

Don't desert your game plan and start betting higher because you are winning big at the moment. Players, dealers, and casino executives may tell you to press your bets while you are on a winning streak, that you're only betting the house's money so you have nothing to lose. But once the chips make the trip from the dealer's chip tray to your side of the table, it's no longer the house's money; it's yours. The first thing to keep in mind is that you don't know what kind of winning streak you are on until it is over. It can end with the very next hand or session, and it can end in disaster. If you are lucky and have a sizeable win at the end of a good trip or a good session, put it in the bank for your next trip. Don't bet over your head just because you have had a streak of luck.

Mistake 3. Betting More to Impress Someone

Let's say you've brought some friends with you to the casino. You've told them about your casino adventures, and they think you are a high-rolling gambler. They occasionally stop by the blackjack table to watch you play. Wanting to impress them, you find yourself edging up your bet size as they chat with you. Don't give in to the temptation to impress others by betting more than you should, or you may find yourself broke in the middle of your trip, and your friends won't be very impressed.

Mistake 4. Playing While Tired

Blackjack is a game of skill and no matter how good you become, you cannot play up to speed if you are tired or rundown.

This particular lesson finally came home to me one night at the Golden Nugget in Las Vegas. It had been a long flight, but my adrenaline was flowing, and I couldn't wait to get to the tables. I was at the tables moments after checking in. After playing for several hours, my body started winding down and the jetlag and lack of sleep started to kick in. My wife, being far more sensible than I am, had gone to bed hours earlier. But I had come to Vegas to play and that's what I intended to do.

The cards were becoming harder to see, but I was convinced I could keep playing with skill. Then, the dealer dealt me an Ace and a Deuce. My hit card was an 8; I had a soft 21. But I didn't see it. I took another hit and my soft 21 became a hard 17. I tucked the cards under my chips and waited for the hand to end. The dealer beat me with an 18.

When she flipped over the cards, my error was exposed. One player rudely pointed it out and suggested that maybe blackjack wasn't my game. At the moment, he was absolutely right. I tucked my tail between my legs and slunk away into the night for some much-needed rest.

Since then, I always make sure I'm well rested before playing. I usually retire to my room after checking in to take a brief nap, followed by a refreshing shower. The tables can wait. Most casinos are open twenty-four hours a day and the games are always there. Don't let your zeal to play overcome your common sense.

Mistake 5. Overtipping

Tipping, or *toking* as it is commonly called in the casinos, can be an expensive overhead. It can be so expensive that it negates whatever can be gained in comps, even at what looks like a conservative rate. Here are some examples:

Kathy's Story

An attractive woman named Kathy joined the players at my table and began making $25 bets. With each bet she made, she placed a $5 chip at

To Toke or Not to Toke?

It is customary for table games players to tip, or *toke*, the dealer, but it is not mandatory. Don't feel pressured into tipping or overtipping if it's not in your game plan.

the edge of the betting square right on the line. The dealer treated the big tipper with deference and respect. When she left the table, Kathy had made more than $300 in wins, but she still left the table a loser. She had put out about $500 in tokes.

Kathy tips were excessively large. We were playing a game that had a house advantage of 0.4 percent. Betting *quarters*—casino slang for $25 chips—Kathy could expect to lose $10 an hour in an average game. With her tips, she was losing $510 an hour. Her story sounds ridiculous, but I was there and saw it happen.

George's Story

My good buddy George engages everybody at the blackjack table in light-hearted conversation and loves the attention he gets from the dealers and the pit crew. His average bet is about $20. He puts out a $1 toke after every win to keep the dealer "on his side." George says that since he only tips after a win, he's tipping with the casino's money, not his own. He also orders a drink every time the cocktail waitress comes by and tips her a dollar when she brings it to him.

George is losing less than Kathy, but he is still paying the dealer far more than he pays any of his employees in his small business. In fact, if one of his employees demanded the same wage George gives the dealer, George would think he was nuts. On average, he is tipping the dealer about $44 an hour and is tipping the waitress another $4 to $5 an hour. He might have the dealer on his side, but the dealer doesn't control the cards, she just hands them out. George has increased his loss rate to five times more than it needs to be and he will never make it up in comps. In fact, with his rate of tipping, he could rent the best suite in the hotel.

Jerry's Story

Jerry believes his tips are quite conservative. His average bet is $5 and he leaves out a fifty-cent tip only after getting blackjack. He knows the dealers are often underpaid and that they rely on tips to make a living. He thinks he's just doing his small part to help them out. But conservative Jerry has doubled his loss rate with that small fifty-cent tip he leaves out after every blackjack. While he can't rent a suite with his tipping money, he is giving up the cost of a meal every day he plays, which is about all he can expect to get in comps at his level of play.

To tip or not to tip is a decision that each player must make for himself. It is not the player's responsibility to make up for the miserable pay that dealers often receive. That should be the casino's responsibility. Judicious toking can be a gracious way to show a dealer your appreciation for a pleasant experience. After all, you are playing for enjoyment, and dealers do make a difference in the casino experience. Although the pit bosses and hosts don't share in the tips earned by dealers or cocktail waitresses, when it comes to earning comps, it's a good thing to be known as a tipper.

I usually toke about 1 percent of my expected win, but I am a card counter who bets more than $5 a hand. I toke to reward the dealer for adding to my enjoyment of the game and because card counters have a reputation for not toking. If I am playing against a dealer who is surly, rude, or in a bad mood, that dealer will get no tokes from me. If I order a drink, I usually tip the cocktail waitress fifty cents. While that may sound cheap, those tokes add up and they cost me money.

I suggest that a basic strategy player who wants to tip only tip a small amount. What is small depends on your level of betting. If you are making $5 bets, put out a fifty-cent tip every hour or so. If you are making $25 bets, perhaps a dollar tip will do. If you are making $100 bets, you might want to toke $5 once or twice during a four-hour session. You may want to consider leaving a toke only if you have had a winning session. Put out a toke near the end of the session, or leave a small tip once you have colored up your chips.

If you choose not to tip at all, that is not a bad choice and don't let dealers hustle you into making tokes you don't want to make. Some dealers are experts at hustling tokes. Some of them may be downright rude about it. They may even imply that tokes can help a player win. This is nonsense, of course. An honest dealer has no control over the cards or your hand. Even a dishonest one isn't likely to possess the skill to cheat a player. Those who do possess such skills aren't going to cheat for a few tokes. If they are caught, they will lose their job and will never get another job in a casino. They might even go to jail.

"Color Me Up"

At the end of a playing session, you can take your chips with you when you leave the table. But if you have many low-denomination chips, you'll want to perform the transaction known as *coloring up*. Simply let the dealer know that you'd like to color up, and she'll exchange your stacks of low-denomination chips for fewer chips with a higher value.

Mistake 6. Chasing Losses

Here's a mistake you will frequently see if you play often enough. A player is in the middle of a bad losing streak and will try to regain what he's lost by increasing his bets. More often than not, he will only increase his losses rather significantly.

When you are in the middle of a bad session, your gut may start churning and you may even feel foolish. You'll certainly hate the idea of leaving the table with a large loss and will want to recoup your losses right away. You may find yourself jacking up your bet. If you do that, you will most likely lose even more and may feel like an even bigger fool when the session is over and your trip bankroll is either gone or reduced to the point where you can't play any longer. Worse yet, you might wind up making a visit to the nearest ATM and go even further into the hole.

Prepare yourself for these losing sessions and trips. They are inevitable and can no more be avoided than death and taxes. Stick with the game plan you have devised. If you have planned to play four hours a day, don't play another four hours trying to turn a loser into a winner. Don't overbet your bankroll chasing losses. While you will have losses, you will also have times when you win big. Keep your perspective and stay in control.

Mistake 7. Drinking Too Much

In Las Vegas and other casino locales, free booze is often made available to players. However, many Midwestern states do not allow this practice. In casinos that do offer free alcoholic drinks, efficient cocktail waitresses ply their trade at each table. While casinos claim this little comp is offered for the players' convenience, one wonders if they mind the benefit of having players whose judgment has been clouded by too much alcohol. I have seen players who were literally too drunk to get off their chairs keep playing, losing bet after bet without really knowing what they were doing.

Of course, free drinks while playing are part of the casino experience and many people enjoy this little comp. These drinks don't have to be alcoholic, however. You can get free soft drinks or bottled water. But if you do want to have an occasional alcoholic drink during play, that's

If you order drink after drink, the alcohol will affect your ability to make the correct plays.

George and the Elevator Tower

A good friend of mine loves the free drinks he gets at the casinos. He is a successful businessman who is usually rational and sober, but there is something about the casinos and the free drinks that causes him to sometimes lose control. I'll call this friend George.

George and his wife, Mary, had just arrived in Tunica, Mississippi, the home of several casinos. After checking in to their room, George headed for the blackjack pit and Mary went to play the slot machines. George ordered a stiff drink and settled in at the table. The cocktail waitress paid plenty of attention to the handsome businessman and made sure his glass was always full. At first, George was winning, so he started increasing his bets. But even after he began to lose, he kept the bet level high, much higher than it should have been.

By the time Mary went to find George at the tables, he had become pretty loud and obnoxious. Even the pit boss was relieved that someone had come to take George off his hands. Between Mary and the pit boss, they talked George into taking a break by bribing him with a free meal at the casino coffee shop.

After ordering their meals, Mary realized George was in no shape to eat. He needed to get to his room and sleep it off. Mary offered to take him to the room, but George insisted on going by himself so Mary could take advantage of the free meal. Since they were in a crowded, well-guarded casino, Mary let him have his way and watched as he stumbled off toward the elevators.

George made it to the elevators, but this particular casino had two elevator towers, and George, of course, got on the wrong one. After wandering around the unfamiliar halls, he got back on the elevator and slumped down in the corner. Finally, some riders notified security, and George was greeted by a couple of concerned security officers.

"Sir," said one of them, "do you know your room number?"

"I don't think so," mumbled George.

"Well, tell us your name and we'll help you find your room."

"My name? Jeez, what is my name?" George slurred, and scratched his head. "Oh, here it is," he slurred, pointing to the embroidered nametag on his company jacket.

Just then, the elevator arrived at the first floor and the doors opened. Fortunately, Mary had been waiting in the elevator lobby. She saw her husband with the security guards and promised the concerned fellows that she'd get him back to the room.

Upon arriving in the room, George pulled off his toupee and tossed it on top of the television, where it promptly slid off and fell on the floor, hidden behind the unit. Mary helped George into the bed, and then returned to the casino for some more play. When she returned to the room later that evening, George was still sound asleep.

The next morning, while Mary was taking a shower, she heard George shouting, "Mary! Mary! I've been robbed!" As he came crashing into the bathroom, he spied his bald head in the mirror. "Being robbed isn't the worst of it," he sobbed. "They stole my hair, too!"

Of course, George hadn't been robbed. He had lost nearly all of his trip money the night before while in a drunken stupor. Mary explained what had happened. George was understandably embarrassed and had learned a costly lesson about drinking while playing. Don't be like George. Keep your drinking under control.

fine. Just be aware that if you order drink after drink after drink, the alcohol will affect your ability to play correctly and cloud your judgment. (For an amusing example of what can happen, see "George and the Elevator Tower" on page 81.) If you want to take advantage of free drinks, it's a good idea to wait until your playing session is nearing an end to order an alcoholic beverage or two.

PITFALLS TO AVOID

Casinos can be likened to minefields. They are purposely designed to trap and entice gamblers into relieving themselves of their money. Many of these traps can be avoided simply by sticking to the game you know and planned to play. But there are some sneaky things casinos do to blackjack that can increase your losses. It pays to be wary while you are in a casino. If something sounds too good to be true, you can bet that it is. The casinos are also not above playing some smoke-and-mirror games. Here are a few of them.

Pitfall 1. The Cut-Card Effect

The cut-card effect has less impact on players who use one bet size than it does on players who vary the size of their bets based on the count.

If you are playing in a single-deck or double-deck game in which the dealer places the cut card in the deck or pack to signify when it is time to shuffle, you should be aware of what has been called the *cut-card effect*. This effect was first documented by David Heath at the Second Gambling Conference in Tahoe in 1973 and has been noted by card counters ever since.

Basically, if a fixed shuffle point is used in single-deck or double-deck games, the player gets fewer rounds if a lot of low cards surface and more rounds if a lot of high cards surface. The reason for this is simple. If low cards are put into play, it will take more cards to make each player's hand. If high cards are put into play, fewer cards will be needed. Thus, with more low cards in play, fewer rounds will be dealt to the fixed shuffle point and more rounds will be dealt if the higher cards are coming out. In a game where more high cards have been played, the last round is likely to be played at a greater disadvantage than normal for the player. In a game where many low cards have been put into play, a player will have been playing at a disadvantage during that time and will not be able to make it up if the high cards are still stuck behind the shuffle card. The player will get fewer blackjacks, with their 3:2 payoff, and the dealer will make more hands by drawing low cards to his stiffs.

The best thing to do when you see a shuffle card being used in single-deck and double-deck games is to not play the game. If it is the best game in the house, you can avoid some of this effect by paying attention to the number of rounds dealt before the shuffle card shows. If you are playing a single-deck game with one other player and the shuffle card is placed at the halfway point in the deck, you should be getting no more than five rounds before the shuffle card is due to show. If you have played five rounds and the shuffle card is not in view yet, sit out the next round. If there are three players, you shouldn't see more than four rounds before the shuffle card appears. Don't play the fifth round if it is offered. With a full table of five or six players and a shuffle card placed at the 50 percent level, more than two rounds of play is suspect. In double-deck games, you can effectively double these numbers at the 50 percent level.

You are more likely to see shuffle cards placed at the 60 to 70 percent level in double-deck games. If the card is placed at the 65 percent level, the shuffle card should be coming out during the twelfth round with one player, during the eighth round with two players, the sixth round with three players, the fifth round with four players, and the fourth round with five players. If you find that you are getting more rounds than you should get, sit out the last round of play.

You can figure out the various places to stop based on where the shuffle card is placed with other configurations. An average round of play uses 2.7 cards for each player and the dealer. In a double-deck game with a shuffle card placed at the 60 percent level, no more than twenty-three hands should be dealt. Divide that number by the number of players plus the dealer, and you should know the number of rounds you should see when the shuffle card appears. Do this in advance and commit the numbers to memory. It is worth the time spent if you feel you must play in a single-deck or double-deck game with a shuffle card. You will have avoided that fatal final round, and you will have had the advantage of playing when the high cards were coming out.

Avoid single-deck and double-deck games that use a shuffle card since this can have a negative effect on the player's advantage.

Pitfall 2. Games That Look Like Single-Deck or Double-Deck Games But Aren't

Some casinos engage in a deceptive practice that is tantamount to cheating. If it isn't cheating, it is certainly misrepresentation. They advertise "hand-held" or "pitch" blackjack games, and sure enough, you will see a dealer holding what looks like a single-deck or double-deck pack in her hands and dealing the cards. Take a closer look. What you will also see in this little charade is a shuffle machine that is holding a pack of cards. The dealer will take out a single deck's or a double deck's worth of cards and deal to the players. As these cards are depleted, she will put them into the shuffle machine. Then, she will take out another pack and deal to the players. This isn't a single-deck or a double-deck game. It is more likely a six-deck or eight-deck game in disguise.

Pitfall 3. Side Bets

In recent years, casinos have devised all sorts of side bets in an attempt to add to the excitement of the game and attract nontraditional players to the tables. I have yet to see a side bet that is worth making at the blackjack tables, besides the insurance bet for card counters. Don't make the side bets. They usually carry a huge house advantage. There is one advantage that can be gained for a basic strategy player trolling for comps at these tables. If you see a table with a side bet that is getting a lot of action from the players, you will be looking at a table with a very slow game. As long as you can avoid the temptation to make the side bet, take advantage of the reduced number of hands you will play and milk it for its extra comp value.

Pitfall 4. Games With Less Than a 3:2 Payoff on a Blackjack

A 2-*for*-1 payoff is just another way to say *even money*. Don't confuse it with a payoff of 2 *to* 1 (2:1), which pays two times the original bet.

This pitfall is most often seen in blackjack machines, but it has also found its way into live blackjack. In the machines, you will see a line that says blackjacks are paid 2 *for 1*. At first glance, it might seem to be a better deal than the usual 3:2 payoff. It isn't. This is just another way of saying you will get an even money payoff. You get the bet you made plus an equal amount on your win, which is exactly what you win on every other winning hand on the machine. 2 *for* 1 is not the same as 2 *to* 1 (2:1), which pays two times your original bet.

A number of casinos in Las Vegas are now offering single-deck games that pay 6:5 for a player's blackjack. This can be deceptive, since 6:5 may sound like more than 3:2. This game is one of the worst rip-offs in blackjack history and is strictly designed for suckers. A payoff at a rate of 6:5 means you get paid $6 for every $5 you bet. In the traditional game of blackjack with a 3:2 payoff, you would get $7.50 for each $5 bet. By playing a game that offers a 6:5 payoff, you are giving up 60 percent of the traditional blackjack bonus. Since a player can expect to receive a blackjack approximately once every twenty hands in a single-deck game, he is losing an additional $4.50 an hour in the sixty-hands-per-hour game. A $10 bettor is giving up $9 an hour to the casino and a $25 bettor is giving the casino $22.50 an hour to play this awful game.

One casino even advertised that it paid a "whopping 6:5" on black-jacks. Believe me, the ones getting "whopped" were the players, not the casino. The 6:5 payoff triples the house advantage over the player. Playing the worst eight-deck game in the casino with traditional rules and a 3:2 payoff on blackjacks is much better than playing this farce of a game.

Another practice that has found its way into some casinos is a single-deck game that is dealt all the way to the bottom. At first glance, this seems like a game that is as good as it can get. It isn't. There is a catch. This game only pays even money on a blackjack, turning it into a big loser for a basic strategy player. It adds an additional 2.3 percent to the casino advantage and puts blackjack into the realm of slot machines.

Blackjack games offered by charitable organizations usually pay only even money on blackjacks. Another disadvantage commonly found in charity games is that a player loses on all pushes. These games are to be avoided at all costs. If you want to make a donation to charity by playing this game, you need to understand that you are playing only for fun. Don't expect to go to a charity game and wind up a winner.

Play "charity" blackjack only if you want to donate your money to a worthy cause.

WHAT YOU SHOULD KNOW ABOUT CASINO CHEATING

Some players are convinced that casinos cheat them on a regular basis. They believe the dealers are stacking the cards—that is, arranging them in an order that is favorable to the house—or that there is someone who pulls a lever or pushes a button that affects the slot machines or roulette wheels. Every time they have a bad losing session, they will blame it on casino cheating. If these players really believe this, why are they bothering to set foot in a casino at all?

Cheating is rare in American casinos. If you think about it, there is really no need for the casinos to cheat. They have an inherent advantage over the average player in every game in the house. Why cheat and take a chance of killing the goose that lays the golden egg? If a casino were caught cheating, it could lose its gaming license. It just isn't worth it. Or so the litany goes.

Why Spoil a Good Thing?

There's really no need for casinos to cheat since they have an inherent advantage over the average player in every game in the house.

Most experts believe that cheating is a rare occurrence, but that doesn't mean it never happens. There are reasons for all those cameras in the ceilings of the casinos, just as there are reasons most gaming commissions require casinos to have someone in surveillance at all times. One of those reasons is to protect against cheaters. Cheaters come to both sides of the table. While it would be foolish for a casino to officially sanction a cheating dealer, that doesn't mean there aren't dealers out there who are foolish enough to cheat.

Dealers and pit bosses are under pressure from above to produce gains for the casino. Casinos obviously want to win as much and as often as possible. If a particular dealer or shift isn't producing as much in wins as the casino wants to see, the job security of those working can be affected. While it is unlikely for a casino to cheat to increase its bottom line, I am not so confident that there aren't dealers and pit bosses that either cheat or encourage cheating from time to time to relieve the pressure from above. I am also not so sure that there aren't some casino executives who, while not openly encouraging this practice, will turn a blind eye to it, assuming that if the cheaters are caught, the blame will rest solely with them and the casino will get away scot-free.

A few years ago, I had been hitting a casino in downtown Las Vegas pretty hard for a few days and had booked a sizeable win. One night, on the midnight shift, I came into the casino and sat down at a table. I continued my winning streak for about fifteen minutes, when the pit boss suddenly appeared and whispered in the dealer's ear. The dealer's response was that it wasn't yet his break time and that he'd wait for the break.

"I told you to leave *now*," the pit boss hissed at him.

The dealer shrugged and gave me an apologetic look, and another dealer was brought to the table. The new dealer had a surly demeanor, and I started losing as soon as he started dealing. After losing my buy in, I decided it was late and time to go to bed. I left the casino without thinking much about the unusual event I had just observed.

Later, I compared notes with some fellow players at that casino and several of them had similar experiences with the same dealer. I can't prove that we were being cheated, but I avoid that pit boss and dealer at all costs.

Whenever a new deck or pack of cards is introduced into the game, the cards should be spread face up one deck at a time in front of the players and thoroughly checked by the dealer.

Some Signs of Cheating

Most of us are not astute enough to recognize a skilled cheater at work. It's also entirely possible that we may never be cheated. However, it doesn't hurt to be aware of some of the signs of cheating.

The cards should always be in full view of the players. Whenever a new deck or pack of cards is introduced into the game, the cards should be spread face up one deck at a time in front of the players and thoroughly checked by the dealer. I have gotten into the habit of checking to make sure that all the aces are in each deck. If you see new cards being brought to the table and not being exposed to the players as described, my advice would be to leave the casino and refuse to play in it as long as this practice exists. If a pit boss examines the cards in play for some reason, the examination should take place in full view of the players. Again, if the pit boss takes cards that are in play out of the sight of the players, leave the casino.

Watch for strange motions by dealers. One of the most common cheating moves is *dealing seconds,* which simply means that the dealer is not dealing the top card off the deck, but is dealing the card under it. The dealer has peeked at the top card and is reserving it for herself or for an accomplice at the table. It will invariably be an Ace or a 10-valued card. Look for dealers who hold their cards high, up by their chest and who have a tendency to turn the cards toward them at certain times, as if they were checking their wristwatch. They will be holding the cards with their thumb on top of the deck, enabling them to slide the top card back and deal the second card. A dealer who is moving her thumb back and forth while dealing the cards should be an immediate suspect. Sometimes, dealers who peek won't actually deal a second but will discard the top card in the discard tray while placing the used cards into the tray. Removing a 10-valued card or an Ace from play is harmful to the players and helpful to the casino.

Peeking can be accomplished by sliding the top card slightly over with the deck turned toward the dealer's face. This motion lasts only for a split second and is not always easy to see. Usually, it is done while something else is happening to attract attention. A dealer might do it while paying off bets or placing cards in the discard tray. Another way a dealer may peek is to bow the card slightly with her thumb, enabling her to see the value of the card. A flash of white can reveal this move. Again, a moving thumb is a telltale sign that you might be playing against a cheating dealer.

CONCLUSION

By following the advice in this chapter, you can reduce your losses and enhance your casino experience. The mistakes and pitfalls described here are easy to avoid. Being aware and vigilant takes a little extra time, but it is well worth it in terms of dollars gained. While drinking, tipping too much, or overbetting to impress someone might be worth a few moments of pleasure or ego gratification, they will not compare to the satisfaction of knowing that you have taken on the casinos and beat them at their own game when your trip is over. The realization that you can avoid casino traps, such as 6:5 games, the cut-card effect, or cheating dealers will gratify your ego in a way that saves you money instead of costing you more.

The next chapter suggests ways to actually make a monetary profit from the casinos without counting cards.

GAINING THE ADVANTAGE WITHOUT COUNTING

I
t is a common belief that only card counters can get the advantage over casinos in the game of blackjack. That is far from the truth. In fact, many, if not most, professional advantage players have found several nontraditional approaches to the game that add to their expectation. Even a casual basic strategy player can look for opportunities that will increase his expectation at the casino, often into the positive realm. While this book is not designed to be a treatise on nontraditional ways to achieve an advantage, it is certainly worth mentioning a few simple tricks that a player might use if and when the opportunity presents itself.

By recognizing situations in which an advantage over the casino can be gained, such as special promotions, match-play coupons, and exploiting dealer mistakes, a basic strategy player can make a profit that goes beyond his gain from comps alone.

PROMOTIONS

For the casual player, the best opportunities arise from promotions and coupons. Blackjack promotions often include special payoffs for certain hands and can be quite valuable. The following are a few of the most common ones.

Blackjack Pays 2:1

The most venerable and one of the most profitable promotions is a 2:1 payoff on blackjacks. This is a game that can be played to an advantage of 2.3 percent just with basic strategy play. The 2:1 payoff on a blackjack means that a player with blackjack will receive $2 for every $1 bet. This is an increase of 33.3 percent over the normal 3:2 payoff, and it makes a negative expectation game a positive one.

If you find such a promotion, play it for all it is worth, even if it is at a casino where you wouldn't normally play. Your potential gain will overcome any loss you might have in comps at your regular casino. (Don't confuse 2:1 with 2 *for* 1, which is not the same payoff.)

Casino Pays on a Tied Blackjack

Normally a dealer's blackjack and a player's blackjack result in a push. However, with this rule, the player's blackjack wins. This rule increases expectation by about 0.3 percent. It might not make a game a positive expectation game, but it will come close, depending on the other rules in effect.

Casino Pays 3:1 on a Suited Blackjack

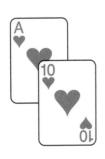

An example of a suited blackjack.

A suited blackjack is one where both cards are of the same suit. For example, a blackjack made up of a 10 of spades and an Ace of spades is a suited blackjack. The 3:1 payoff on a blackjack means that a player with blackjack will receive $3 for every $1 bet. This bonus adds about 0.43 percent to your expectation.

Bonuses for Certain Card Combinations

Sometimes casinos offer a special bonus for a 21 combination such as 7-7-7 or 6-7-8. These bonuses might also be tied to a certain suit combination. The payoffs and variations are all over the board. Usually, these bonuses aren't large enough to go out of your way to play, but if they are offered in a place where you'd play anyway, they can certainly add to your expectation.

COUPONOMY

Couponomy is a term coined by Anthony Curtis, the publisher of the *Las Vegas Advisor*. It is used to describe the use of casino coupons that offer special deals to players. It is worthwhile to check out the coupons that are available through different sources—especially if you're a $5 bettor. These coupons are often more valuable to low-stakes bettors because they can permit a small bettor to receive comps and bonuses that he wouldn't normally get with his level of play.

Valuable coupons can be found in casino funbooks, which you can pick up at the players club booth. They can also be found in advertisements and gambling magazines. In fact, you can get a variety of very valuable coupons by subscribing to some publications. For example, *Casino Player* offers subscribers a good package of coupons. They are, however, from casinos all around the country and, depending on where you play, might not be useful to you. The *Las Vegas Advisor* has the best coupon package for Las Vegas casinos that I've come across. It usually includes good meal offers, special promotion plays, and free rooms.

Playing Other Casino Games

If you are going to spend time in the casinos playing blackjack, you may run across favorable opportunities that can be found in other casino games. Since the real bottom line for an astute player is to glean the largest gain possible while gambling, you may find it worthwhile to take advantage of non-blackjack opportunities that may pop up from time to time.

Casinos sometimes offer promotions that can make other games worthwhile play. The promotion most frequently seen offers some multiple of points for machine play. Since many casinos offer cash back for accrued points, these promotions can turn negative expectation games into positive ones. For example, a casino near my home offers triple points if you play on Monday through Thursday. This casino normally offers 0.25 percent cash back for machine play, which is pretty anemic by most standards. With triple points, the 0.25 percent cash back becomes 0.75 percent, which is excellent. This same casino also offers 9/6 Jacks or Better video poker. This game has a 0.5 percent advantage for the house if the proper strategy is played. With 0.75 percent cash back, it becomes a positive game. If one considers the comps that can also be gleaned from this play, it makes video poker an attractive gaming option. If these kinds of promotions are of interest, you might want to obtain a good book on video poker strategies in order to take advantage of such an opportunity.

Coupons can also be found in local newspapers in casino locales. It is a good idea to get a local paper when visiting a casino location. In addition to coupons, there may be ads that can lead you to good promotional opportunities that you might not learn about any other way.

Match-Play Coupons

The most valuable coupons allow you to increase the size of your bet and your potential payoff without having to put extra money on the table.

The most valuable coupons include coupons that allow you to increase the size of your bet and your potential payoff without having to put extra money on the table. These are called *match-play coupons*. These coupons typically match the amount of money you bet on a particular round in a table game. Depending on the maximum bet permitted, these coupons can be quite valuable. If you have a match-play coupon that is worth $5, that means you can make a $5 bet and place the coupon along with your bet in the betting square. If you win, the dealer will payoff your bet as if it were a $10 bet, meaning that you will get a return of $10 plus your original $5 bet if you win a hand.

Free Ace Coupon

Another valuable coupon is a *free Ace coupon*. You present this coupon to the dealer when you place your bet and it will be treated as if it were an Ace. The dealer will deal you one card to complete your original hand. Then, you can proceed with your play decisions as usual.

Other Valuable Coupons

Other valuable coupons I've come across offer a 2:1 or even a 3:1 payoff on the first blackjack a player receives after presenting the coupon to the dealer.

All of the coupons mentioned above usually have a maximum bet limit. Their ultimate value depends on your level of betting. For example, if you are a $100 bettor, a $5 match-play coupon isn't going to be of much worth to you; however, it can be very valuable to a $5 bettor or even to a $25 bettor.

Discarded coupons and funbooks often litter the casinos, and they might be worth picking up. You might even ask other players if you can use their coupons if they aren't going to use them. Some casinos have a limitation on how many coupons a player can use in a day, but they don't strictly enforce those rules.

TOURNAMENT PLAY

To attract customers, most casinos offer tournaments from time to time for various games. In tournaments, players usually play with a set amount of "play money" determined by the casino. So, if there is no entry fee for the tournament, the only investment is your time. But even tournaments that require an entry fee may be lucrative.

When you are considering entering a tournament, the first thing to consider is the cost of the tournament versus the benefits that can be gained by being in the tournament. As part of the tournament package, participants are usually entitled to a variety of comps, such as free rooms, meals, apparel, and other gifts. A good tournament package should be equal to or better in value than the cost of the tournament entry fee. Also, when evaluating the cost versus the benefits, consider the prizes for that tournament, which may be quite substantial.

A successful blackjack tournament player does not have to be a card counter, but he should, of course, have the basics of blackjack down. There will be times, however, when a tournament player will throw basic strategy out the window and rely on luck, doubling down on blackjacks or other unlikely hands, splitting 5s, or hitting on hands that one would normally stand on. This is because the tournament player's goal is to win enough chips to make it to the next round and eventually place in the money or even win the tournament. If this means departing from basic strategy on a play because it is the only way to gain the lead or finish in the money, then such a departure is the best play.

How to play successfully in tournaments can be the subject of a book in and of itself. In fact, Stanford Wong has written one. It's called *Casino Tournament Strategy*, and covers blackjack, craps, baccarat, and keno tournament strategy.

OTHER ADVANTAGE PLAYS

There is a shadow world out there inhabited by advantage players who have become the elite of the gambling world. Many of them believe that garden-variety card counting is no longer a viable way to make a living and have expanded their repertoire to include a host of tricks. In black-jack, these tricks include *hole-carding* and *sequencing,* which are discussed in the following sections.

Advantage players are always willing to explore any game the casinos offer to see if an advantage can be gleaned from it. They even consider games that had been given up for naught by advantage players of previous generations. Although they sometimes miss the mark, they can often find advantages in the most unlikely places. For example, one fellow I know, whom I'll call Fred, happened by the Big Six Wheel one day as he was cruising through a casino. On its face, the Big Six Wheel is one of the worst bets in the casino, with a house advantage that can be as high as 24 percent depending on the bet. The casino was doing a Big Six Wheel promotion that day and was allowing the players to spin the wheel. Fred wandered over to the table and placed a bet. When he spun the wheel, he realized that he could make the wheel land in a specific area. That was all he needed to know. He could affect the randomness of the game with his spin and he went to town. He hit it for all it was worth and spent the next couple of hours winning cash at an astounding rate. Finally, a casino executive came over and told Fred that she was ending the promotion. The fun was over, but it had been a glorious two hours for Fred.

Even without a promotion such as this, it is sometimes possible to gain the advantage in Big Six Wheels by scouting out dealers who consistently pull the wheel for a certain number of spins. If the dealer's spin can be predicted, a player can place his bets in the area where the wheel is likely to land. These advantage players have discovered that this is not really a random game. Players like Fred are always on the lookout for these kinds of events and can find advantages in the most unlikely places.

Hole-Carding

One of the most common methods of gaining a non-counting advantage at the tables is called *hole-carding.* Hole-carders scout out dealers who accidentally flash their hole card. Obviously, knowing what the dealer's hole card is offers a tremendous advantage. With a shortage of expert dealers due to the proliferation of casinos over the last two decades in the United States, there are many dealers who make this mistake.

If hole-carding is something you want to try, it's a good idea to observe the habits of the various dealers on duty before joining a game. Once you find a dealer who flashes her hole card, the best place to observe this flash is usually from the center position at the table. However, that won't always be the case. It really depends on the dealer's motions. Playing against a dealer who is right-handed or left-handed may make a difference in the ideal position.

By the way, you don't have to confine hole-carding to blackjack. Knowing the dealer's hole card is an advantage in most table games that use playing cards.

Closely related to hole-carding is watching for dealers who expose the next card to be dealt before the deal. Knowing what the next card is provides another valuable opportunity for an observant player. In *The Theory of Blackjack*, Peter Griffin lists the value of each card if it is the first card in a player's hand. This is too involved to go into here, but if you're interested in knowing more, check out Peter Griffin's book.

While taking advantage of exposed hole cards or the next card to be dealt may sound like cheating, it is not. A player is simply using information that the dealer makes available to him. In fact, the courts have determined that using such information is not cheating. However, if you were to use a confederate who could observe these things at a vantage point away from the table and communicate them to you by surreptitious means, that would be considered cheating.

> While taking advantage of exposed hole cards or the next card to be dealt may sound like cheating, it is not. A player is simply using information that the dealer makes available to him.

Sequencing

Another trick that some players use is tracking or *sequencing* certain cards through the pack and figuring out where that card is likely to appear in the pack after the next shuffle. Most shuffles are not purely random, and cards that are close to one another sometimes tend to stay close after the shuffle. Usually, sequencing trackers are looking for the Aces. Suppose an Ace of clubs is accompanied by a 5 of hearts. After the next shuffle, the sequencer will watch for the 5 of hearts to appear and will expect to see the Ace soon and bet accordingly.

Most advantage methods take time and practice to learn, but some of them can be used just because a player is in the right place at the right time. Being observant and aware of your surroundings while in the casino can occasionally pay big dividends. For the player who is interested in exploring alternative methods of play, there are two good books in print that go into detail on this kind of play: *Beyond Counting* by James Grosjean and *Get the Edge at Blackjack* by John May.

CONCLUSION

With the information contained in this chapter, a casual player can become an advantage player from time to time. Casinos are often full of opportunities that the average tourist never realizes. By being on the lookout for such opportunities and being able to recognize them when they happen, you can turn such chances into profits that you may never had found otherwise.

PART TWO

THE CARD COUNTER

CARD COUNTING

If you have read and studied the first part of this book and want to take your play to the next level, card counting might be for you. If you skipped Part One, go back and learn basic strategy. Just as you had to crawl before you could get up and walk, you must know basic strategy before you can successfully count cards. Once you know basic strategy, you're ready to proceed.

Card counting is often misunderstood by the general public. Many people think that it's illegal or a sophisticated form of cheating. It is neither. A card counter does what any good card player tries to do in just about any kind of card game. He keeps track of the cards played and adjusts his betting and playing strategies accordingly. A good poker player or bridge player does the same thing and no one accuses him of breaking the law or cheating. Card counters are simply taking advantage of the information presented to them and to every other player at the table. Casinos are in business to make a hefty profit, and the last thing they want in their casinos are players who consistently win. So they encourage the view that counters are cheaters engaged in illegal activity and harass anyone they suspect of being a card counter. Despite this, no one in the United States has ever been arrested or prosecuted for counting cards.

Another commonly held misconception is that a person must have great mathematical abilities or a photographic memory to successfully count cards. Not so. If you can add and subtract single digits and do the simple division you learned in elementary school, you can master the mechanics of card counting. But you must be willing to learn, to practice, and to put your skills to the test in a crowded, noisy casino.

This chapter takes a brief look at the history of card counting and what makes it work. Then it introduces and explains the most popular card-counting system in use today along with advice on learning and using the system. If you take the time to seriously study and learn the material presented, you will be able to turn a game with an inherent advantage to the house into one that you can play at your advantage.

THE HISTORY OF BLACKJACK CARD-COUNTING SYSTEMS

In 1956, the *Journal of the American Statistical Association* published the article "The Optimum Strategy in Blackjack" by Roger Baldwin, Wilbert Cantey, Herbert Maisel, and James McDermott. These mathematicians are known today as the developers of the first mathematically derived basic strategy for blackjack. This article got the attention of Edward O. Thorp, an MIT mathematics professor, who went on to use the findings of Baldwin and colleagues as a basis for his own system. He was assisted by IBM computer expert Julian Braun.

With his groundbreaking book *Beat the Dealer*, mathematics professor Edward O. Thorp brought basic strategy and card counting to the public's attention.

Then, in 1962, with his groundbreaking book *Beat the Dealer*, Thorp brought basic strategy and card counting to the public's attention. In the first edition of the book, he introduced the Ten-Count System, a card-counting system that, when used properly, could give a player the advantage in blackjack. Although Thorp's system was difficult to use, it did work. By 1964, *Beat the Dealer* was on the *New York Times* bestseller list. On March 27, 1964, *Life* magazine ran a twelve-page article about Thorp's work.

Needless to say, Las Vegas casinos went into a panic and changed the rules of the game to shift the advantage back to the house. Instead of the 3:2 payoff on blackjacks, they made the payoff even money. They also eliminated the rules that allow players to double down or split pairs. The new version of blackjack was so unfavorable that no one wanted to play it. Not too much time passed before the casinos finally gave in and reinstated the old rules.

To this day, casinos tinker with the rules of blackjack in an attempt to make it the unbeatable game they once thought they had. But because it *is* a game in which players in the know can break even or possibly beat, it is one of the most popular table games in casinos—even more popular than craps and roulette. Because blackjack lures unskilled players who mistakenly think the advantage is in their favor, casinos have actually benefited from Thorp's work more than anyone else has.

As other players used Thorp's system, some developed their own refinements based on his ideas. For example, in 1963, Harvey Dubner developed the High-Low Point Count System, which has come to be known as the Hi-Lo System of card counting. Thorp included Dubner's system in the second edition of *Beat the Dealer*, published in 1966. This is the system you will learn in this book.

WHAT TO EXPECT FROM A CARD-COUNTING SYSTEM

A card-counting system allows a player to do two things that will give him an advantage: 1) modify basic strategy based on the count (see Chapter 7), and 2) raise or lower his bet based on the count (see Chapter 8). Modifying basic strategy based on the count adds value to the player's game, but unless he has found a very good well-penetrated single-deck game, strategy modification alone won't put him over the top. Although it's also possible to make a profit by *flat betting*—that is, sticking to one bet size without raising or lowering the amount—and making the appropriate strategy adjustments based on the count in well-penetrated single-deck games, these days such games are as rare as flies at a frog convention. Therefore, the single most important thing that card counting does for a player is tell him when to raise his bets. By keeping track of the cards, a player knows when he has the advantage over the house, he knows what the size of his advantage is, and he knows the amount to bet given the size of the advantage.

> A card-counting system allows a player to do two things that will give him an advantage: 1) modify basic strategy based on the count, and 2) raise or lower his bet based on the count.

THE BASIS FOR CARD-COUNTING SYSTEMS

As Thorp revealed, when the ratio of 10-valued cards to non-10-valued cards is more than 1:2.25 (the ratio in a fifty-two-card deck), the advantage swings away from the house and to the player. As the ratio of high cards to low cards increases, the player's advantage increases with it. If a player can recognize when this happens, he can increase his bet, thereby gaining an overall advantage over the house. This is the basis for all card-counting systems.

Thorp's Ten-Count System requires a player to count 10-valued cards and what Thorp calls *others*—that is, non-10-valued cards. In a single-deck game, there are sixteen 10s and thirty-six "others." Using this system, a player starts his count with two numbers: 16 (representing the 10s) and 36 (representing the "others"). For each "other" card that is dealt out, the player drops the second number by one. In other words, if six "others" were dealt out, the second number would drop by 6 to 30. If, at the same time, one 10-valued card were dealt, the first number would drop to 15. The player's new count would be 15/30. The ratio of 10s to non-10s would be 1:2. The advantage would be in the player's favor and he would raise his bet.

For most players, Thorp's system is too difficult to use. Keeping track of 10s and non-10s separately and mentally computing the ratio is not an easy task while playing blackjack. Although Dubner's Hi-Lo System is based on Thorp's findings, it is a much simpler system to use. In fact, the Hi-Lo System is so easy to use and accurate that it is still the most popular card-counting system in use today. It has become the standard against which all other systems are compared and the system that is most often used as a reference by blackjack players and authors.

The Effects of Discards

As you've probably figured out, as cards are removed from the deck, the odds of the game are affected. For example, with a few Aces out of play, the odds of getting a blackjack decrease; with a lot of low cards out of play, the odds of the dealer's busting on hands totaling 12 to 16 increase; and with a lot of 10-valued cards out of play, the odds of a player's getting a pat hand (a total of 17, 18, 19, 20) decrease—just to mention some of what goes on as cards are removed.

Each card has a different value to the player in terms of how drastic the effects of removal are. The most valuable out-of-play cards to the player are 5s. Following that in order are 4s, 6s, 3s, and 2s. Out-of-play

7s add value to the player, while out-of-play 8s are completely neutral. Out-of-play 9s have a slight detrimental effect on the player, and out-of-play 10s and Aces hurt the player the most.

Table 6.1 illustrates the impact discarded cards have on a player's *per-hand expectation*—that is, what percentage of money a player can expect to win or lose in the long run on each hand. As you can see from this table, the effects of removal are quite significant when the house advantage is a half a percent or less.

The figures in Table 6.1 are based on a single deck. Obviously, as more decks are added, the effects of removal become diluted. However, if you were to calculate the effects of removal on a per-deck basis, the outcome would be the same. For example, if you were playing in a six-deck game, the effect of removing one Ace would be divided by six at the start of the shoe. Similarly, the effect of removing one 4 from a double-deck game at the beginning of play with a new pack would be one-half of what it is for a single-deck game.

Out-of-Play Cards	Change in Player's Expectations
Ace	−.61 percent
2	+.38 percent
3	+.44 percent
4	+.55 percent
5	+.69 percent
6	+.46 percent
7	+.28 percent
8	0 percent
9	−.18 percent
10	−.51 percent

Table 6.1

The Effects of Out-of-Play Cards in Single-Deck Games

When considering the standard rules of blackjack, including a 3:2 payoff on a player's blackjack, a player's ability to double down and split hands, and the dealer's requirements to hit her hand until she reaches 17 or greater, it is easy to understand how the removal of cards has an effect on the game. For example, if all the Aces have been discarded or played, a player cannot get a blackjack and reap the benefits of the 3:2 payoff. (The fact that a player's blackjack gets 3:2 while the house only gets even money from the player on a dealer's blackjack is what makes blackjack a nearly even game.) Clearly, removing Aces has a drastic effect on the player's expectation.

An excess of low cards remaining in the deck means that the dealer is not going to bust on her stiff hands as often because she will be drawing lower cards from the deck. Many low cards remaining in the deck also means that a player is likely to get a stiff hand more often. Moreover, low cards interfere with successful double downs and splits.

Although an excess of high cards results in more pat hands for both the player and the dealer, it also means that the dealer is more likely to bust when she hits to her stiff hand. Unlike the dealer, a player can choose not to hit stiffs when hitting would be to his disadvantage. Also, an excess of 10-valued cards means that a player is more likely to be successful when he doubles down or splits.

The effects of removal described above provide the basis for any card-counting system. Using this information, each card is assigned a positive, negative, or neutral value. As cards are removed and discarded during play, the count reflects the change in the per-hand expectation, as well as in the composition of the deck, pack, or shoe. Thus, if the count indicates that an excess of Aces or 10-valued cards are left in play, the player should bet more than he would in a neutral or negative count. And, because he has information about the composition of the cards remaining in play, he can vary basic strategy.

THE HI-LO CARD-COUNTING SYSTEM

Running Count
The total point value of the cards seen as they are played.

The Hi-Lo System is based on a simple plus-minus count. As certain cards are played on the table, the player either adds 1 or subtracts 1 from a *running count* that starts at 0 and divides that number by the number of decks or fraction of decks still in play to get the *true count*. As the count changes, the bet is adjusted accordingly, as discussed in Chapter 8. When the count is positive, the player has the advantage; when the count is negative, the house has the advantage. Obviously, when the player has the advantage, he should increase his bet, and when the house has the advantage, the player should decrease his bet. Ideally, the player should bet nothing when he has a disadvantage, but

True Count
The running count divided by the fraction or number of decks left in play.

practically speaking, that isn't always possible without drawing attention to the fact that he's counting cards.

The value, or *tag*, for each card in the Hi-Lo System is shown in Table 6.2 below.

Card	Value	Card	Value
2	+1	7	0
3	+1	8	0
4	+1	9	0
5	+1	10, J, Q, K	−1
6	+1	Ace	−1

Table 6.2
Card Values in the High-Low Point Count System

Hi-Lo is known as a *balanced count*. This is because if you add up the values of all the +1 cards, they balance with the negative values of all of the −1 cards. There are twenty +1 cards per deck, twenty −1 cards per deck, and twelve cards with no value. As you can see, the 8 has no value, which corresponds with its effects of removal discussed earlier. The 7, which has a lesser positive value in terms of removal than 2 through 6, isn't counted, nor is the 9, which has a slight negative value.

Hi-Lo is also known as a *level-one* and a *single-parameter* count, which means that aside from the cards given no value, it assigns the same corresponding positive and negative value—in this case +1 and −1—to the cards being counted. It is a single-parameter count because it does not require a player to keep any side counts of cards not given a value in the basic counting system.

There are multilevel systems that assign differing, non-corresponding values to different cards as well as systems that require a player to keep side counts of cards not assigned a value in the basic system. These are "multilevel" and "multiparameter" counts. They can often be more efficient and more powerful than level-one single-parameter counts, but they are also more difficult to use.

In Hi-Lo, as in other counting systems, a positive (or plus) count indicates the deck is rich in high cards and is favorable to the player. A negative (or minus) count indicates the deck is heavy in low cards and is unfavorable to the player. For each 1-point increase in the true count (see "Keeping True Count" on page 110), the player's advantage grows by approximately a half of a percent.

The advantage that level-one counts such as Hi-Lo have over their bigger and stronger multilevel brothers is that they are easier to use. They are less taxing on the mind and many players who might make costly errors with more difficult counting systems will be able to use a level-one system accurately and efficiently. But of course there is a tradeoff of efficiency for simplicity. See "No System Is Perfect" on page 107 for more information.

Keeping a Running Count

To learn the Hi-Lo System, you must first learn how to keep a running count quickly and accurately. Begin by memorizing the card values found in Table 6.2 on page 105. Then, you'll need to practice by counting actual cards.

Although you may not use them all in the very beginning, start with at least six decks of standard playing cards. If you are close to a casino, you may be able to buy used decks in packs of twelve at a reduced rate from the casino gift shop. This may seem like a lot of cards, but as you practice counting, you will find a use for all of them. Although there are computer programs to help a player learn to keep count, there is no substitute for handling and observing actual cards.

Practice Drills for Keeping a Running Count

The most basic exercise is to count the cards in the deck one card at a time, using the values in Table 6.2. When you reach the end of the deck, you should have a count of 0. Hold the deck face down and count each card as it is turned over, or hold the deck face up and count each card as you move through the deck. Keep practicing this exercise until you can count the deck in thirty seconds or less.

A variation of this exercise is to remove a card from the deck without looking at it. Then, count the deck and see if you can determine if the unseen card is a high card, a low card, or a neutral card. If your count is +1, it should be a high card. If it is –1 it should be a low card, and if it is 0, it should be a neutral card. If you are incorrect, continue to work on your accuracy.

No System Is Perfect

There is no known card-counting system that provides perfect *playing efficiency*—that is, the accuracy of a counting system in providing information about the correct playing decision given the composition of the deck as predicted by the system. However, the closer to 100 percent a system is, the more accurate it is for predicting the perfect play.

While someone could theoretically devise a "perfect" system that reflects the true value of each card, most of us would never be able to use it. The best card-counting system for playing efficiency allows a card counter to play at about 70 percent of the perfect playing strategy for each hand. But this system is a difficult-to-master multilevel count, which is why it is not in widespread use.

The Hi-Lo System has a playing efficiency of 51 percent. If you're thinking that 51 percent sounds low, don't despair: The bulk of the money in card counting is made from variations in betting amounts. What makes this system so valuable is that it has *a betting correlation* of 97 percent. The term *betting correlation* describes the accuracy of a counting system in predicting when it is time to raise or lower your bet based on the count and the composition of the cards remaining in play. The Hi-Lo System, with its 97 percent accuracy, is comparable to just about every other decent system in use today, and it surpasses many.

This isn't to say that higher level counts aren't good systems. In the hands of a good player who has the ability to use them, many higher-level counts can bring in the money faster than level-one counts. Advanced Omega II Count, a system featured in Bryce Carlson's book *Blackjack for Blood*, is a proven winner. Hi-Opt 2 is another multilevel count that has been shown to be an effective money winner.

If you believe you can take card counting even further after learning the Hi-Lo System, then by all means explore one of these higher-level counts. A person such as this author, who, as Dirty Harry once said, "knows his limitations," is better served to keep it simple.

Once you're comfortable counting down the deck, play a few one-hand rounds against yourself as the dealer, keeping a running count as you play. To add a bit of realism to this exercise, ask someone to deal to you. After you have played several hands but have not made it all the way through the deck, check your accuracy by counting down the remaining cards in the deck. After adding your running count to the count of the unseen cards, you should have a count of 0. If not, continue practicing.

As you become more used to keeping a running count, you will notice that you tend to look at pairs of cards that cancel each other out. For example, a hand with a 10 (–1) and a 6 (+1) has a value of 0.

Whether or not they cancel each other out, you should still be able to count the cards two at a time; after all, this is how you will see them most often in the casino. When I was learning how to count, I'd spread out a deck of cards face down, two at a time. Then, as I turned the pairs over, I would count them. If I counted out all twenty-six pairs correctly, the end count would be 0.

Another exercise to help you count cards in pairs is to deal out the cards face up to seven players and the dealer with your eyes closed. Be sure to place the dealer's upcard in the position it would be placed on the table at a casino. Open your eyes, scan the table, and try to pick up the count as rapidly as possible. This should take only a few seconds. As you become more skilled, not only will you be canceling out pairs, but you will also be canceling out other variations. For example, if you see a pair of 10s in one hand and a 5-6 in another, the count is 0 for those four cards.

When you've become proficient at counting cards by twos and scanning a table of hands, try counting three-card hands by modifying the exercises described above.

Tips for Keeping a Running Count

Since we tend to think in words, reducing the syllables of the words you use to keep track of the running count shortens the time it takes to think it out. For example, when I am card counting, I use the term *bad* for negative counts, instead of *minus,* and simply do away with the word *plus* for positive counts. So a count of *minus two* (three syllables) is simply *bad two* (two syllables) and a count of *plus two* (two syllables) is simply *two* (one syllable). Thus, I have saved myself the time it takes to pronounce several syllables in my head. Try this out for yourself, or come up with your own syllable-saving system.

It is important that as you are learning to count you do not move your lips. This may sound silly, but it is something we often do unconsciously. It is a good idea to have someone watch you while you count to make sure you aren't giving yourself away.

Loose Lips...
Be sure not to move your lips as you are learning to count. It's a hard habit to break and it's a dead give-away to an alert dealer or pit boss.

Counting Order

When playing in a casino, the order in which you count the cards

Card-Counting Distractions

Casinos are full of distractions. The bells and whistles of the slot machines can bring on a form of near insanity. One particular type of slot machine that drives me especially crazy is based on the television game show *Wheel of Fortune*. The machine shouts "Wheel! ...of! ...Fortune!" just like the game-show audience. This is followed by the show's theme music. I have more than once been tempted to find the nearest fire ax and hack the machine to pieces.

Other distractions include cocktail waitresses, chatty players and dealers, obnoxious drunks, tobacco smoke, and the constant flow of people moving through the casino. So, when you are practicing card counting at home, it's a good idea to include some distractions. Turn up the volume on the television and/or radio. If you have small children or grandchildren, encourage them to play near you while you practice counting. Many casinos run the air conditioning full blast, so try doing that at home if you can afford the energy bill. The point is to try to re-create the distracting aspect of the casino atmosphere in your home while you are practicing.

depends on whether the game is dealt face up or face down. Described below are the counting orders that work for me. You may wish to begin with my system. Then, as you become more practiced, you can develop your own if you wish.

In a face-down game, first count the cards in your own hand. Then, count the dealer's upcard and each of the hit cards as they are dealt to you and the other players. If a player has a blackjack or exposes his cards for a double or a split, count them as they are exposed. Next, count the dealer's remaining cards when her hand is exposed, and then count her hit cards, if any. Once the hand is complete, the dealer will turn each player's hand face up before collecting the cards. As the dealer turns over the players' hands, she places the original face-down hand closest to her and above the hit cards. Count these cards as they are turned over.

In face-up games, wait until all the original hands are dealt, then count the cards on the table, including the dealer's upcard. Waiting until all the hands are dealt is usually less confusing than trying to count them one at a time. This also leaves you time to talk with other players and the dealer, and not appear as if you are constantly studying the cards. If you have become proficient at counting the cards in pairs, you should have no difficulty waiting until all of the hands are on the table. Then, count subsequent cards as they are dealt.

Keeping True Count

Once you have learned to keep the running count with ease, move on to keeping a true count. As mentioned earlier, the true count is the running count divided by the number or fraction of decks left in play. Keeping the true count in a level-one system such as Hi-Lo is essential to being able to identify the proper betting strategies, especially in multiple-deck games. This is discussed more fully in Chapter 8.

You can make your true count as accurate as you wish. As you'll learn below, you can divide your running count by the number of remaining whole decks, by the half deck, or even by the quarter deck if you can handle the necessary calculations. Studies have shown that an exact calculation of the true count doesn't add much, if anything, to a player's expectation; however, a more accurate true count will probably result in slightly less risk to the player because he will be more accurate in his *bet sizing*—that is, varying the size of his bet according to the advantage. In multiple-deck games, a true count kept to the nearest whole deck should be quite adequate.

True Count in Single-Deck Games

If you are playing single-deck games, your true count will always be calculated using fractions. For example, if you have a running count of +3 and three-quarters of the cards are left in play, your true count would be +4 (+3 divided by $3/4$ = 4). If you recall from grade school, this is figured like this: $3/1 \div 3/4$. To divide fractions, flip each fraction and multiply the top and bottom figures: $3/1 \times 4/3 = 12/3 = 4$. If a half deck is left in play, your true count would be +6 (+3 divided by $1/2$ = 6). If you have a negative running count, use the same figures but simply attach a negative value to the number. In other words, a running count of –3 with three-quarters of a deck left would be a true count of –4.

It is fairly easy to estimate a single deck to the nearest quarter deck. Since you may not be able to see the approximate number of cards remaining in the dealer's hand, concentrate on the cards in the discard tray and make your estimate from there. If you see a quarter deck in the discard tray, you know that three-quarters of a deck is left. (See "Practice Drills for Keeping a True Count" on page 111 for a few training drills to perfect your skills in determining the number of cards in the discard tray.)

True Count in Multiple-Deck Games

In multiple-deck games, a true count is kept by dividing mostly whole numbers. A running count of +9 with four decks left in play would give you a true count of 2.25 (9 ÷ 4 = 2.25). When your true count includes a fraction, round the number down, not up. For example, if your true count is 2.5 or 2.25, play the hand as if it was a +2 if you are on the positive side and as if it were a –3 if you are on the negative side. This leads to a safer betting pattern and strategy deviation. You certainly don't want to prematurely put out a big bet, and you don't want to make an important strategy deviation if the count isn't really at the proper level.

Using the discard tray to estimate the remaining cards in play is particularly important in multiple-deck games due, in part, to the larger numbers of cards being dealt. (A running count of +8 means something totally different if there are five decks remaining to be played than it does if there are two decks remaining to be played.) Also, it is often difficult to estimate the number of cards remaining in a shoe. They are at a slanted angle and tend to spread out in the shoe as cards are removed. Some casinos even cover the top of their shoes, making it impossible to see the remaining cards in the shoe. In hand-held double-deck games, the dealer holds the cards in her hand, so it's difficult to see how many are left. Therefore, being able to estimate the number of cards in the discard tray is essential in keeping an accurate true count for multiple-deck games.

A very small number of casinos cover their discard trays as well. If you run into such circumstances and still want to play the game, you can estimate the number of cards that have been dealt by multiplying the number of hands (including the dealer's hand) in each round by 2.7. Obviously, this can be a difficult calculation to do in your head. I don't recommend practicing these calculations unless you know you'll be playing in games with a concealed discard tray on a regular basis. It is worth knowing, however, in case you happen across a game with a covered discard tray and wish to play.

Practice Drills for Keeping a True Count

A good exercise to prepare yourself for keeping a true count in single-deck games is to practice dividing the running count by fractions of one-quarter, one-half, and three-quarters.

The +5 True Count

As you learn the betting and playing strategies in this part of the book, you will come to recognize that by the time you get to a +5 true count, you should have your maximum bet out. This count is at the outside range of just about all of the playing strategies recommended in this book. In effect, you don't really need to worry about calculating an exact true count once you have hit a +5.

Table 6.3 can help you memorize the outcome of these calculations. If the running count is negative, simply assign a negative value to the true count. This table includes running counts up to 5, which is as high as the strategy deviations for single-deck play goes in this book. You could form similar tables for multiple-deck games if you wish to increase your accuracy estimating the true count. How far you take this is up to you.

Table 6.3
Calculating the True Count in a Single-Deck Game

Running Count	Fraction of Deck Left in Play	True Count
1	three-quarters	1.3
1	one-half	2
1	one-quarter	4
2	three-quarters	2.6
2	one-half	4
2	one-quarter	8
3	three-quarters	4
3	one-half	6
3	one-quarter	12
4	three-quarters	5.3
4	one-half	8
4	one-quarter	16
5	three-quarters	6.6
5	one-half	10
5	one-quarter	20

You will find your purchase of several decks of cards worthwhile when you begin learning to estimate the number of decks remaining in play. To learn quarter-deck estimations for single-deck play, divide a deck by quarters, and become familiar with the size of a quarter-deck stack, a half-deck stack, and a three-quarter-deck stack by sight. If you use two decks of cards, you can make three stacks of cards at each level. You might want to tape the various sized stacks together and set them side by side so you can get used to what each level looks like.

For estimating the cards in multiple-deck games, use several decks of cards. Make a whole-deck stack, a one-and-a-half-deck stack, a two-deck stack, and so on, by half decks until you get to six or eight decks. Set them up where you will see them often, maybe on top of your television or on the kitchen table; look at them whenever you walk by. If, like me, you often find yourself staring into the fridge waiting for something tasty to pop out at you, putting the stacks of cards on one of the refrigerator shelves might work, too.

Making various stacks of several decks will take more than just the twelve decks originally discussed. You may need to invest in fifty or sixty decks of cards if you want to take your stack making this far. You can avoid the need to purchase this many cards by using construction paper or cardboard, as described below, to make flashcards.

A regulation deck of casino cards is $\frac{5}{8}$ of an inch thick and $2\frac{1}{2}$ inches wide. (A half deck is $\frac{5}{16}$ of an inch thick.) To make flashcards, use these measurements to cut out various sizes of stacks by the half deck from construction paper or thin cardboard. Paste the various sized cutouts onto index cards or appropriately sized pieces of construction paper, which should be a different color from the cutout. Write the size of the deck on the back of the card. Go through the flashcards, estimating the size of the stack and checking the back for accuracy.

Putting Your New Skills to the Test

If you have engaged in the various practice drills outlined above and

A regulation deck of casino cards is $\frac{5}{8}$ of an inch thick and $2\frac{1}{2}$ inches wide.

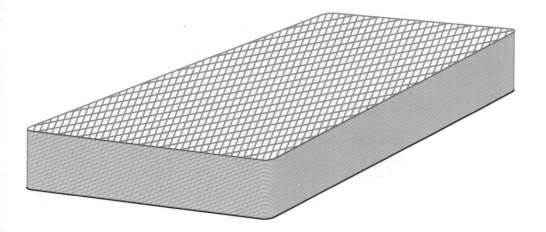

think you know what you're doing, you'll probably be in for a shock when you actually go to a casino to put it into practice. Stanford Wong once told me that he learned to count as a youth and was well prepared to count when he turned twenty-one and entered a casino for the first time. As Stanford Wong has proven throughout his career as a card counter, he is the exception to the rule. I suspect that most people are more like me.

I thought I was ready the first time I tried counting in the casino. I was well versed in basic strategy and had been playing in the casinos for some time before I tried counting. I did all of the practice drills, and I was sure I could handle the game in a real casino. The truth is, I was shaking like a leaf that first time. I was afraid the pit would catch me. I'd left all of my hard-won confidence at the casino door. I sat down at a six-deck game with a full table of players. I hadn't played three hands before I lost the count. No matter how hard I tried to pick it back up, I just couldn't do it. Shoe after shoe, I found myself distracted and losing concentration. The cocktail waitress would come by, the players wanted to kibitz, and every time the pit boss looked my way I thought I'd been nailed. That first night, I never did manage to keep the count throughout an entire shoe. I left the casino shaken and unsure of myself. I doubted if I would ever be able to successfully count cards.

A lot of players have had that kind of experience. The successful card counters are the ones who don't give up. They go back to the woodshed, as musicians say, and keep on practicing. If you think about it, you were probably just as nervous the first time you tried to drive a car. Odds are, you didn't do so well at that either. You may have even flunked your first driving test. You didn't give up then, and if you have an experience similar to the one I had, you don't have to give up on card counting either. Tenacity is one hallmark of a successful player. Be tenacious and don't surrender to your fears.

PRACTICE PRACTICE PRACTICE

The successful card counters are the ones who don't give up. They go back to the woodshed, as musicians say, and keep on practicing.

CONCLUSION

Knowing basic strategy and *how* to count cards is only part of becoming a successful card counter. These are only the basics, and even if you've mastered them, you are still only at the threshold of the house of card counting. To be a successful card counter, you must be able to keep the count of the cards played, while figuring out the proper play for your card total, while conversing with the dealer and the other play-ers. You also must know the proper betting level for your bankroll, as well as for the game you're playing. And you have to do all this in a manner that doesn't alert the pit boss that you're a card counter. You must be mindful of the pit boss's body language and know the signs that the casino is on to you. You must be able to distinguish normal attention from *heat*—a form of pressure casinos put on card counters to intimidate them.

You must be able to accept painful losing streaks without becoming so frustrated and doubtful that you quit playing blackjack all together. You must think in the long term and see the game for what it is: one long playing session punctuated by sleep, work, other activities, and family time. On top of all of that, you must not become so obsessed that you neglect your responsibilities. If you think you can handle all of this, you might make it as a card counter. Read on to learn more.

BASIC STRATEGY VARIATIONS FOR THE CARD COUNTER

As you've learned, card counting serves two purposes: The first and most important is knowing when to raise the bet based on the count, which is discussed in Chapter 8. The second is knowing when to make basic strategy variations based on the count. This is the topic of this chapter.

Even with the basic strategy variations set forth in this chapter, you will still be using basic strategy a large majority of the time. If you were to add up the frequency of the conditions that may call for a variation and multiplied them by the percentage of time the count would actually call for you to depart from basic strategy for those plays, you'd find that departure from basic strategy occurs less than 1 percent of the time. Although that may seem somewhat insignificant, using basic strategy variations at the appropriate time has value. Here's an example:

Suppose you are playing in a six-deck game with S17 and you have a 7-4, and the dealer's upcard is an Ace. Basic strategy tells you to stand in those circumstances. You'll probably come across a player who doubles down on that hand and wins. And you might think to yourself, "I could have doubled my money if I'd just had enough courage to double down on that same hand." However, in *Professional Blackjack,* Stanford Wong reveals that your long-term gain from hitting the 7-4 is 0.147 times your original bet. Meanwhile, your long-term gain from doubling the same hand is only 0.127. In other words, if you were betting $10, you would earn an average profit of $1.47 for that hand, while doubling it gains you a profit of $1.27, which is 13.6 percent *less* than you'd earn by sticking to basic strategy.

However, in this chapter, you'll learn to double down on that hand whenever the true count is +1 or higher. Such a play will add a small percentage; in this case, your expectation will go from 0.147 to 0.148. True, that's a small change, but you'll be making this play when you are making larger bets (see Chapters 8 and 9 for betting recommendations). It is just one of eighteen variations in basic strategy that are recommended in this chapter. All together, these variations can add more than 33 percent to the gain you'd expect from playing basic strategy alone in a six-deck game. They can be even more valuable in single-deck and double-deck games.

Let's take a close look at these eighteen variations, known as the Illustrious 18. Then we'll take a look at the Fab Four, a basic strategy variation for games with the option to surrender.

THE ILLUSTRIOUS 18

The value of making strategy variations depends on the card-counting system in use, the number of decks in play, and the depth of penetration. In the rare well-penetrated single-deck game, the gain that can be had from altering basic strategy plays based on the count with perfect play can be as high as 66 percent more than the expected gain from playing basic strategy alone. In other words, if a player expects to make $100 an hour using basic strategy in such a game, he could expect to make $166 an hour if he played all the count-based basic strategy variations perfectly. In multiple-deck games, the gain from proper bet sizing is greater than the gain from perfect play. However, one could roughly expect to make an additional 41 percent with absolutely perfect playing variations. If he had an expectation of $100 an hour from basic strategy play alone, he could expect to earn about $141 an hour using perfect play. In order to achieve this level of perfection, the player would have to memorize *hundreds* of playing variations and apply them with 100 percent accuracy. Fortunately, Don Schlesinger recognized that there comes a point of diminishing returns. He boiled down the important variations to what he calls the *Illustrious 18* and presented them in his book *Blackjack Attack*. These eighteen plays are listed in Table 7.1 on page 119.

> The value of making strategy variations depends on the card-counting system in use, the number of decks in play, and the depth of penetration.

Table 7.1 The Illustrious 18 Strategy Variations

	In Single-Deck Games	In Double-Deck Games	In Shoe Games
Insurance?	Take insurance if the count is equal to or greater than +1.4	Take insurance if the count is equal to or greater than +2.4	Take insurance if the count is equal to or greater than +3
16 versus dealer's 10-valued card	Stand at 0 or higher	Stand at 0 or higher	Stand at 0 or higher
15 versus dealer's 10-valued card	Stand at +4 or higher	Stand at +4 or higher	Stand at +4 or higher
A pair of 10-valued cards versus dealer's 5*	Split at +5 or higher	Split at +5 or higher	Split at +5 or higher
A pair of 10-valued cards versus dealer's 6*	Split at +5 or higher; If H17, split at +4 or higher	If S17, split at +4 or higher; If H17, split at +4 or higher	If S17, split at +4 or higher
10 versus dealer's 10	Double at +3 or higher	Double at +4 or higher	Double at +4 or higher
12 versus dealer's 3	Stand at +3 or higher	Stand at +3 or higher	Stand at +2 or higher
12 versus dealer's 2	Stand at +4 or higher	Stand at +4 or higher	Stand at +4 or higher
11 versus dealer's Ace	If S17, double at −1 or higher; If H17, double at −2 or higher	If S17, double at 0 or higher; If H17, double at −1 or higher	If S17, double at +1 or higher; If H17, double at 0 or higher
9 versus dealer's 2	Double at +1 or higher	Double at +1 or higher	Double at +1 or higher
10 versus dealer's Ace	Double at +2 or higher	Double at +3 or higher	If S17, double at +4 or higher; If H17, double at +3 or higher
9 versus dealer's 7	Double at +4 or higher	Double at +4 or higher	Double at +4 or higher
16 versus dealer's 9	Stand at +5 or higher	Stand at +5 or higher	Stand at +5 or higher
13 versus dealer's 2	Hit at 0 or less	Hit at 0 or less	Hit at 0 or less
12 versus dealer's 4	Hit at +1 or less	Hit at 0 or less	Hit at 0 or less
12 versus dealer's 5	Hit at 0 or less	Hit at −1 or less	Hit at −1 or less
12 versus dealer's 6	If S17, hit at +1 or less; If H17, hit at −2 or less	If S17, hit at 0 or less; If H17 hit at −3 or less	If S17, hit at −1 or less; If H176 hit at −3 or less
13 versus dealer's 3	Hit at −1 or less	Hit at −2 or less	Hit at −2 or less

*Splitting 10s against 5s or 6s is a valuable play, but a player needs to consider that such a play can call unnecessary attention from dealers and pit bosses, as well as upsetting his fellow players at the table. If this sort of attention is unwanted, the player may not want to split 10s.

Strategy variations for negative counts have relatively little overall value, so you will see that there are only a few negative-count variations in the Illustrious 18. This stems primarily from the fact that a player should be either betting the minimum or not betting at all in negative counts (see Chapter 8).

Out of all the strategy variations shown in Table 7.1, insurance is by far the most valuable. Using the Hi-Lo System, a player should take insurance if the count is +3 or higher in multiple-deck games, +2.4 or higher in double-deck games, and +1.4 or higher in single-deck games. If this is the only strategy variation you use, you have captured about 33 percent of the gain you can get from the entire Illustrious 18.

The next two most important plays in Illustrious 18 are standing on a 16 versus a dealer's 10, which should be done at a count of 0 or higher and standing on a 15 against a dealer's 10 at counts of +4 or higher. These three plays alone get you 60 percent of the overall gain from the Illustrious 18. (The first twelve get you 90 percent of the gain.)

A detailed explanation of Illustrious 18 is included in Don Schlesinger's *Blackjack Attack*. Stanford Wong's *Professional Blackjack* has fairly complete strategy numbers for the Hi-Lo System if you want to expand your repertoire of strategy variations even further.

THE FAB FOUR

While the Illustrious 18 describes variations from basic strategy for any game, a game where surrender (discussed in Chapter 1) is offered gives a player the opportunity to use a few more strategy variations to enhance his profits at the table.

Don Schlesinger coined the blackjack term *Fab Four*, which describes the top-four late-surrender plays based on the Hi-Lo System. These

Table 7.2 Fab Four Late-Surrender Plays

Surrender when...		
Player's Hand Is	and Dealer's Upcard Is	at True Count
15	9	+3
15	10	0
15	Ace	+2 (in S17)
		−1 (in H17)
14	10	+4

plays are made when the true count is 0 or higher. The Fab Four variations for multiple-deck games are shown in Table 7.2 on the previous page.

CONCLUSION

The Illustrious 18 and the Fab Four are valuable additions to the card-counter's tool chest. When practicing at home, it's wise to keep a copy of these plays handy and refer to them whenever the need arises. Once they are committed to memory, you can use them to your financial advantage in the casino. However, as pointed out in this chapter, a majority of the gain that can be obtained from card counting comes with betting strategies. That's what the next chapter is all about.

MONEY MANAGEMENT FOR THE CARD COUNTER

The biggest problem facing a card counter isn't casino surveillance, suspicious pit bosses, or private security agencies. The biggest problem is money. I have heard many stories about card counters who lost their bankrolls and had to start over from scratch.

Part of this problem no doubt comes from the fact that many of the classic card-counting books were written at a time when single-deck games were the norm, and they do not go into detailed discussions on risk of ruin, nor do they give appropriate betting advice for today's multiple-deck "monsters."

Overbetting their bankrolls is a tremendous problem for card counters. They either don't know what the risk of ruin is for the game being played or they change games without changing their betting levels and wind up playing to a far greater risk of ruin than they believe.

I often read the posts on Stanford Wong's BJ21.com website (www.bj21.com). Player after player posts messages about having lost his bankroll. Others describe their woefully inadequate betting strategies for the games they play. There are also folks who post comments like "Why do you waste your time playing blackjack when all you can expect is an overall gain of 1 or 2 percent?" And some people wonder why they don't win every time they play blackjack. From these posts and others like them, it is obvious that there is a vast pool of ignorance when it comes to matters involving bankroll and how the blackjack advantage can be gained.

This chapter includes in-depth discussions of the long run and the short run, bankroll, risk of ruin, how to avoid complete ruin, protecting your bankroll, and styles of betting that can be used by a card counter. There are a number of new terms introduced in this chapter, so be sure to read the inset "Money Management Terms" below before you get started.

THE BLACKJACK ADVANTAGE: THE LONG RUN AND THE SHORT RUN

The advantage to a blackjack player is never very large in terms of pure percentage. A player who wins consistently at a rate of 1 to 2 percent does very well, indeed. When people who aren't in the know see figures like 1 or 2 percent, they tend to compare that to current interest rates. It isn't the same thing.

Money Management Terms

The term *bankroll* can refer to your *total* bankroll (the total amount of money you're willing to risk playing blackjack) or to a *trip* bankroll (the total amount of money you bring with you to play in the casinos for a single trip).

The term *base betting unit,* or simply *unit,* refers to the smallest amount of money you would bet on a single hand. It could be $5 or $100 or any other amount, but it boils down to the base bet you are making.

A *bet spread* is the range in which you will be making your bets. For example, a bet spread of 1–4 means you are betting anywhere from 1 to 4 units on a single hand during the course of your play. If you are using a $10 betting unit, then your bet spread would range from $10 to $40. The term *betting ramp* is used to describe the

steepness of a player's bet spread. For example, a player using a 1–12 bet spread might bet 1 unit in negative or neutral counts, 2 units at a +1 count, 4 units at a +2 count, 8 units at a +3 count, and 12 units at a +4 count. A steeper betting ramp might be 1 unit to 6 units to 12 units.

In any case, the bets described in this chapter are the initial bets made on a single hand. They do not include the additional bets that you might make when doubling down or splitting hands. In an extreme case, you could start with 12 units on one hand and wind up splitting and doubling from that hand to the point where you have a total of 96 units bet. You'd still be using a 1–12 bet spread, since that only describes the beginning bet on the hand and not the possible total that could be bet in such a circumstance.

Many typical games can yield an earning's rate of about 1.25 percent of the total amount of money that is bet. If a player were in such a game and had an average bet of $100, he could expect to earn $125 an hour in a typical 100-hands-per-hour game. In a four-hour session, this player would have an earning's expectation of $500. If his largest bet were $500, he would be wise to bring $6,000 to the table for such a session. Viewing that $6,000 as an investment, he is getting a return of 8.33 percent for his money *in four hours*. If that player were to play 500 hours per year, he would have an earnings expectation of $62,500. A bankroll of $100,000 would have a very low risk of ruin for such a player, and he would be looking at an annual return of 62.5 percent on his $100,000 investment. There are very few investment possibilities that can boast that kind of return on the investor's money.

The kind of return on your money described above is an example of what can occur in the long run. In the short run, anything is possible. A four-hour session such as the one in the preceding paragraph can earn a player $500, but three standard deviations for that session could see the player in the range of minus $6,000 to plus $7,000. This is a game with more swings than a city full of playgrounds.

So when can a player expect to be in the long run? This is a widely debated subject among blackjack theorists, but a good rule of thumb would be when a player has played enough to overcome three standard deviations of possible loss. This would vary greatly depending upon the quality of the games played, the player's bet spread and ramp, and the style of play being used, but 300,000 hands should cover most situations. This is 3,000 hours of play at an-average-hands-per-hour rate of 100. While this is a lot of hands, it is certainly possible for a player to play that number of hands in a lifetime. A professional player can reach that number in four years or less, depending on how much he plays.

For a casual player, 300,000 hands may sound insurmountable. Some may reason that if it takes that many hands to get into the long run and be assured of a profit, then card counting may not be worth the time it takes to learn it. It is worthwhile to note that even in the short run, the counter has the advantage in any honest game. He is the favorite, whether it is for one session of play or for a thousand sessions of play. A competent card counter can expect to come out ahead or break even in eight hours of play approximately 56 percent of the time.

A competent card counter can expect to come out ahead or break even in eight hours of play approximately 56 percent of the time.

BANKROLL

In Part One, the emphasis was placed on the size of a bankroll for a single trip or playing session. While this approach makes sense for a casual, recreational player who knows that he's playing at a disadvantage and hopes to make up his losses in comps, it does not make sense for a serious card counter. The card counter is not playing to earn comps. He is playing the game for hard cash and expects to win. To do that, the card counter needs to understand his risk of ruin—what he considers an acceptable risk of ruin and what betting plan is needed to meet or beat that risk.

The Effect of Risk of Ruin on Bankroll Size

A card counter should establish a starting bankroll that has an acceptable risk of ruin for him and build on that bankroll with his winnings until he has reached a point that satisfies his tolerance of risk and his earning goals.

Card counters evaluate risk of ruin in terms of percentages. If the bankroll is X, how often can a counter expect to lose his entire bankroll in a given number of hands? A 5 percent risk of ruin means the player has one chance in twenty of losing all of his bankroll if he doesn't resize his bets. With computer aids—for example, Auston's Blackjack Risk Manager 2002, Dunbar's Risk Analyzer Spreadsheet 2.3, and the risk calculator in the software program CVCX by Casino Vérité or on BJMath.com—a risk of ruin figure is easily calculated for whatever set of conditions is put into the computer.

The problem with any risk of ruin calculations is, none of us will play the same game the same way all of the time. We will make human errors, we won't find the exact same conditions that we enter into a computer program, and we'll probably play a variety of games. Risk of ruin for the same bankroll can vary wildly depending on the games being played. We add to this by using cover plays and cover bets (as discussed in Chapter 11), both of which can change the expected value of the game and the standard deviation—figures that are essential to computing risk of ruin.

In terms of a total playing bankroll, a card counter needs to think in long-run terms. He should establish a starting bankroll that has an acceptable risk of ruin for him and build on that bankroll with his winnings until he has reached a point that satisfies his tolerance of risk and his earning goals. Some ideas for establishing a bankroll are discussed a little later in this chapter.

What constitutes an acceptable risk of ruin varies widely from player to player. If a player has a bankroll that can be replenished regularly, he may wish to play to a higher risk of ruin for that specific bankroll than a player who has a bankroll that cannot be easily replaced. Professional players who rely on playing blackjack for a living prefer to have the smallest risk of ruin possible. Even a one in twenty chance of losing their entire bankroll is too great; most would prefer a 1 percent risk of ruin or less.

Using a 5 percent risk of ruin as an acceptable risk for a non-professional player, a good rule of thumb for sizing a total bankroll is to use an amount equal to 100 of a player's largest bets. It is best to size your bankroll and determine your betting units by using that top bet in your calculations. For example, if your big bet is $100 and you are engaged in a game where a 1–4 bet spread is recommended, your base betting unit can be $25. If you are in a game where a 1–12 bet spread is recommended, you should resize your base betting unit to approximately 1/12 of your top bet of $100, making it $8. That way, your risk of ruin should not change substantially—unless you're playing in the very worst of games (game selection is the primary topic in the next chapter).

The Effect of Standard Deviation on Bankroll

Standard deviation was discussed in Part One in relation to flat betting, and the SD per hand was given as 1.14. However, if you are a card counter who is using a bet spread, the SD numbers will vary significantly. As the size of the bet spread increases, so does the SD per hand. In games where a counter is using a large spread, such as 1–12 units, the SDs can go above 3, and with a backcounting, or Wonging, style of play (in which you enter a game only on favorable counts), SDs can go above 5. As a result of these variations in SD, one can find himself either significantly above or below expectation during any set period of time at the tables.

Most of the time, a player will find that he is below his all-time high. Then, he will establish a new all-time high and will soon find himself below that one as well. If his game selection is good and he plays properly, his bankroll will grow, but not at an even rate. He'll find himself taking three steps forward and two steps back all of the time.

It's difficult for players who use a bet spread to compute the SD per hand without the aid of a computer program. The rules, number of decks, penetration level, bet spread, and betting ramp all have an effect on the SD per hand. Nevertheless, here are approximate SD numbers for the play-all style approach using generic bet spreads:

One deck (1–4 units). 2.35

Two decks (1–8 units). 3.00

Four decks (1–8 units). 3.50

Six decks (1–12 units). 3.75

Eight decks (1–12 units). 3.50

A card counter must be prepared for huge bankroll swings. While we often express expectation in terms of hourly rates of earnings, counting cards isn't like working a nine-to-five job and punching a time clock. Standard deviation gets in the way of consistent week-in and week-out earnings.

BUILDING A STARTING BANKROLL

You can build a starting bankroll by saving every extra dollar that comes your way. You can work a second job or you can work overtime simply for the purpose of building a bankroll. Someone who trusts you might be willing to share the risk for a share of your profits. However, anyone who becomes involved by contributing to your bankroll must understand that this is a very risky investment and that the money invested could be lost. You can also begin building a bankroll by starting small and trusting to luck. I have a very lucky friend who once built a $20,000 bankroll with a starting bankroll of $800.

Some players solve the bankroll dilemma by latching on to a team and playing with the team's bankroll. (See "Becoming a Team Player" below.) Another option is to form a partnership. There are a variety of ways to use a partner. The advantage of a partner is a shared bankroll. With a joint bankroll, you can play to the same risk with two players as you would with one. You are just getting in more hands in a shorter

Becoming a Team Player

A team player usually has some experience playing and counting before he even thinks about joining a team. If he is new to the scene, he probably won't even know how to find a team to join. If you're interested in becoming a team player, one of the best ways to become known to those who manage teams is to join Internet discussion groups. Once you have established some level of trust and have learned about some of the teams, you might be able to arrange meetings with members of the group.

Most teams have rigorous entry standards. They may test you to determine your level of skill. You will probably be asked to sign an agreement that sets forth the requirements the team has, how you will be paid, and even the specific types of games you are expected to play. These agreements can include a provision that allows the team mangers to subject you to a lie detector test at any time. If you join a team, you will be a suspect until you can prove your trustworthiness. It goes with the territory.

period of time than you would by going solo. To get the most out of a shared bankroll, partners shouldn't play at the same table. That increases their risk when compared with playing separately. Of course, it is vital that both partners are skilled in their play and that both of them know how to select a good game. Trust is essential. Many a friendship has been destroyed over partnership arrangements in blackjack.

Whatever you do, be sure not to go into debt trying to build a bankroll—especially not with a credit company or a bank. Borrowing money from friends and family is also risky business. If you can't pay them back, you may very well lose your friends or negatively affect your lifelong relationships.

PROTECTING YOUR TRIP BANKROLL FROM THEFT, CONFISCATION, OR LOSS

A Twist on Partnerships

Your blackjack partner doesn't necessarily have to know how to count cards. He can watch you play from a distance and join the game by a prearranged signal from you when the count becomes favorable. Then, he can play with a preset bet until you signal him that the count has taken a nosedive. Of course, two players can only do so much of this in one casino before rousing the pit crew's attention.

A very real risk of ruin is the possibility that your bankroll will be stolen by thieves, confiscated by legal authorities, or even simply lost. Card counters must, by necessity, carry fairly large amounts of cash. A trip bankroll can run into several thousand dollars, which would be quite a haul for any aspiring mugger. Even if you are a low-stakes bettor, you will find yourself carrying hundreds of dollars in cash. It is important to take a few commonsense measures to protect it.

Traveler's checks are a good way to protect your bankroll from thieves during travel to your casino destination, but there are two problems with this once you arrive: 1) You may be required to show your identification at the cashier's cage to cash a traveler's check. If you want to keep your identity to yourself to avoid being recognized as a card counter, you won't want to produce your ID for inspection. 2) After cashing the checks, you'll still wind up having lots of cash on you.

Another way to avoid carrying large amounts of cash during travel is to arrange for a line of credit with a casino prior to your trip. Since you will be required to submit a credit application and subject your bank accounts to review, there is an obvious tradeoff of privacy for security in this case, too.

Some of my acquaintances have established bank accounts in casino locales, particularly Las Vegas, and keep their excess cash in these accounts. Since these banks are not in any way connected to the casinos, their privacy remains intact. You, too, might want to consider doing this to avoid carrying cash during your travels. Another good idea is to wire yourself your trip bankroll before arriving at your destination and wire any profits back to your bank before returning home.

If you do choose to travel with cash and you are staying in a hotel, use one of their safe-deposit boxes to keep your money safe. In most casino hotels, this can be arranged at the cashier's cage or at the front desk. Keep most of your cash in the safe-deposit box and carry just enough for short-term playing sessions. After a losing session, you can go to the safe-deposit box to replenish your bankroll.

Be sure not to flash your cash while you are in the casino. I keep my "walking-around" money in a money clip that I carry in my front pocket. When I take it out, I keep it covered as much as possible and don't put it in full view of passers-by. You would be wise to do the same.

Be wary of potential thieves who sometimes hang out around the cashier's cage waiting for someone to cash in a large number of chips or coins. Usually, once such a thief has spotted a cash-rich victim, he'll phone an accomplice waiting near the exit. So, if you must take a lot of cash out of the cage, don't leave the casino immediately. Wander about for a while—go to the coffee shop or to the lounge for a snack or a drink. Visit the restroom. (Most thieves won't wait forever and will seek out a more ready mark if they think you are going to stay in the casino awhile longer.) If you have driven to the casino, use valet parking. Even in Las Vegas, where millions of lights turn night into day, and with its excellent police department and private casino security officers, people do get mugged, especially in parking garages.

Wearing a money belt—an around-the-waist fabric pouch—is a good way to conceal a large amount of cash on your body. However, the belt should be donned in privacy to avoid advertising its location. An acquaintance of mine keeps a fabric money bag near his groin on the assumption that a thief won't search that part of his body for money.

A wonderful idea that I got from a fellow player is to carry a "give-up wallet." This is a decoy wallet in which you put a few bucks, a few photos, and some expired credit cards that have been cut in half and placed in the slot just so the top half is showing. Then, if confronted by a thief or even if hit by a pickpocket, you can give up the decoy wallet.

In addition to theft, a player can be faced with legal confiscation of his cash. Unfortunately, in our society today, legal authorities need to be on the lookout for drug dealers and terrorists, both of whom tend to carry around large amounts of cash. As a result, people who carry large amounts of cash equal to or greater than $10,000 are subject to legal confiscation of their money in the United States by lawful authorities. It is a travesty of American liberty for anyone who is carrying large amounts of cash to automatically be considered a suspected criminal, but it is a fact of life. It can cost a lot in legal fees to recover this money. I am aware of at least one person who failed to recover a large amount of money that was confiscated during a routine traffic stop.

With increased airport security after the 9/11 tragedy, the possibility of being found with a large amount of cash during a routine passenger check has grown considerably. In such times, arranging credit, carrying traveler's checks, or wiring money ahead is something that gamblers who carry a lot of cash have to consider.

As far as physically losing your bankroll is concerned, you must make a concerted effort to safeguard your money. Before I knew better, I'd lose bills or chips by filling my pockets too full with too many items. So, take a lesson from me and keep your belongings well organized and accessible, and your cash and chips should be safe.

BET SPREADS AND BETTING RAMPS

The more decks that are in play, the greater the bet spread needs to be. This is because a player generally has to overcome the larger house

---

Betting Approaches

There are a few ways counters can approach blackjack that can affect the steepness of their bet spreads. These include the play-all style of play, in which a player enters a game and plays through the negative counts while waiting for the positive counts; Wonging, or backcounting, in which a player enters a game only on favorable counts; and semi-Wonging, or exit strategy, in which a player exits a game when the count becomes unfavorable. (See Chapter 10.)

The play-all approach is best used in single-deck and double-deck games and only in the best of multiple-deck games. However, some people prefer the play-all style and even may accept marginal game conditions to play this way. They simply aren't comfortable lurking in the pit area, watching the games, and jumping into the game when the count is favorable. It upsets other players and, sometimes, it's strictly prohibited.

A player can make a decent profit using a 1–2 or 1–3 bet spread in a single-deck game and can play profitably using a 1–4 or 1–6 bet spread in double-deck games. But once he moves to multiple-deck games, he must widen the spread considerably.

advantage inherent in multiple-deck games and is often stuck making "waiting bets" of minimum size at neutral or negative counts. When the count swings to the player's advantage, he must make larger bets to overcome the bets he made at a disadvantage.

A player can make a decent profit using a 1–2 or 1–3 bet spread in a single-deck game and can play profitably using a 1–4 or 1–6 bet spread in double-deck games. But once he moves to multiple-deck games, he must widen the spread considerably. A 1–4 spread using the play-all style of play is not going to generate a profit in multiple-deck games. He needs at least a 1–8 bet spread to make any appreciable profit, and a 1–12 bet spread is what it takes to even begin to approach the potential profit of hand-held games.

For our purposes, I recommend the following generic bet spreads:

- 1–4 units for single-deck games

- 1–8 units for double-deck and four-deck games

- 1–12 units for six- and eight-deck games

Of course, the way you bet makes all the difference in how much profit you earn and how much risk you take. There is no one method that fits all games and all conditions. Although most players use a generic betting ramp that is geared to the number of decks in play, this method is not always the most effective. It does, however, have an advantage: It is easy to remember and is one less thing to distract a counter while at the tables. (If you are interested in optimal betting ramps, see the game-simulation tables in Chapter 9.)

Tables 8.1 to 8.3 present generic betting ramps for the play-all style and Wonging and semi-Wonging strategies. They are not necessarily the optimal betting ramps, but they are easy to use and remember.

ADJUSTING YOUR BASE BETTING UNIT FOR DIFFERENT GAMES

Many counters don't think of their bankroll in terms of units. Instead, they think in terms of big bets. By using that method of bankroll sizing, a player who uses a 1–4 spread at single-deck games with a unit of $25 and a top bet of $100 would not play a multiple-deck game with the

Table 8.1 Betting Ramps for the Play-All Style

True Count	One Deck	Two Decks	Four Decks	Six Decks	Eight Decks
<0	1 unit	1 unit	1 unit	1 unit	1 unit
+1	2 units	1 unit	1 unit	1 unit	1 unit
+2	4 units	2 units	2 units	2 units	2 units
+3	4 units	4 units	4 units	4 units	4 units
+4	4 units	6 units	8 units	6 units	6 units
+5	4 units	8 units	8 units	12 units	12 units

Table 8.2 Betting Ramps for the Semi-Wonging Style of Play

True Count	One Deck	Two Decks	Four Decks	Six Decks	Eight Decks
<0	0 units	0 units	0 units	0 units	0 units
0	1 unit	1 unit	1 unit	1 unit	1 unit
+1	2 units	1 unit	1 unit	1 unit	1 unit
+2	4 units	2 units	2 units	2 units	2 units
+3	4 units	4 units	4 units	4 units	4 units
+4	4 units	6 units	8 units	6 units	6 units
+5	4 units	8 units	8 units	12 units	12 units

Table 8.3 Betting Ramps for the Wonging Style of Play

True Count	One Deck*	Two Decks*	Four Decks	Six Decks	Eight Decks
<0	0 units	0 units	0 units	0 units	0 units
0	0 units	0 units	0 units	0 units	0 units
+1	2 units	2 units	1 unit	1 unit	1 unit
+2	4 units	4 units	2 units	2 units	2 units
+3	4 units	6 units	4 units	4 units	4 units
+4	4 units	8 units	8 units	6 units	6 units
+5	4 units	8 units	8 units	12 units	12 units

*Using the Wonging strategy in single-deck or double-deck games is a very effective method, but it also brings on excessive heat from the pit and a good deal of resentment from fellow players.

same unit. For a double-deck game, using a top bet of 8 units, he will adjust his base betting unit downward to $10 or $15 to keep his top bet close to the $100 limit. In a six-deck game, he will adjust his unit down to an amount between $5 and $10. This is a useful approach to determine the proper bet size for a variety of games. You might be a $25 bettor at single-deck tables, but find that being a $5 bettor in multiple-deck games is the best way to keep your risk of ruin in order. Of course, your earnings per hour will also be reduced as you reduce the size of your base betting unit.

READJUSTING YOUR BASE BETTING UNIT AND RESIZING YOUR BANKROLL

If you are starting with a small bankroll and your base betting unit is $5, you will certainly want to increase that amount as soon as possible. This is partly because games starting at the $25 level are usually more favorable to the players. In many casinos, games with better rules are only found at the higher denomination tables. These tables also tend to be less crowded than lower denomination tables, and it is far easier to score good comps at tables with minimums of $25 or more. While you could continue to play at a $5 table using $5 as your base betting unit, the spread required to earn money proportional to your increased bankroll would no doubt catch the unwanted attention of either the pit boss or surveillance personnel.

When should you resize your bankroll? I suggest keeping your unit at your original level until you have reduced your risk of ruin to at least 5 percent. Then, increase that unit by $5 when you can play at that level with a 5 percent risk of ruin. Keep playing at that level, until you can increase it by another $5 and still play with a 5 percent risk of ruin. Once you get to the $25 base betting unit level, however, you should not resize again until you can play with a 1 percent risk of ruin or less.

DETERMINING THE NUMBER OF BIG BETS FOR SHORT PERIODS OF PLAY

Any card counter who intends to put in a significant number of hours playing blackjack should be thinking in terms of total bankroll. However, if he is betting $25 units or higher, he might not want to take his entire bankroll with him when taking a trip to a casino locale. To achieve a very low risk of ruin, a bankroll of eighteen big bets should be sufficient for a typical weekend's worth of play. Table 8.4 can help you determine the bankroll you'll need based on the projected length of playing time. Using the table as a guide, if you plan to play a total of four hours, you should bring an amount of money equal to at least twelve big bets. In other words, if your big bet is $50, you'll need a bankroll of $600 for four hours of play. This approximates a 5 percent risk of ruin in most playable games.

Hours of Play	Number of Big Bets	Hours of Play	Number of Big Bets
4	12	24	24
8	16	28	26
12	18	32	28
16	20	36	29
20	22	40	30

Table 8.4
Bankroll Calculator for Short Periods of Play

The High Cost of Tipping and Other Expenses

Although tipping and other expenses were discussed in Part One, this subject is worth another mention. Tips directly affect your expected value, as well as your risk of ruin. For example, tipping just $1 per hour in a double-deck game with S17, DAS, and 70 percent penetration can increase your required bankroll from 1,172 units to 1,206 units with a top bet of $100 for a 1 percent risk of ruin. That would require a 2.9 percent increase in your bankroll just to cover the risk. It would also reduce your earnings by 2.8 percent. Tipping is a personal decision, but you should be aware of its effect on your bankroll.

Travel costs to and from casinos are also a drain on your bankroll. These can be anything from the cost of driving to the nearest local casino to the expense of airline tickets, hotel rooms, meals, rental cars, taxi fares, tips, or entertainment expenses incurred while visiting a gaming town. If you are a recreational player, you may keep these expenses separate from your blackjack bankroll and simply chalk them up to the cost of a vacation. If you are engaged in the more serious pursuit of profit, you can't ignore the effect of these costs on your bankroll. They are the equivalent of fixed expenses to a business. Unfortunately, these fixed costs are not tax deductible for gamblers. You must deduct these fixed costs from your bankroll and consider the remainder your actual playing bankroll if you want to have a true picture of your risk of ruin.

KEEPING RECORDS OF YOUR PLAYING SESSIONS

Be sure to keep good records of your playing sessions. This serves several purposes: 1) You know where you stand in terms of your bankroll; 2) You can examine your losing and winning sessions and consider where you might be making mistakes in playing choices; 3) You can identify those casinos and casino personnel who are difficult, helpful, or neutral; and, 4) You will have a record for tax purposes.

I take a loose-leaf notebook with me on my gambling trips in which I record a number of things about my play, usually right before going to bed. I also carry a memo pad in my pocket to make notes immediately after a playing session. As a card counter, you should assume you are being watched, so don't write in your notebook or memo pad inside the casino.

In my notebook, I record the date, the casino's name, the shift, the rules, the penetration, and the amount of my wins or losses for the session. If it is pertinent, I make notes on the dealer or the pit crew. For example, I might write, "Sally at the Stardust gives 75 percent penetration on the double-decker," or "Mary, the pit boss on swing shift at Treasure Island, paid close attention to my play and called surveillance." Such notes can be valuable to you as your playing career progresses. Record keeping should be a part of your regular routine. Here's a sample entry:

Date: June 16

Casino: Treasure Island

Shift: Afternoon 1 p.m.-5 p.m.

Type of Game/Rules: 6 deck/S17, DAS

Penetration: 83%

Wins/Losses: plus $60

Comments: Pit boss (Mary) was paying close attention to my play.

Comps and the Card Counter

Comps are an important part of a counter's game. Free lodging and meals can add significantly to a player's bottom line. The less he spends on living expenses, the more profits he has.

The difference between a basic strategy player and a card counter is that a card counter is not playing for comps. He is playing for money. The comps come with the game, but they are not the reason a counter enters the casino. It is very easy for a counter to forget this. Counters are no different from most other folks. The idea of getting a freebie is attractive and getting the VIP treatment at a first-class resort can be a big boost to the ego. Counters often play for stakes high enough to get the best. They are offered suites, side trips to vacation resorts, airfare, and more. This kind of treatment is difficult to resist.

However, it has been the downfall of many a counter and his bankroll. Counters who fall for this most attractive of casino traps find themselves overbetting their bankrolls just to get the next highest level of comps or, even worse, camping out at a single casino for hours on end to qualify for the high-roller treatment.

Some players feel that counters shouldn't take comps at all because this puts them on the pit's radar screen. Then, it'll be just a matter of time before the counter gets the toss. They say, get in, put in your time, and get out with as little fuss as possible. Pay for your expenses out of your winnings. In effect, comp yourself. However, I believe that any player who makes $25 bets or more should ask to be rated and take the comps that come his way. A player who is playing for those stakes will stand out more by refusing to be rated. What a player should not do is play one minute longer than he planned or play in a game that has deteriorated just to get a comp. It is better to give up an hour's worth of estimated value to pay for a room than it is to get barred, overbet your bankroll, or play a game with poor conditions.

CONCLUSION

This chapter covered handling and protecting your money and discussed the basics of risk of ruin. You can't play blackjack without money at hand, and knowing the proper amount to bet is an essential part of the game. As expressed in this chapter, just knowing how much money is needed for betting isn't enough. A card counter can lose his money in other ways as well. Overtipping and the possibility of either losing your money through carelessness or by robbery are very real threats.

The next chapter provides another building block for a card counter's arsenal, and it is perhaps the most important of them all if profit is your motive. Just as a wise investor knows that all investments are not the same, a wise card counter knows that all games aren't the same, and does his best to choose the game that will give him the greatest return.

GAME
SELECTION

A blackjack player who knows how to play basic strategy, how to count, how to make the proper strategy variations, and how to bet still isn't ready to walk into a casino and put his hard-earned money at risk. All of that knowledge can be for naught if the player isn't wise in his game selection. It isn't just a matter of looking at the expectation or the rules and choosing the game that looks good on paper. It's about taking all of the factors into consideration.

This chapter begins by offering some practical advice about the factors that can affect the quality of the game, including the all-important penetration level, game speed, and casino tolerance. Just as important as selecting a game is knowing when to quit a game, so this chapter also covers that important topic. Then, it sets forth a series of game-simulation tables that can be used to analyze the comparative value of different game conditions. Regardless of the style of play or betting ramp you choose, you can use these tables as a guide for selecting the best games when using the Hi-Lo System.

FACTORS TO CONSIDER WHEN SELECTING A GAME

A card counter should be as selective about what games he chooses as a gourmand is about the meals he eats. When a card counter goes to a casino locale, he should already have a plan of action. He should know where to find the good games, and he should plan to spend a good portion of his time scouting out each casino he visits. The best source for up-to-date gaming conditions in most of North America is Stanford Wong's *Current Blackjack News*, a gaming magazine that includes a comprehensive listing of the games, the rules, penetration estimates, expectation figures for each game, the number of tables in each casino listed, and the table limits.

Even with the newest issue of *Current Blackjack News* in hand, there is no substitute for scouting out a casino before you play. When you enter a casino, check out the different pit areas. Watch the dealers to see who is offering the best penetration. If you don't know what rules are in play, ask a dealer or a pit boss. Look for tables that meet your criteria for rules, penetration, and number of players. If you don't see what you want, especially in Las Vegas or in any area with a number of casinos, move on to the next place. This all takes time, but it is time well spent.

Various methods have been devised to measure the value of games. For instance, Don Schlesinger's *Blackjack Attack* has contributed much to game and system evaluation by introducing grading methods such as the *desirability index* and *SCORE*. He attempts to balance the risk with the potential profit of the game. His methods should be taken seriously by any card counter. But even with a specific method for measuring the value of a game, you will need to be on the lookout for certain conditions, each of which is discussed below. (See "The Best and the Worst" on page 144 for some specifics on game selection.)

Casino Tolerance

The pressure that casinos put on card counters is called *heat*. The amount of heat a counter perceives should be a part of his game selection. High-stake counters often pass on single-deck games because these games require a significant increase in bets when the count goes up. This makes a single-deck game especially vulnerable to "counter catchers," or so the conventional wisdom tells us. But for a player who has a top bet of $100 or less, heat shouldn't be a major factor at most casinos. In fact, quite a few casinos won't pay undue attention to bettors who keep their bets below $200. There are exceptions to the rule, of course. See Chapter 11 for more on casino heat.

Game Speed

Unlike the comp player, a card counter wants to find a game in which he can play as many hands per hour as possible. Instead of looking for crowded tables, he gravitates toward the empty tables where a fast heads-up game (that is, one player against the dealer) can be found. By the way, there are few things more frustrating to a card counter than sitting down at an empty table only to be joined by a lurker who was too shy to open up an empty table himself, especially if the counter is playing two hands.

Low Minimum Bet

Generally speaking, single-deck games offer the most bang for the buck. Single-deck games with $25 minimums can often mean good playing conditions, good comps, and a reasonable chance of finding empty tables. If your maximum bet doesn't exceed $100, you might want to specialize in single-deck games—assuming you can find them. (If you do decide to play single-deck games, be sure to take the level of penetration and number of players at the table into account.)

Penetration

Penetration is one of the most important factors to consider when evaluating a game. Games with good rules and poor penetration usually don't measure up to games with mediocre rules and good penetration. For example, single-deck games with H17 and D10 are generally accompanied by poor or mediocre penetration these days. If you find such a game and it isn't well penetrated—that is, if thirty-five or more cards aren't dealt—it isn't a good choice. For the best value as far as single-deck games are concerned, look for empty or nearly empty single-deck games that deal to the rule of six. (See "The Rule of Six" on page 142.)

A good double-deck game should have penetration of at least 67 percent (seventy cards). The minimum you should seek in rules at this level of penetration is H17 and DAS. Even then, the game isn't a great choice, but it will do if that's all you can find. At 75 percent penetration, just about any double-deck game becomes a good game. At this level of penetration, with a 1–8 bet spread, a double-deck game should be chosen over any single-deck game that deals to the rule of six—with the possible exception of the rare single-deck game with S17, DAS, and LS.

While not very common these days, a four-deck game with 75 percent penetration can be an acceptable game if it offers, at the very least, S17 and DAS. If you find such a game, be sure to choose it over most six-deck games, unless fantastic penetration (83 percent or better) is being offered.

Good penetration in six-deck games starts at 83 percent (that's five out of six decks). But even then, the only six-deck game that can even compare to the better single- and double-deck games is one with S17, DAS, and LS. If you are lucky enough to find a six-deck game with 92 percent penetration (that's five and a half decks out of six decks), you can get a passable game if it offers S17 and DAS. With that same level of penetration, you can get a good game with S17 and LS; H17, DAS, and LS; or H17 and LS. You can get a quite good game with S17, DAS, and LS.

The Rule of Six

In single-deck games, the rule of six simply means that five rounds are dealt to a single player, four rounds are dealt to two players, three rounds are dealt to three players, and two rounds are dealt to four players. Some casinos employ the rule of six for up to four players and then deal at least two rounds to five or more players. However, many casinos strictly apply the rule of six and deal only one round to five or more players. A game that offers one round and then a shuffle isn't worth playing.

It's generally believed that rule-of-six games offer penetration of 50 percent, but that's not necessarily the case. A heads-up game will see an average of 27 cards prior to the shuffle, but a game with two players will see an average of 32.4 cards, or 62.3 percent penetration. That level of penetration is quite good in a single-deck game.

The number of players in a game that's dealt to the rule of six makes a difference in the expected value of the game. More than three players at a single-deck table usually makes for a game that's not worth playing—unless that game has five or more players and two rounds are being dealt before the shuffle. With these conditions, a player can make a good per-hand profit but at the expense of game speed.

In general, the best configuration of players at a single-deck game that's dealt to the rule of six is two. In fact, if you are playing in a heads-up game at a single-deck table, play two hands with a spread of 1–3 units or even 1–2 units. The extra expected value from playing a game with better penetration will make up for the smaller bet size. Also, since casino personnel are less likely to take notice of a change in bet size from $25 to $75 than from $25 to $100, you'll probably get less heat.

As for eight-deck games, the pickings are pretty much nonexistent. However, if you are Wonging or semi-Wonging (see Chapter 10), you might find a playable game if it is well penetrated to at least the 81 percent level with S17, DAS, and LS.

Rules

Although not as important as penetration, rules are still important. All things being equal, a card counter should choose a game that offers DAS. In fact, it isn't worth playing in a multiple-deck game that doesn't offer DAS—unless it is very well penetrated (75 percent or greater). If you are faced with games of only four decks or more, look for those that offer, at the very least, S17 and DAS—unless the game offers outstanding penetration of 83 percent or greater. Even with such deep penetration, however, you can probably find a better game elsewhere.

Use of the Shuffle Card

In hand-held games, avoid games that use a shuffle card, also called a *cut card*. As you may recall from Chapter 4, if a fixed shuffle point is used in single-deck or double-deck games, the players get fewer rounds if a lot of low cards surface and more rounds if a lot of high cards surface. This is known as the *cut-card effect*. Some card counters don't mind the use of a shuffle card since it makes it more difficult for a dealer to shuffle the deck prematurely. (See "Avoid Preferential Shuffling" on page 63.) In general, however, it's best to avoid games with a shuffle card.

Sadly, for a conventional counter, if the only game in town is a lousy game, the best solution is to find another town. If you are serious about card counting, then you should be serious about making money from the game. If the game you have closest to you won't allow you to do that at a decent rate, you either have to make the hard choice not to play or admit that you are more interested in the action than you are in making money.

WHEN TO QUIT A SESSION

A good player not only knows when to get into a game, but also when to quit and when not to quit a particular session. Much of the gambling

The Best and the Worst

All things being equal, a deeply dealt single-deck game at a table with two players is the best game for a card counter while an eight-deck game with lousy rules and poor penetration is the worst. But all things are *not* equal. As this chapter points out, there are many factors to take into consideration when evaluating a game. So, keeping that in mind, the following is a general list of the five best and the five worst games for low-stakes bettors (a max bet of $200 or less) and for high-stakes bettors (a max bet over $200). Games that are not commonly found in the United States are not included in these lists, nor are games that should be avoided at all costs, such as Spanish 21.

For Low Stakes

Games to Play

1. Single deck, S17, 50 percent penetration or better, with three or fewer players

2. Single deck, H17, 50 percent penetration or better, with three or fewer players

3. Double deck, S17, DAS, 60 percent penetration or better

4. Double deck, H17, DAS, 75 percent penetration or better

5. Six deck, S17, DAS, LS, 83 percent penetration or better

Games to Avoid

1. Any eight-deck H17 game

2. Any six-deck H17 game

3. Any eight-deck or six-deck game with less than 75 percent penetration

4. Any double-deck game with 50 percent penetration or less

5. Any single-deck game in which the dealer deals one hand between shuffles

For High Stakes

Games to Play

1. Six deck, S17, DAS, LS, 83 percent penetration or better

2. Double deck, S17, DAS, 60 percent penetration or better (but watch out for heat)

3. Double deck, H17, DAS, 60 percent penetration or better (but watch out for heat)

4. Six deck, S17, DAS, LS with 75 percent penetration or better, using Wonging or semi-Wonging

5. Eight deck, S17, DAS, LS, with 88 percent penetration or better, using Wonging or semi-Wonging

Games to Avoid

1. Any single-deck game (a card-counter trap)

2. Double-deck, S17, DAS, LS (another card-counter trap)

3. Any six-deck game with less than 75 percent penetration unless using Wonging or semi-Wonging

4. Any eight-deck game with less than 88 percent penetration that doesn't offer LS

5. Any eight-deck game with less than 81 percent penetration

literature is devoted to recommending stop losses and win goals, which require that you leave a game when you've lost or won × amount of money. While a stop loss or a win goal might have some psychological effect on a player, it does nothing to add to or subtract from his overall results in a lifetime of play. If you have been hammered really hard in a session and it affects your play, you might want to leave the table, but this is not the same thing as a stop loss. Similarly, if you have won enough money to attract unwanted attention from the pit, you also might want to leave the table, but this should not be confused with a win goal. Ideally, if you are in a good game (barring the reasons to quit listed below), you should play it as long as you have money in your pocket or credit on the books, or as long as your game plan says you should play.

The following are my top ten reasons for leaving a game or quitting a session:

1. The game conditions have deteriorated. This can occur, for example, when a new dealer takes over and doesn't penetrate the deck as deeply as the previous dealer or when more players join the table in a single-deck game.

2. From the attention you're getting, you suspect that the pit might be on to you.

3. You hit a preset time limit. For card counters, time limits are valuable tools in the battle against the casino (see Chapter 11).

4. You have hit a preset win *limit*. This isn't done in an effort to preserve your winnings but rather to avoid heat.

5. You're tired. Tired players make mistakes, and those mistakes can turn a good game into a very bad one.

6. You're not feeling well. If you're ill, your game won't be up to par.

7. You've made other plans with family and/or friends, and they're waiting for you. Remember, you're also a player in the game of life, and that game is more important than any blackjack game, no matter how good the conditions are. Standing up people you care for can have its very own negative expectation. Other card counters might understand, but those who don't play the game probably won't.

8. You have to check out of your hotel or catch a plane. If you are in a great game, you might want to weigh the potential earnings in the game against the cost of a late checkout or rescheduling a flight. And don't forget number 7.

9. You've consumed too many alcoholic beverages. This will affect your ability to play a good game perhaps even more than being tired or sick.

10. Your spouse says it's time to quit!

DETERMINING THE QUALITY OF VARIOUS GAMES

The tables you'll find on pages 150–177 have multiple purposes. In addition to helping you compare the relative quality of various games in terms of earning potential balanced with the risk involved, they can be used to determine bet size, bet spreads, betting ramps, and strategies for a variety of games.

The information presented in the tables is based on computer-generated game simulations. The number of players in the simulations is two players for single-deck games, three players for double-deck games, and four players for all multiple-deck games—with a total bankroll of $10,000 and a constant risk of ruin of 5 percent.

You'll find tables for single-deck, double-deck, four-deck, six-deck, and eight-deck games with rule combinations that are most likely to be found in today's casinos. A few games that are included are provided only for comparison purposes. You'll know which ones they are by the data presented. Wonging and semi-Wonging styles of play are included only for multiple-deck games, since these strategies attract too much attention in single- and double-deck games. Some games, particularly multiple-deck games with certain rules, are not included in the tables because they simply aren't worth playing. You won't find data for single-deck games or double-deck games with surrender, since this option is practically nonexistent in these games.

Each table includes various games within a certain category. For example, Table 9.1 is labeled "Single-Deck Games." In this table, you will find specific descriptions, such as "Single Deck, H17, D10, 26/52 (50% Penetration)." This portion of the table is obviously a simulation of a single-deck game in which the dealer hits soft 17 (H17), with doubles limited to 10 and 11 (D10), and with twenty-six out of fifty-two cards dealt, or 50 percent penetration. (In tables for more than two decks, the penetration fraction is given in number of decks rather than number of cards.)

Single-deck and double-deck games have been set up with four columns, while multiple-deck games have been set up with six columns. Here is a breakdown of what you will find in each column:

1. The true count.

2. The optimum betting ramp for the game, using a spread of 1–4 units for single-deck games, 1–8 units for double- and four-deck games, and 1–12 units for six- and eight-deck games.

3. This column lists near-optimum bets—that is, bets that correspond to the optimum bet to the nearest whole unit.

4. The "traditional" betting ramp, which reflects the generic betting ramps in Chapter 8.

5. Betting ramps for Wonging. The player comes into the game at true counts of +2 for the four-deck game and +1 for the six- and eight-deck games. A player would only play when the count is at that level or greater and would exit the game once the count had fallen below that level. (This column is included only for multiple-deck games.)

6. Betting ramps spreads for semi-Wonging. Using this strategy, a player could approach a freshly shuffled multiple-deck game and play it as long as the true count remains at 0 or above. As soon as the count falls below 0, the player would exit the game and seek another one. (This column is included only for multiple-deck games.)

The last four rows included for each set of game conditions listed below the heading *Game Results* provide some important information. *EV per 100 hands* indicates the expected value in terms of units for each 100 hands played in the play-all style or observed in the Wonging and semi-Wonging styles of play. The next row, *5 Percent ROR* shows the number of units one would need to play to a 5 percent risk of ruin with a $10,000 bankroll. The necessary unit size expressed in dollar amounts is reflected in the row *Unit Size*. Last, *Earnings per 100 hands* indicates the earnings that could be expected per 100 hands played or observed using the unit size set forth in the row above. It is this bottom row that can be used to compare games and betting styles.

As you review the tables, keep the following points in mind.

• About the Betting Amounts—While the tables show the exact bet one would make in a given situation, no one can make a bet of $9.37 at the blackjack table (see Table 9.4, six-deck H17, DAS, LS, 83 percent penetration). To use these tables as a guide for betting, divide your bankroll by the number of units listed for each game and style of betting and round them to the nearest whole unit or even to the nearest $5 unit. While there's no reason you can't bet odd amounts, such as $9 or $13.50, doing so will slow down the dealer whiles she figures out the payouts for blackjacks or insurance.

• About the Risk of Ruin—The dollar figures for bets given in the tables are designed for a 5 percent risk of ruin with a $10,000 bankroll. Risk of ruin is not linear in nature. If the table for the game you are playing says you need 554 units, dropping to 277 units will not increase your risk of ruin to 10 percent. In fact, it will increase your risk of ruin far beyond 10 percent. By the same token, increasing your number of units will not decrease your risk of ruin. If you want to design a bankroll for a different risk of ruin, it would be a good idea to create your own game-simulation tables using computer software such as Blackjack Risk Manager 2002 (BJRM 2002) or CVCX.

Short of buying the software, here is a formula you can use to play to some different risk of ruin levels. If you want to decrease your risk of ruin to 1 percent, multiply the number of units in the 5 percent ROR row by 1.54. For example, if you were considering a double-deck game with H17, DAS rules at the 70/104 (67 percent) penetration range (see Table 9.2), using the near optimum betting ramp, you would multiply 763 times 1.54. You would need a total of 1,175 units to play to a 1 percent risk of ruin. If you wanted to go in the other direction, you would divide the number of units in the 5 percent ROR row. For a 10 percent risk of ruin, divide by 1.3, for a total of 586 units. If you are really daring and are willing to play to a 15 percent risk of ruin, divide the 5 percent ROR number by 1.58. In the example given, you could play to a 15 percent risk of ruin with 483 units. You can use this formula for any of the games listed.

• About the Bet Spreads—The tables reflect a 1–4 bet spread for single-deck games, a 1–8 bet spread for double- and four-deck games, and a

1–12 spread for six- and eight-deck games. In the case of single- and double-deck games, these are the spreads that will earn the most profit for a player without immediate pit attention. Other smaller spreads can be used, but their earnings will be smaller and the risk will not be reduced by a similar amount. A player can make a profit in most single-deck games using a spread as small as 1–2, and a profit can be made in double-deck games with a spread of 1–4. Larger spreads than the ones mentioned would earn very good profits in these games, but the pit would take immediate notice.

For multiple-deck games, the spread given is designed to generate at least a decent profit. Smaller spreads reduce the profit to the point that the games are not worth playing. A 1–4 or 1–6 bet spread in six- or eight-deck games will get little if any profit. A larger spread can get a larger profit. Using a 1–16 or greater spread will produce more hourly earnings. The tradeoff is in additional risk and a greater chance of being recognized as a counter by the pit.

• About Game Speed—One flaw in the game-simulation tables is that they don't take into account game speed, and that is no small consideration for a card counter. Suppose you are in a casino that offers two games, one of them a six-deck game with S17, DAS, and LS. The other game is a double-deck game with S17 and DAS, but no surrender. The six-deck game is penetrated to five decks (83 percent) and the double-deck game is penetrated to seventy cards (67 percent). At first glance, the double-deck game looks like the obvious choice, with its earning potential of $49.76 per 100 hands played. However, when you are making your decision, all of the double-deck tables are crowded, and if you can find a seat, you will be playing in a slow, crowded, hand-held game. In the meantime, the six-deck games have plenty of open seats, and you can get a heads-up game at one of the tables. You can get more than 200 rounds per hour at the near-empty six-deck game, while you can expect to get only about 50 rounds at the crowded double-deck game. Assuming you adjust your unit size to the fixed risk of ruin rate of 5 percent, you can make about $30 an hour at the double-deck game as opposed to about $70 an hour at the six-deck game. The game that looked better on paper is not the game you want to play. If there are several six-deck tables and using a Wonging or semi-Wonging style is practical, the six-deck game might be the better choice under any circumstances, unless you can get that double-deck table all to yourself.

Table 9.1   **Single-Deck Games**

H17, D10, 26/52 (50% Penetration)			
True Count	**Optimum Betting Ramp**	**Near Optimum Betting Ramp**	**Traditional Betting Ramp**
</=0	1	1	1
+1	1.9	2	2
+2 and up	4	4	4
Game Results			
EV per 100 hands	0.85	0.86	0.86
5 percent ROR	895	891	891
Unit size	$11.17	$11.22	$11.22
Earnings per 100 hands	$9.50	$9.65	$9.65
H17, D10, 31/52 (60% Penetration)			
True Count	**Optimum Betting Ramp**	**Near Optimum Betting Ramp**	**Traditional Betting Ramp**
</=0	1	1	1
+1	1.1	1	2
+2	3.2	3	4
+4 and up	4	4	4
Game Results			
EV per 100 hands	1.45	1.43	1.55
5 percent ROR	526	518	569
Unit size	$19.01	$19.31	$17.57
Earnings per 100 hands	$27.56	$27.61	$24.23
H17, D10, 35/52 (67% Penetration)			
True Count	**Optimum Betting Ramp**	**Near Optimum Betting Ramp**	**Traditional Betting Ramp**
</=0	1	1	1
+1	1	1	2
+2	2.9	3	4
+4 and up	4	4	4
Game Results			
EV per 100 hands	1.72	1.73	1.85
5 percent ROR	451	453	497
Unit size	$22.17	$22.08	$20.12
Earnings per 100 hands	$38.13	$38.20	$37.22

H17, D10, 39/52 (75% Penetration)			
True Count	**Optimum Betting Ramp**	**Near Optimum Betting Ramp**	**Traditional Betting Ramp**
</=0	1	1	1
+1	1	1	2
+2	2.2	2	4
+4	3.9	4	4
+5 and up	4	4	4
Game Results			
EV per 100 hands	2.27	2.26	2.46
5 percent ROR	344	345	395
Unit size	$29.07	$28.99	$25.32
Earnings per 100 hands	$65.99	$65.52	$62.99
H17, 26/52 (50% Penetration)			
True Count	**Optimum Betting Ramp**	**Near Optimum Betting Ramp**	**Traditional Betting Ramp**
</=0	1	1	1
+1	2.2	2	2
+2 and up	4	4	4
Game Results			
EV per 100 hands	1.44	1.42	1.42
5 percent ROR	582	582	582
Unit size	$17.18	$17.18	$17.18
Earnings per 100 hands	$24.74	$24.40	$24.40
H17, 31/52 (60% Penetration)			
True Count	**Optimum Betting Ramp**	**Near Optimum Betting Ramp**	**Traditional Betting Ramp**
</=0	1	1	1
+1	1.5	2	2
+2	3	3	4
+4 and up	4	4	4
Game Results			
EV per 100 hands	2.05	2.07	2.20
5 percent ROR	396	403	431
Unit size	$25.25	$24.81	$23.20
Earnings per 100 hands	$51.76	$51.36	$51.04

H17, 35/52 (67% Penetration)			
True Count	Optimum Betting Ramp	Near Optimum Betting Ramp	Traditional Betting Ramp
</=0	1	1	1
+1	1.3	1	2
+2	2.9	3	4
+4 and up	4	4	4
Game Results			
EV per 100 hands	2.35	2.35	2.52
5 percent ROR	357	358	392
Unit size	$28.01	$27.93	$25.51
Earnings per 100 hands	$65.83	$65.64	$64.29
H17, 39/52 (75% Penetration)			
True Count	Optimum Betting Ramp	Near Optimum Betting Ramp	Traditional Betting Ramp
</=0	1	1	1
+1	1.1	1	2
+2	2.3	2	4
+4	3.7	4	4
+5 and up	4	4	4
Game Results			
EV per 100 hands	2.89	2.90	3.18
5 percent ROR	285	288	328
Unit size	$35.09	$34.72	$30.49
Earnings per 100 hands	$101.40	$100.69	$96.95
H17, DAS, 26/52 (50% Penetration)			
True Count	Optimum Betting Ramp	Near Optimum Betting Ramp	Traditional Betting Ramp
</=0	1	1	1
+1	2.2	2	2
+2 and up	4	4	4
Game Results			
EV per 100 hands	1.69	1.68	1.68
5 percent ROR	487	482	482
Unit size	$20.53	$20.75	$20.75
Earnings per 100 hands	$34.70	$34.85	$34.85

H17, DAS, 31/52 (60% Penetration)			
True Count	**Optimum Betting Ramp**	**Near Optimum Betting Ramp**	**Traditional Betting Ramp**
</=0	I	I	I
+1	1.6	2	2
+2	3	3	4
+4 and up	4	4	4
Game Results			
EV per 100 hands	2.31	2.33	2.47
5 percent ROR	361	366	392
Unit size	$27.70	$27.32	$26.51
Earnings per 100 hands	$63.99	$63.66	$63.01
H17, DAS, 35/52 (67% Penetration)			
True Count	**Optimum Betting Ramp**	**Near Optimum Betting Ramp**	**Traditional Betting Ramp**
</=0	I	I	I
+1	1.5	2	2
+2	2.9	3	4
+4 and up	4	4	4
Game Results			
EV per 100 hands	2.62	2.66	2.80
5 percent ROR	329	336	360
Unit size	$30.40	$29.76	$27.78
Earnings per 100 hands	$79.64	$79.17	$77.78
H17, DAS, 39/52 (75% Penetration)			
True Count	**Optimum Betting Ramp**	**Near Optimum Betting Ramp**	**Traditional Betting Ramp**
</=0	I	I	I
+1	1.2	I	2
+2	2.3	2	4
+4	3.6	4	4
+5 and up	4	4	4
Game Results			
EV per 100 hands	3.13	3.16	3.47
5 percent ROR	265	269	306
Unit size	$37.44	$37.17	$32.68
Earnings per 100 hands	$118.11	$117.47	$113.40

S17, 26/52 (50% Penetration)			
True Count	**Optimum Betting Ramp**	**Near Optimum Betting Ramp**	**Traditional Betting Ramp**
</=0	I	I	I
+I	2.2	2	2
+2 and up	4	4	4
Game Results			
EV per 100 hands	1.74	1.73	1.73
5 percent ROR	481	477	477
Unit size	$20.79	$20.96	$20.96
Earnings per 100 hands	$36.17	$36.27	$36.27
S17, 31/52 (60% Penetration)			
True Count	**Optimum Betting Ramp**	**Near Optimum Betting Ramp**	**Traditional Betting Ramp**
'</=0	I	I	I
+I	1.6	2	2
+2	3	3	4
+4 and up	4	4	4
Game Results			
EV per 100 hands	2.35	2.37	2.51
5 percent ROR	347	351	377
Unit size	$28.82	$28.49	$26.53
Earnings per 100 hands	$67.72	$67.52	$66.58
S17, 35/52 (67% Penetration)			
True Count	**Optimum Betting Ramp**	**Near Optimum Betting Ramp**	**Traditional Betting Ramp**
</=0	I	I	I
+I	1.5	2	2
+2	2.8	3	4
+4 and up	4	4	4
Game Results			
EV per 100 hands	2.65	2.70	2.85
5 percent ROR	315	324	346
Unit size	$31.75	$30.86	$28.90
Earnings per 100 hands	$84.14	$83.33	$82.37

S17, 39/52 (75% Penetration)			
True Count	**Optimum Betting Ramp**	**Near Optimum Betting Ramp**	**Traditional Betting Ramp**
</=0	1	1	1
+1	1.2	1	2
+2	2.3	2	4
+4	3.5	4	4
+5 and up	4	4	4
Game Results			
EV per 100 hands	3.14	3.19	3.50
5 percent ROR	256	261	297
Unit size	$39.06	$38.31	$33.67
Earnings per 100 hands	$122.66	$122.22	$117.85
S17, DAS, 26/52 (50% Penetration)			
True Count	**Optimum Betting Ramp**	**Near Optimum Betting Ramp**	**Traditional Betting Ramp**
</=0	1	1	1
+1	2.2	2	2
+2	3.8	4	4
+4 and up	4	4	4
Game Results			
EV per 100 hands	1.97	1.98	1.98
5 percent ROR	422	425	425
Unit size	$23.70	$23.53	$23.53
Earnings per 100 hands	$46.68	$46.59	$46.59
S17, DAS, 31/52 (60% Penetration)			
True Count	**Optimum Betting Ramp**	**Near Optimum Betting Ramp**	**Traditional Betting Ramp**
</=0	1	1	1
+1	1.7	2	2
+2	2.9	3	4
+4 and up	4	4	4
Game Results			
EV per 100 hands	2.59	2.63	2.78
5 percent ROR	319	323	347
Unit size	$31.35	$30.96	$28.82
Earnings per 100 hands	$81.19	$81.42	$80.12

S17, DAS, 35/52 (67% Penetration)			
True Count	**Optimum Betting Ramp**	**Near Optimum Betting Ramp**	**Traditional Betting Ramp**
</=0	1	1	1
+1	1.6	2	2
+2	2.8	3	4
+4 and up	4	4	4
Game Results			
EV per 100 hands	2.91	2.97	3.13
5 percent ROR	294	300	321
Unit size	$34.01	$33.33	$31.15
Earnings per 100 hands	$98.97	$98.99	$97.50
S17, DAS, 39/52 (75% Penetration)			
True Count	**Optimum Betting Ramp**	**Near Optimum Betting Ramp**	**Traditional Betting Ramp**
</=0	1	1	1
+1	1.3	1	2
+2	2.3	2	4
+4	3.4	3	4
+5 and up	4	4	4
Game Results			
EV per 100 hands	3.38	3.29	3.78
5 percent ROR	240	237	281
Unit size	$41.67	$42.19	$35.59
Earnings per 100 hands	$140.84	$138.81	$134.53

Table 9.2 Double-Deck Games

H17, 52/104 (50% Penetration)			
True Count	**Optimum Betting Ramp**	**Near Optimum Betting Ramp**	**Traditional Betting Ramp**
</=0	1	1	1
+1	2	2	1
+2	5.8	6	2
+3	8	8	4
+4	8	8	6
+5 and up	8	8	8
Game Results			
EV per 100 hands	1.43	1.44	0.88
5 percent ROR	1421	1434	1184
Unit size	$7.04	$6.97	$8.45
Earnings per 100 hands	$10.07	$10.04	$7.44
H17, 62/104 (60% Penetration)			
True Count	**Optimum Betting Ramp**	**Near Optimum Betting Ramp**	**Traditional Betting Ramp**
</=0	1	1	1
+1	1.6	2	1
+2	4.4	4	2
+3	6.9	7	4
+4	8	8	6
+5 and up	8	8	8
Game Results			
EV per 100 hands	1.99	1.85	1.53
5 percent ROR	1019	983	864
Unit size	$9.81	$10.17	$11.57
Earnings per 100 hands	$19.52	$18.81	$17.70
H17, 70/104 (67% Penetration)			
True Count	**Optimum Betting Ramp**	**Near Optimum Betting Ramp**	**Traditional Betting Ramp**
</=0	1	1	1
+1	1.5	2	1
+2	3.9	4	2
+3	5.6	6	4
+4	8	8	6
+5 and up	8	8	8

Game Results			
EV per 100 hands	2.47	2.51	2.09
5 percent ROR	829	845	727
Unit size	$12.06	$11.83	$13.76
Earnings per 100 hands	$29.79	$29.69	$28.76

H17, 78/104 (75% Penetration)			
True Count	Optimum Betting Ramp	Near Optimum Betting Ramp	Traditional Betting Ramp
</=0	1	1	1
+1	1.3	1	1
+2	3.2	3	2
+3	4.6	5	4
+4	6.7	7	6
+5 and up	8	8	8

Game Results			
EV per 100 hands	2.92	2.94	2.73
5 percent ROR	663	669	629
Unit size	$15.08	$14.95	$15.90
Earnings per 100 hands	$44.03	$43.95	$43.41

H17, DAS, 52/104 (50% Penetration)			
True Count	Optimum Betting Ramp	Near Optimum Betting Ramp	Traditional Betting Ramp
</=0	1	1	1
+1	2.6	3	1
+2	5.6	6	2
+3	8	8	4
+4	8	8	6
+5 and up	8	8	8

Game Results			
EV per 100 hands	1.78	1.83	1.13
5 percent ROR	1184	1209	950
Unit size	$8.45	$8.27	$10.53
Earnings per 100 hands	$15.04	$15.13	$11.90

H17, DAS, 62/104 (60% Penetration)			
True Count	Optimum Betting Ramp	Near Optimum Betting Ramp	Traditional Betting Ramp
</=0	1	1	1
+1	2.1	2	1
+2	4.5	5	2
+3	6.7	7	4
+4	8	8	6
+5 and up	8	8	8
Game Results			
EV per 100 hands	2.36	2.41	1.81
5 percent ROR	895	916	751
Unit size	$11.17	$10.92	$13.32
Earnings per 100 hands	$26.36	$26.32	$24.11
H17, DAS, 70/104 (67% Penetration)			
True Count	Optimum Betting Ramp	Near Optimum Betting Ramp	Traditional Betting Ramp
</=0	1	1	1
+1	1.9	2	1
+2	4	4	2
+3	5.5	6	4
+4	7.7	8	6
+5 and up	8	8	8
Game Results			
EV per 100 hands	2.81	2.86	2.38
5 percent ROR	745	763	657
Unit size	$13.42	$13.11	$15.22
Earnings per 100 hands	$37.71	$37.49	$36.22
H17, DAS, 78/104 (75% Penetration)			
True Count	Optimum Betting Ramp	Near Optimum Betting Ramp	Traditional Betting Ramp
</=0	1	1	1
+1	1.6	2	1
+2	3.4	3	2
+3	4.6	5	4
+4	6.5	7	6
+5 and up	8	8	8

Game Results			
EV per 100 hands	3.27	3.32	3.05
5 percent ROR	611	624	579
Unit size	$16.37	$16.03	$17.27
Earnings per 100 hands	$53.53	$53.22	$52.67

S17, 52/104 (50% Penetration)			
True Count	Optimum Betting Ramp	Near Optimum Betting Ramp	Traditional Betting Ramp
</=0	1	1	1
+1	2.6	3	1
+2	5.5	6	2
+3	8	8	4
+4	8	8	6
+5 and up	8	8	8
Game Results			
EV per 100 hands	1.83	1.88	1.18
5 percent ROR	1108	1141	881
Unit size	$9.03	$8.76	$11.35
Earnings per 100 hands	$16.52	$16.47	$13.39

S17, 62/104 (60% Penetration)			
True Count	Optimum Betting Ramp	Near Optimum Betting Ramp	Traditional Betting Ramp
</=0	1	1	1
+1	2.2	2	1
+2	4.4	4	2
+3	6.4	6	4
+4	8	8	6
+5 and up	8	8	8
Game Results			
EV per 100 hands	2.39	2.33	1.85
5 percent ROR	842	822	713
Unit size	$11.88	$12.17	$14.03
Earnings per 100 hands	$28.39	$28.36	$25.96

S17, 70/104 (67% Penetration)			
True Count	**Optimum Betting Ramp**	**Near Optimum Betting Ramp**	**Traditional Betting Ramp**
</=0	1	1	1
+1	1.9	2	1
+2	3.9	4	2
+3	5.3	5	4
+4	7.4	7	6
+5 and up	8	8	8
Game Results			
EV per 100 hands	2.82	2.78	2.43
5 percent ROR	697	688	624
Unit size	$14.35	$14.53	$16.03
Earnings per 100 hands	$48.47	$40.39	$38.95
S17, 78/104 (75% Penetration)			
True Count	**Optimum Betting Ramp**	**Near Optimum Betting Ramp**	**Traditional Betting Ramp**
</=0	1	1	1
+1	1.7	2	1
+2	4.5	5	2
+3	6.3	6	4
+4	8	8	6
+5 and up	8	8	8
Game Results			
EV per 100 hands	3.31	3.27	3.09
5 percent ROR	582	577	554
Unit size	$17.18	$17.33	$18.05
Earnings per 100 hands	$56.87	$56.67	$55.77
S17, DAS, 52/104 (50% Penetration)			
True Count	**Optimum Betting Ramp**	**Near Optimum Betting Ramp**	**Traditional Betting Ramp**
</=0	1	1	1
+1	2.9	3	1
+2	5.3	5	2
+3	7.6	8	4
+4	8	8	6
+5 and up	8	8	8

Game Results			
EV per 100 hands	2.15	2.16	1.43
5 percent ROR	946	945	744
Unit size	$10.57	$10.58	$13.44
Earnings per 100 hands	$22.73	$22.85	$19.22

S17, DAS, 62/104 (60% Penetration)

True Count	Optimum Betting Ramp	Near Optimum Betting Ramp	Traditional Betting Ramp
</=0	1	1	1
+1	2.5	3	1
+2	4.5	5	2
+3	6.3	6	4
+4	8	8	6
+5 and up	8	8	8

Game Results			
EV per 100 hands	2.75	2.81	2.13
5 percent ROR	760	775	633
Unit size	$13.16	$12.90	$15.80
Earnings per 100 hands	$36.19	$36.25	$33.65

S17, DAS, 70/104 (67% Penetration)

True Count	Optimum Betting Ramp	Near Optimum Betting Ramp	Traditional Betting Ramp
</=0	1	1	1
+1	2.2	2	1
+2	4	4	2
+3	5.3	5	4
+4	7.1	7	6
+5 and up	8	8	8

Game Results			
EV per 100 hands	3.16	3.12	2.72
5 percent ROR	634	627	570
Unit size	$15.77	$15.95	$17.54
Earnings per 100 hands	$49.83	$49.76	$47.71

S17, DAS, 78/104 (75% Penetration)			
True Count	**Optimum Betting Ramp**	**Near Optimum Betting Ramp**	**Traditional Betting Ramp**
</=0	1	1	1
+1	1.9	2	1
+2	3.5	4	2
+3	4.6	5	4
+4	6.2	6	6
+5 and up	8	8	8
Game Results			
EV per 100 hands	3.65	3.71	3.40
5 percent ROR	540	549	515
Unit size	$18.52	$18.21	$19.42
Earnings per 100 hands	$67.60	$67.56	$66.03

Table 9.3 **Four-Deck Games**

	HI7, DAS, 2.5/4 (63% Penetration)				
True Count	**Optimum Betting Ramp**	**Near Optimum Betting Ramp**	**Traditional Betting Ramp**	**Wong**	**Semi-Wong**
<0	1	1	1	0	0
0	1	1	1	0	1
+1	1	1	1	1	1
+2	5.38	5	2	2	2
+3	8	8	4	4	4
+4 and up	8	8	8	8	8
Game Results					
EV per 100 hands	1.12	1.10	0.76	1.54	1.35
5 percent ROR	1885	1837	1600	704	851
Unit Size	$5.31	$5.44	$6.25	$14.20	$11.75
Earnings per 100 hands	$5.94	$5.99	$4.75	$21.87	$15.86
	HI7, DAS, 3/4 (75% Penetration)				
True Count	**Optimum Betting Ramp**	**Near Optimum Betting Ramp**	**Traditional Betting Ramp**	**Wong**	**Semi-Wong**
</=0	1	1	1	0	1
+1	1	1	1	1	1
+2	3.24	3	2	2	2
+3	6.26	6	4	4	4
+4 and up	8	8	8	8	8
Game Results					
EV per 100 hands	1.73	1.71	1.56	2.39	2.23
5 percent ROR	1131	1118	1057	637	708
Unit Size	$8.84	$8.94	$9.46	$15.70	$14.12
Earnings per 100 hands	$15.30	$15.30	$14.76	$37.52	$31.49

H17, DAS, 3.5/4 (88% Penetration)					
True Count	**Optimum Betting Ramp**	**Near Optimum Betting Ramp**	**Traditional Betting Ramp**	**Wong**	**Semi-Wong**
<0	1	1	1	0	0
0	1	1	1	0	1
+1	1	1	1	1	1
+2	2.1	2	2	2	2
+3	3.98	4	4	4	4
+4	6.18	6	8	8	8
+5	7.79	8	8	8	8
+6 and up	8	8	8	8	8
Game Results					
EV per 100 hands	2.69	2.67	2.84	3.70	3.57
5 percent ROR	752	662	713	514	547
Unit Size	$12.95	$15.11	$14.02	$19.46	$18.28
Earnings per 100 hands	$34.84	$40.33	$39.83	$72.00	$65.26
S17, DAS, 2.5/4 (63% Penetration)					
True Count	**Optimum Betting Ramp**	**Near Optimum Betting Ramp**	**Traditional Betting Ramp**	**Wong**	**Semi-Wong**
<0	1	1	1	0	0
0	1	1	1	1	1
+1	1.99	2	1	2	1
+2	5.52	6	2	4	2
+3	8	8	4	8	4
+4 and up	8	8	8	8	8
Game Results					
EV per 100 hands	1.54	2.07	1.61	1.64	1.52
5 percent ROR	1446	1093	803	660	756
Unit Size	$6.92	$9.15	$12.45	$15.15	$13.23
Earnings per 100 hands	$10.65	$18.94	$20.05	$24.85	$20.11

S17, DAS, 3/4 (75% Penetration)					
True Count	Optimum Betting Ramp	Near Optimum Betting Ramp	Traditional Betting Ramp	Wong	Semi-Wong
<0	1	1	1	0	0
0	1	1	1	1	1
+1	1.22	1	1	2	1
+2	3.81	4	2	4	2
+3	5.72	6	4	8	4
+4 and up	8	8	8	8	8
Game Results					
EV per 100 hands	2.11	2.13	1.87	2.52	2.43
5 percent ROR	954	964	881	604	724
Unit Size	$10.48	$10.37	$11.35	$16.56	$13.81
Earnings per 100 hands	$22.12	$22.10	$21.33	$41.73	$33.56

S17, DAS, 3.5/4 (88% Penetration)					
True Count	Optimum Betting Ramp	Near Optimum Betting Ramp	Traditional Betting Ramp	Wong	Semi-Wong
<0	1	1	1	0	0
0	1	1	1	0	1
+1	1	1	1	1	1
+2	2.50	3	2	2	2
+3	3.57	4	4	4	4
+4	5.38	5	8	8	8
+5	6.92	7	8	8	8
+6 and up	8	8	8	8	8
Game Results					
EV per 100 hands	2.98	3.06	3.23	3.92	3.84
5 percent ROR	558	583	626	485	508
Unit Size	$17.92	$17.15	$15.97	$20.62	$19.69
Earnings per 100 hands	$50.41	$52.49	$51.60	$80.83	$75.61

Table 9.4 **Six-Deck Games**

H17, DAS, 4/6 (67% Penetration)					
True Count	**Optimum Betting Ramp**	**Near Optimum Betting Ramp**	**Traditional Betting Ramp**	**Wong**	**Semi-Wong**
<0	1	1	1	0	0
0	1	1	1	0	1
+1	2.7	3	1	1	1
+2	11.1	11	2	2	2
+3	12	12	4	4	4
+4	12	12	6	6	6
+5 and up	12	12	12	12	12
Game Results					
EV per 100 hands	1.25	1.25	0.27	1.05	0.75
5 percent ROR	3097	3097	3465	746	1176
Unit Size	$3.23	$3.23	$2.89	$13.40	$8.50
Earnings per 100 hands	$4.04	$4.04	$0.78	$14.07	$6.38
H17, DAS, 4.5/6 (75% Penetration)					
True Count	**Optimum Betting Ramp**	**Near Optimum Betting Ramp**	**Traditional Betting Ramp**	**Wong**	**Semi-Wong**
</=0	1	1	1	0	1
+1	1.9	2	1	1	1
+2	7.8	8	2	2	2
+3	12	12	4	4	4
+4	12	12	6	6	6
+5 and up	12	12	12	12	12
Game Results					
EV per 100 hands	1.68	1.70	0.76	1.58	1.31
5 percent ROR	2081	2087	1685	717	935
Unit Size	$4.81	$4.79	$5.93	$13.95	$10.70
Earnings per 100 hands	$8.08	$8.14	$4.51	$22.04	$14.02

True Count	H17, DAS, 5/6 (83% Penetration)				
	Optimum Betting Ramp	Near Optimum Betting Ramp	Traditional Betting Ramp	Wong	Semi-Wong
<0	1	1	1	0	0
0	1	1	1	0	1
+1	1.5	2	1	1	1
+2	5.6	6	2	2	2
+3	9.1	9	4	4	4
+4	12	12	6	6	6
+5 and up	12	12	12	12	12
Game Results					
EV per 100 hands	2.24	2.27	1.47	2.32	2.08
5 percent ROR	1435	1456	1153	668	786
Unit Size	$6.97	$6.87	$8.67	$14.97	$12.72
Earnings per 100 hands	$15.61	$15.59	$12.74	$34.73	$26.46

True Count	H17, DAS, 5.5/6 (92% Penetration)				
	Optimum Betting Ramp	Near Optimum Betting Ramp	Traditional Betting Ramp	Wong	Semi-Wong
<0	1	1	1	0	0
0	1	1	1	0	1
+1	1.1	1	1	1	1
+2	4	4	2	2	2
+3	6.1	6	4	4	4
+4	9.4	9	6	6	6
+5 and up	12	12	12	12	12
Game Results					
EV per 100 hands	3.07	3.06	2.63	3.54	3.32
5 percent ROR	943	946	849	591	654
Unit Size	$10.60	$10.57	$11.78	$16.92	$15.29
Earnings per 100 hands	$32.54	$32.34	$30.98	$59.90	$50.76

True Count	H17, DAS, LS, 4/6 (67% Penetration)				
	Optimum Betting Ramp	Near Optimum Betting Ramp	Traditional Betting Ramp	Wong	Semi-Wong
<0	1	1	1	0	0
0	1	1	1	0	1
+1	3.3	3	1	1	1
+2	9.4	9	2	2	2
+3	12	12	4	4	4
+4	12	12	6	6	6
+5 and up	12	12	12	12	12
Game Results					
EV per 100 hands	1.72	1.68	0.54	1.27	1.02
5 percent ROR	1928	1893	1631	578	813
Unit Size	$5.19	$5.28	$6.13	$17.30	$12.30
Earnings per 100 hands	$8.93	$8.87	$3.31	$21.97	$12.55

True Count	H17, DAS, LS, 4.5/6 (75% Penetration)				
	Optimum Betting Ramp	Near Optimum Betting Ramp	Traditional Betting Ramp	Wong	Semi-Wong
</=0	1	1	1	0	1
+1	2.6	3	1	1	1
+2	7.4	7	2	2	2
+3	12	12	4	4	4
+4	12	12	6	6	6
+5 and up	12	12	12	12	12
Game Results					
EV per 100 hands	2.26	2.25	1.10	1.88	1.65
5 percent ROR	1457	1452	1094	563	696
Unit Size	$6.86	$6.89	$9.14	$17.76	$14.37
Earnings per 100 hands	$15.50	$15.50	$10.05	$33.39	$23.71

H17, DAS, LS, 5/6 (83% Penetration)					
True Count	Optimum Betting Ramp	Near Optimum Betting Ramp	Traditional Betting Ramp	Wong	Semi-Wong
<0	1	1	1	0	0
0	1	1	1	0	1
+1	2	2	1	1	1
+2	5.6	6	2	2	2
+3	9.1	9	4	4	4
+4	12	12	6	6	6
+5 and up	12	12	12	12	12
Game Results					
EV per 100 hands	2.87	2.89	1.89	2.72	2.50
5 percent ROR	1067	1076	840	532	612
Unit Size	$9.37	$9.29	$11.90	$18.80	$16.34
Earnings per 100 hands	$26.89	$26.85	$22.49	$51.14	$40.85
H17, DAS, LS, 5.5/6 (92% Penetration)					
True Count	Optimum Betting Ramp	Near Optimum Betting Ramp	Traditional Betting Ramp	Wong	Semi-Wong
<0	1	1	1	0	0
0	1	1	1	0	1
+1	1.5	2	1	1	1
+2	4	4	2	2	2
+3	6.1	6	4	4	4
+4	8.7	9	6	6	6
+5	11.7	12	12	12	12
+6 and up	12	12	12	12	12
Game Results					
EV per 100 hands	3.67	3.72	3.20	4.08	3.89
5 percent ROR	717	730	652	478	521
Unit Size	$13.95	$13.70	$15.34	$20.92	$19.19
Earnings per 100 hands	$51.20	$50.96	$49.09	$85.35	$74.65

| S17, DAS, 4/6 (67% Penetration) | | | | | |
True Count	Optimum Betting Ramp	Near Optimum Betting Ramp	Traditional Betting Ramp	Wong	Semi-Wong
<0	1	1	1	0	0
0	1	1	1	0	1
+1	4.1	4	1	1	1
+2	9.9	10	2	2	2
+3	12	12	4	4	4
+4	12	12	6	6	6
+5 and up	12	12	12	12	12
Game Results					
EV per 100 hands	1.73	1.73	0.55	1.15	0.97
5 percent ROR	2159	2164	1683	674	900
Unit Size	$4.63	$4.62	$5.94	$14.84	$11.11
Earnings per 100 hands	$8.01	$7.99	$3.27	$17.07	$10.78
S17, DAS, 4.5/6 (75% Penetration)					
True Count	Optimum Betting Ramp	Near Optimum Betting Ramp	Traditional Betting Ramp	Wong	Semi-Wong
<0	1	1	1	0	0
0	1	1	1	0	1
+1	3.1	3	1	1	1
+2	7.6	8	2	2	2
+3	11.4	11	4	4	4
+4	12	12	6	6	6
+5 and up	12	12	12	12	12
Game Results					
EV per 100 hands	2.15	2.15	1.06	1.70	1.53
5 percent ROR	1615	1621	1197	659	792
Unit Size	$6.19	$6.17	$8.35	$15.17	$12.63
Earnings per 100 hands	$13.31	$13.27	$8.85	$25.79	$19.32

S17, DAS, 5/6 (83% Penetration)					
True Count	Optimum Betting Ramp	Near Optimum Betting Ramp	Traditional Betting Ramp	Wong	Semi-Wong
<0	1	1	1	0	0
0	1	1	1	0	1
+1	2.4	2	1	1	1
+2	5.9	6	2	2	2
+3	8.8	9	4	4	4
+4	12	12	6	6	6
+5 and up	12	12	12	12	12
Game Results					
EV per 100 hands	2.71	2.71	1.78	2.46	2.31
5 percent ROR	1207	1208	943	624	701
Unit Size	$8.29	$8.28	$10.60	$16.03	$14.27
Earnings per 100 hands	$22.47	$22.44	$18.87	$39.43	$32.96
S17, DAS, 5.5/6 (92% Penetration)					
True Count	Optimum Betting Ramp	Near Optimum Betting Ramp	Traditional Betting Ramp	Wong	Semi-Wong
<0	1	1	1	0	0
0	1	1	1	0	1
+1	1.8	2	1	1	1
+2	4.2	4	2	2	2
+3	6	6	4	4	4
+4	8.7	9	6	6	6
+5	11.3	11	12	12	12
+6 and up	12	12	12	12	12
Game Results					
EV per 100 hands	3.42	3.42	2.97	3.71	3.58
5 percent ROR	815	817	745	558	601
Unit Size	$12.27	$12.24	$13.42	$17.92	$16.64
Earnings per 100 hands	$41.96	$41.86	$39.86	$66.48	$59.57

S17, DAS, LS, 4/6 (67% Penetration)				
True Count	**Optimum Betting Ramp**	**Near Optimum Betting Ramp**	**Traditional Betting Ramp**	**Wong**	**Semi-Wong**
<0	1	1	1	0	0
0	1	1	1	0	1
+1	3.9	4	1	1	1
+2	8.7	9	2	2	2
+3	12	12	4	4	4
+4	12	12	6	6	6
+5 and up	12	12	12	12	12
Game Results					
EV per 100 hands	2.12	2.15	0.79	1.37	1.21
5 percent ROR	1524	1542	1104	530	678
Unit Size	$6.56	$6.49	$9.06	$18.87	$14.75
Earnings per 100 hands	$13.91	$13.95	$7.16	$25.85	$17.85

S17, DAS, LS, 4.5/6 (75% Penetration)				
True Count	**Optimum Betting Ramp**	**Near Optimum Betting Ramp**	**Traditional Betting Ramp**	**Wong**	**Semi-Wong**
<0	1	1	1	0	0
0	1	1	1	0	1
+1	3.1	3	1	1	1
+2	7	7	2	2	2
+3	10.8	11	4	4	4
+4	12	12	6	6	6
+5 and up	12	12	12	12	12
Game Results					
EV per 100 hands	2.60	2.61	1.37	1.99	1.85
5 percent ROR	1187	1188	869	526	614
Unit Size	$8.42	$8.42	$11.51	$19.01	$16.29
Earnings per 100 hands	$21.89	$21.98	$15.77	$37.83	$30.14

S17, DAS, LS, 5/6 (83% Penetration)					
True Count	Optimum Betting Ramp	Near Optimum Betting Ramp	Traditional Betting Ramp	Wong	Semi-Wong
<0	1	1	1	0	0
0	1	1	1	0	1
+1	2.5	3	1	1	1
+2	5.6	6	2	2	2
+3	8.5	9	4	4	4
+4	11.6	12	6	6	6
+5 and up	12	12	12	12	12
Game Results					
EV per 100 hands	3.21	3.33	2.18	2.84	2.72
5 percent ROR	922	957	721	504	557
Unit Size	$10.85	$10.45	$13.87	$19.84	$17.95
Earnings per 100 hands	$34.83	$34.80	$30.24	$56.35	$48.82
S17, DAS, LS, 5.5/6 (92% Penetration)					
True Count	Optimum Betting Ramp	Near Optimum Betting Ramp	Traditional Betting Ramp	Wong	Semi-Wong
<0	1	1	1	0	0
0	1	1	1	0	1
+1	1.8	2	1	1	1
+2	4.1	4	2	2	2
+3	5.9	6	4	4	4
+4	8.2	8	6	6	6
+5	10.9	11	12	12	12
+6 and up	12	12	12	12	12
Game Results					
EV per 100 hands	3.97	3.96	3.51	4.24	4.13
5 percent ROR	634	635	589	455	486
Unit Size	$15.77	$15.75	$16.98	$21.98	$20.58
Earnings per 100 hands	$62.61	$62.37	$59.60	$93.20	$85.00

Table 9.5 Eight-Deck Games

S17, DAS, 6/8 (75% Penetration)

True Count	Optimum Betting Ramp	Near Optimum Betting Ramp	Traditional Betting Ramp	Wong	Semi-Wong
<0	1	1	1	0	0
0	1	1	1	0	1
+1	3.7	4	1	1	1
+2	9.3	9	2	2	2
+3	12	12	4	4	4
+4	12	12	6	6	6
+5 and up	12	12	12	12	12
Game Results					
EV per 100 hands	1.62	1.61	0.55	1.16	0.96
5 percent ROR	2111	2114	1691	671	915
Unit Size	$4.74	$4.73	$5.91	$14.90	$10.93
Earnings per 100 hands	$7.68	$7.62	$3.25	$17.28	$10.49

S17, DAS, 6.5/8 (81% Penetration)

True Count	Optimum Betting Ramp	Near Optimum Betting Ramp	Traditional Betting Ramp	Wong	Semi-Wong
<0	1	1	1	0	0
0	1	1	1	0	1
+1	3.1	3	1	1	1
+2	7.6	8	2	2	2
+3	12	12	4	4	4
+4	12	12	6	6	6
+5 and up	12	12	12	12	12
Game Results					
EV per 100 hands	1.95	1.97	0.92	1.58	1.38
5 percent ROR	1724	1742	1302	664	829
Unit Size	$5.80	$5.74	$7.68	$15.06	$12.06
Earnings per 100 hands	$11.31	$11.31	$7.07	$23.79	$16.64

S17, DAS, 7/8 (88% Penetration)					
True Count	**Optimum Betting Ramp**	**Near Optimum Betting Ramp**	**Traditional Betting Ramp**	**Wong**	**Semi-Wong**
<0	1	1	1	0	0
0	1	1	1	0	1
+1	2.4	2	1	1	1
+2	5.5	6	2	2	2
+3	9.3	9	4	4	4
+4	12	12	6	6	6
+5 and up	12	12	12	12	12
Game Results					
EV per 100 hands	2.29	2.29	1.47	2.16	1.98
5 percent ROR	1300	1300	1027	630	734
Unit Size	$7.69	$7.69	$9.74	$15.87	$13.62
Earnings per 100 hands	$17.61	$17.61	$14.32	$34.28	$26.97
S17, DAS, LS, 6/8 (75% Penetration)					
True Count	**Optimum Betting Ramp**	**Near Optimum Betting Ramp**	**Traditional Betting Ramp**	**Wong**	**Semi-Wong**
<0	1	1	1	0	0
0	1	1	1	0	1
+1	3.7	4	1	1	1
+2	8.7	9	2	2	2
+3	12	12	4	4	4
+4	12	12	6	6	6
+5 and up	12	12	12	12	12
Game Results					
EV per 100 hands	2.03	2.06	0.77	1.36	1.19
5 percent ROR	1534	1567	1137	535	693
Unit Size	$6.52	$6.38	$8.80	$18.69	$14.43
Earnings per 100 hands	$13.24	$13.14	$6.78	$25.42	$17.17

S17, DAS, LS, 6.5/8 (81% Penetration)					
True Count	**Optimum Betting Ramp**	**Near Optimum Betting Ramp**	**Traditional Betting Ramp**	**Wong**	**Semi-Wong**
<0	1	1	1	0	0
0	1	1	1	0	1
+1	3.3	3	1	1	1
+2	7.3	7	2	2	2
+3	11	12	4	4	4
+4	12	12	6	6	6
+5 and up	12	12	12	12	12
Game Results					
EV per 100 hands	2.41	2.37	1.22	1.85	1.69
5 percent ROR	1253	1234	922	530	634
Unit Size	$7.98	$8.10	$10.85	$18.87	$15.77
Earnings per 100 hands	$19.23	$19.20	$13.24	$34.91	$26.25

S17, DAS, LS, 7/8 (88% Penetration)					
True Count	**Optimum Betting Ramp**	**Near Optimum Betting Ramp**	**Traditional Betting Ramp**	**Wong**	**Semi-Wong**
<0	1	1	1	0	0
0	1	1	1	0	1
+1	2.7	3	1	1	1
+2	5.8	6	2	2	2
+3	9	9	4	4	4
+4	12	12	6	6	6
+5 and up	12	12	12	12	12
Game Results					
EV per 100 hands	2.85	2.88	1.84	2.50	2.35
5 percent ROR	998	1010	768	508	577
Unit Size	$10.02	$9.90	$13.02	$19.69	$17.33
Earnings per 100 hands	$28.56	$28.51	$23.96	$49.23	$40.73

Learning From the Game Results

When you begin to study the simulation tables, a lot of valuable information will pop out at you. For starters, you can clearly see that penetration is king. In every instance, the significant difference between well-penetrated games and poorly penetrated games is obvious. Look at Table 9.4. The six-deck S17, DAS game with poor penetration (4/6; 67 percent penetration) has the potential to earn $7.99 per 100 hands using near optimum bets. Now look at the six-deck S17, DAS game with excellent penetration (5.5/6; 92 percent penetration). This game has the potential to earn $41.86 per 100 hands—that's over 400 percent more than the poorly penetrated game!

You can also see how important it is to carefully consider your betting unit for each game you approach. Remember, the simulations assume a player has a static bankroll size and wants to maintain the same risk of ruin regardless of the game he is playing. Given these assumptions, a player with a $10,000 bankroll wouldn't play with $25 units at a six-deck table, but he could easily play with such units in most single-deck games. See Table 9.1, for example. A player in a single-deck game with H17 and 60 percent penetration can afford a $25 betting unit. However, if he wants to maintain a 5 percent risk of ruin and play in a game that uses more than one deck, he will have to adjust his betting unit accordingly. As game conditions improve, the betting unit increases. In addition, better game conditions offer more opportunities to play at positive counts, thus more opportunities to play with larger bets.

You'll also see that the difference between optimum or near-optimum betting and traditional betting grows larger as the number of decks increases, making a proper betting ramp more important. However, as the quality of the game improves with better rules and penetration, optimum betting and traditional betting begin to converge. Take a look at Table 9.4, for example. In the six-deck H17, DAS game with 4/6 (67 percent penetration), you can see the traditional betting ramp wins a paltry 78 cents per 100 hands while the optimum betting ramp can potentially generate more than five times as much profit. Now, look further down the table. The same game with 5.5/6 (92 percent penetration) has the potential to earn $32.54 at the optimum betting level and $30.98 at the traditional level, a much smaller difference. (If the games available to you are marginal games, pay close attention to the betting ramp used in the game-simulation tables and try to bet as close to optimum as possible.)

The tables also express the value of the rules. A player who uses the play-all approach can see sizeable differences between S17 and H17 games. See Table 9.1, for example. The single-deck H17 game with 31/52 (60 percent penetration) has the potential to earn $51.36 per 100 hands, while the same game with S17 has the potential to earn $67.52 per 100 hands.

The DAS rule is quite valuable as well. Take a look at Table 9.2 and compare the game with S17 and 75 percent penetration to the game with S17, DAS, and 75 percent penetration. With an optimum bet spread, the game without DAS generates an earnings potential of $56.87 per 100 hands. If you add DAS, you can see an increase in earnings potential of more than 18 percent to $67.60.

The value of the late surrender option is illustrated in Table 9.4. Compare the six-deck S17, DAS game with 83 percent penetration to the one with S17, DAS, LS and 83 percent penetration. The game without late surrender shows an earnings potential of $22.47 per 100 hands with optimum betting, while the game with late surrender shows potential earnings of $34.83 per 100 hands. When using the semi-Wonging style of play in that same game with late surrender, the profit jumps to $48.82 per 100 hands, and when using the Wonging style of play, it jumps to $56.35. Meanwhile, in the game without the late surrender option, Wonging generates a potential profit of $39.43 and semi-Wonging generates a potential profit of $32.96 per 100 hands. Obviously, late surrender means more to a card counter than it does to a basic strategy player.

As you can see from Tables 9.3, 9.4, and 9.5, the Wonging and semi-Wonging style of play can turn an otherwise unplayable game into a decent one and can increase profits by a considerable margin. I don't recommend playing any of the eight-deck games in the tables unless you are using one of these strategies. Table 9.5 clearly illustrates my reasons. Look at the game with S17, DAS, LS and 81 percent penetration. Using a play-all approach, a counter has a 100-hand expectation of $19.23. By semi-Wonging, he can raise his expectation to $26.25 and Wonging brings it up to $34.91. This is not great by the standards for games with fewer decks, but it's certainly a vast improvement over playing all hands. For players who play in areas where eight-deck games are prevalent, these strategies are well worth using.

CONCLUSION

This chapter has provided you with some valuable information regarding game selection, but in the end, it's up to each player to decide which games to play. Choosing a game that pays $20 an hour and playing it for 100 hours per year might satisfy one player, especially if he views his time in the casino as having an intrinsic entertainment value to him. Another, more hard-nosed player might think this is chicken feed and would only want to go for the games that generate the big bucks. A return of 50 percent on his money per year might be what he needs to even consider spending the time and taking the risks associated with playing blackjack.

In any event, if a player is offered a variety of games, he should choose the one with the best value. However, if he is faced with games that are so pitiful they aren't worth the time it takes to drive to the casino and back, the following chapter should be of special interest.

BACKCOUNTING AND EXIT STRATEGY
(WONGING AND SEMI-WONGING)

A player's advantage at positive counts shrinks and the disadvantage at negative counts grows as the number of decks in play increases. What's more, when playing in multiple-deck games, a player spends more time in negative counts. In fact, in a six-deck game with 75 percent penetration, a player can find himself in neutral or negative counts about 73 percent of the time! This means that a larger bet spread is required to offset the disadvantage of having more decks in play. One way to reduce this need is to use the style of play called *backcounting,* or *Wonging.* Named for Stanford Wong, this method of play requires a player to enter a game only at positive counts. Another way to mitigate the disadvantage of multiple decks in play is to use an exit strategy, in which a player departs the table at a pre-set point in the count. I like to call this method *semi-Wonging.* Semi-Wonging reduces the number of hands a counter ends up playing in negative counts.

Although previous chapters have touched upon Wonging and semi-Wonging, this chapter examines both styles of play in depth and includes a comprehensive set of tables that can be used to compare the relative value of different games using these styles of play. The tables in this chapter can also be used to determine the proper bet sizes and expected earnings for various bet spreads using these approaches.

WONGING (BACKCOUNTING)

The Father of Backcounting

The backcounting style of play was popularized by the accomplished blackjack player Stanford Wong and eventually became known in blackjack circles as *Wonging.*

Although Stanford Wong didn't invent backcounting, he was an early practitioner and advocate of this method of play. Having been popularized by and associated so closely with him, backcounting eventually became known in blackjack circles as *Wonging,* and counters who used the method became known as *Wongers.* Use of the Wonging style of play simply means that a player joins a game only in positive counts, assuming of course that midshoe entry is permitted.

The counter stands behind the table or at some other vantage point where he can count the cards as they are played. Some players back count more than one table at a time. Attentive counters with excellent eyesight can even back count several tables by using the mirrors that are often found in casinos. Wongers generally wait until the count is +2 or better in multiple-deck games. Once the count is favorable, the player enters the game and plays until the count drops to an unfavorable level or until the shuffle comes. As soon as the advantage turns back to the house, the Wonger quits playing at that table and searches for a positive count at another table.

A player who is Wonging can play with a much smaller bet spread than he would if he were using a play-all approach. If he is absolutely disciplined about playing only in advantageous situations, he can even flat bet.

Some play-all counters believe they have sole right to any good counts at a table because they've played through the bad counts. Chances are these players will resent you for getting in on that juicy count without having put in the time. So, if you plan to become a Wonger, make sure you have thick skin.

SEMI-WONGING (EXIT STRATEGY)

With the semi-Wonging style of play, a player leaves a table when the count gets to a pre-set point and goes in search of another. Obviously, this works best in a large casino with many tables. You may even want to do a little *mini-Wonging*—that is, back count the tables next to you and enter if the count is favorable when you exit the table you're at. Although your exit point is a decision you'll need to make, a good time to leave a game is at a count of less than 0. If you leave at counts of less than 0 in a six-deck game, you will have avoided playing at least one-third of the negative expectation hands you would have played if you were using a play-all style and more if you are in a game with decent penetration. You will also be avoiding playing those hands that have the worst expectation. At a count of –1, your per-hand expectation is about –0.5 percent; at –2, it's about –1 percent; and it keeps going down-hill from there. If you are consistent about exiting at bad counts, you can turn a marginal game into a playable game and increase your earnings by 50 percent or more, and significantly reduce your risk of ruin.

It's become common for casinos to place no-midshoe entry rules on certain games. As the name of the rule suggests, you cannot enter a game until after the next shuffle. Although you can't employ Wonging in these games, you can put your exit strategy to good use.

WONGING AND SEMI-WONGING GAME SIMULATIONS

It's been estimated that Wongers can get in about twenty-five to twenty-seven hands per hour. There is little doubt that this style of play will earn the most money, if conditions permit. A player can be quite creative with his bet spread and still stay within a reasonable risk of ruin. A traditional 1–12 unit bet spread in a shoe game can attract unwanted attention if a player is using large bets that top out at $500 or more. With backcounting, other bet spreads that can earn nearly as well as the larger spread can be used.

To familiarize you with the tables you'll find later in the chapter, let's take a look at a game that is commonly found around the United States: a six-deck game with S17 and DAS. Tables 10.1 and 10.2 on pages 184 and 185 show some betting schemes that a Wonger and semi-Wonger might choose to use in this game. Once again, these schemes are based on a $10,000 total bankroll with a 5 percent risk of ruin. Each column includes the bet spread, unit size, number of units needed for a 5 percent risk of ruin, and the potential hourly profit for various levels of penetration. These tables assume that a player will get in three times as many hands when using the semi-Wonging style of play than he would when using a strict Wonging strategy.

As you can see from Table 10.1, a 1–4 spread is the most effective given the parameters of the simulation. Of course, this is a marginal game, and a player can do much better if he picks a game with better

Table 10.1
**Wonging Bet Spreads
for Six-Deck Games,
S17, DAS**

	S17, DAS				
	1–1 unit	1–2 units	1–4 units	1–6 units	1–8 units
Penetration: 4/6 (67%)					
Unit Size	$66.23	$45.25	$35.21	$25.39	$21.69
Units Needed	151	221	284	379	461
Hourly Profit	$21.86	$27.15	$33.45	$34.04	$34.27
Penetration: 4.5/6 (75%)					
Unit Size	$68.97	$46.73	$35.71	$26.6	$21.65
Units Needed	145	214	280	375	462
Hourly Profit	$24.14	$29.91	$36.07	$36.80	$36.81
Penetration: 5/6 (83%)					
Unit Size	$80.65	$52.91	$39.32	$28.99	$23.20
Units Needed	124	189	254	345	431
Hourly Profit	$34.68	$42.33	$52.36	$53.92	$54.06
Penetration: 5.5/6 (92%)					
Unit Size	$99.01	$63.69	$45.66	$33.22	$26.39
Units Needed	101	157	219	301	379
Hourly Profit	$55.45	$66.87	$83.10	$86.04	$87.09

conditions. Several more tables are included later in the chapter based on games with more favorable conditions, but first let's take a look at the same game using the semi-Wonging strategy in Table 10.2.

You'll notice that Table 10.2 doesn't show a bet spread smaller than 1–4. This is because anything smaller does not generate enough profit given these particular circumstances. Also, making a large jump in bet size, such as from 1 unit at a 0 count to 4 or 8 units at +1 count carries too much risk to be profitable with a fixed bankroll. Making an intermediate jump to a large bet at a +2 count doesn't produce as well as the incremental jumps set forth in these simulation results.

The tables in this chapter were designed to illustrate the relative value of employing the Wonging and semi-Wonging styles of play for various sets of circumstance. Once again, the figures are based on the

	S17, DAS	
	1–4 units	1–8 units
Penetration: 4/6 (67%)		
Unit Size	$17.51	$14.75
Units Needed	571	678
Hourly Profit	$14.01	$18.14
Penetration: 4.5/6 (75%)		
Unit Size	$15.87	$13.77
Units Needed	630	726
Hourly Profit	$12.70	$17.63
Penetration: 5/6 (83%)		
Unit Size	$19.76	$16.05
Units Needed	506	623
Hourly Profit	$21.93	$29.85
Penetration: 5.5/6 (92%)		
Unit Size	$25.38	$19.42
Units Needed	394	515
Hourly Profit	$39.85	$53.41

Table 10.2 Semi-Wonging Bet Spreads for Six-Deck Games, S17, DAS

proper bet sizes and betting units needed to play to a 5 percent risk of ruin with a $10,000 bankroll.

Clearly, you will not be able to play in a casino with the exact betting units shown, but you can approximate that unit to the nearest whole-dollar figure and adjust your bankroll accordingly. For example, the game illustrated in Table 10.1 shows a betting unit of $35.71 and a total number of betting units of 280 needed. If you were to use a $35 betting unit instead, you would need a bankroll of $9,800 to maintain your 5 percent risk of ruin. Your expected earnings would be $35.35 per 100 hands observed. This profit figure is obtained by dividing the earnings figure ($36.07) by the unit figure ($35.71) and multiplying the result by the unit you will use in actual play. Here's the math: ($36.07 ÷ $35.71) × $35.00 = $35.35.

You can use a similar calculation to determine the unit size and expected earnings for different-sized bankrolls. For example, if you want to play to a 5 percent risk of ruin with a $17,000 bankroll, you'll need to divide your total bankroll by the number of units recommended. Keeping with the above example, you would figure it like this: $17,000 ÷ 280 = $60.71. In actual play, your unit would be rounded down to $60. Your expected earnings would be $60.60: ($36.07 ÷ $35.71) × $60 = $60.60. By keeping with the 280 betting unit figure, you could compute the required bankroll for any size bet you wish to use as your base betting unit.

The examples given for Tables 10.1 and 10.2 should prepare you to put Tables 10.3 to 10.9 on the following pages to good use. Also, if you are presented with a variety of choices, you can compare the information in the tables to determine which game conditions to choose and which style you might want to try.

HI7, DAS	1–1 unit	1–2 units	1–4 units	1–6 units	1–8 units
Penetration: 2.5/4 (63%)					
Unit Size	$41.15	$27.47	$22.57	$17.33	$14.20
Units Needed	243	364	443	577	704
Hourly Profit	$11.11	$14.56	$19.80	$21.32	$21.87
Penetration: 3/4 (75%)					
Unit Size	$52.63	$34.25	$26.11	$19.53	$15.70
Units Needed	190	292	383	512	637
Hourly Profit	$19.47	$25.35	$33.94	$36.52	$37.52
Penetration: 3.5/4 (88%)					
Unit Size	$74.63	$46.08	$33.44	$24.51	$19.46
Units Needed	134	217	299	408	514
Hourly Profit	$41.05	$49.77	$65.88	$70.10	$72.00

SI7, DAS	1–1 unit	1–2 units	1–4 units	1–6 units	1–8 units
Penetration: 2.5/4 (63%)					
Unit Size	$48.78	$31.15	$24.63	$18.66	$15.15
Units Needed	205	321	406	536	660
Hourly Profit	$15.61	$18.69	$23.64	$24.63	$24.85
Penetration: 3/4 (75%)					
Unit Size	$59.88	$38.02	$28.09	$20.79	$16.56
Units Needed	321	263	356	481	604
Hourly Profit	$25.15	$31.18	$39.33	$41.37	$41.73
Penetration: 3.5/4 (88%)					
Unit Size	$82.64	$50.25	$35.84	$26.04	$20.62
Units Needed	121	199	279	384	485
Hourly Profit	$50.41	$59.30	$75.62	$79.16	$80.83

Table 10.3 Wonging Bet Spreads for Four-Deck Games

1–1 spread. Bet 0 units at all counts below +1, 1 unit at all counts of +1 and above

1–2 spread. Bet 1 unit at +1, 2 units at +2 or higher

1–4 spread. Bet 1 unit at +1, 2 units at +2, 3 units at +3, 4 units at +4 or higher

1–6 spread. Bet 1 unit at +1, 2 units at +2, 4 units at +3, 6 units at +4 or higher

1–8 spread. Bet 1 unit at +1, 2 units at +2, 4 units at +3, 8 units at +4 or higher

Table 10.4
Wonging Bet Spreads for Six-Deck Games

I–I spread. Bet 0 units at all counts below +1, 1 unit at all counts of +1 and above

I–2 spread. Bet 1 unit at +1, 2 units at +2 or higher

I–4 spread. Bet 1 unit at +1, 2 units at +2, 3 units at +3, 4 units at +4 or higher

I–6 spread. Bet 1 unit at +1, 2 units at +2, 4 units at +3, 6 units at +4 or higher

I–8 spread. Bet 1 unit at +1, 2 units at +2, 4 units at +3, 8 units at +4 or higher

H17, DAS	I–I unit	I–2 units	I–4 units	I–6 units	I–8 units
Penetration: 4/6 (67%)					
Unit Size	$43.86	$30.67	$24.63	$18.83	$15.53
Units Needed	228	326	406	531	644
Hourly Profit	$8.33	$13.19	$17.49	$18.64	$18.95
Penetration: 4.5/6 (75%)					
Unit Size	$45.05	$32.36	$25.45	$19.27	$15.70
Units Needed	222	309	393	519	637
Hourly Profit	$10.81	$15.21	$19.60	$20.62	$20.88
Penetration: 5/6 (83%)					
Unit Size	$56.82	$38.02	$28.90	$21.55	$17.33
Units Needed	176	263	346	464	577
Hourly Profit	$18.18	$23.19	$30.35	$32.11	$32.58
Penetration: 5.5/6 (92%)					
Unit Size	$71.94	$47.17	$34.60	$25.38	$20.20
Units Needed	139	212	289	394	495
Hourly Profit	$30.93	$39.15	$51.21	$54.06	$55.15

H17, DAS, LS	I–I unit	I–2 units	I–4 units	I–6 units	I–8 units
Penetration: 4/6 (67%)					
Unit Size	$57.80	$40.49	$32.05	$24.51	$20.08
Units Needed	173	247	312	408	498
Hourly Profit	$16.76	$21.86	$27.88	$29.66	$29.72
Penetration: 4.5/6 (75%)					
Unit Size	$60.98	$42.02	$33.00	$24.69	$20.12
Units Needed	164	238	303	405	497
Hourly Profit	$18.90	$24.37	$31.02	$31.85	$32.19
Penetration: 5/6 (83%)					
Unit Size	$72.99	$48.78	$36.63	$27.10	$21.74
Units Needed	137	205	273	369	460
Hourly Profit	$28.47	$36.10	$45.79	$47.70	$48.05

Penetration: 5.5/6 (92%)					
Unit Size	$90.09	$59.17	$43.10	$31.35	$25.00
Units Needed	111	169	232	319	400
Hourly Profit	$45.95	$57.99	$74.56	$77.43	$79.00

Table 10.4
continued

S17, DAS					
	1–1 unit	1–2 units	1–4 units	1–6 units	1–8 units
Penetration: 4/6 (67%)					
Unit Size	$51.55	$35.84	$28.01	$20.96	$17.24
Units Needed	194	279	357	477	580
Hourly Profit	$13.92	$17.92	$22.41	$22.85	$23.10
Penetration: 4.5/6 (75%)					
Unit Size	$54.64	$37.45	$28.65	$21.46	$17.30
Units Needed	183	267	349	466	578
Hourly Profit	$15.85	$20.22	$24.64	$25.32	$25.09
Penetration: 5/6 (83%)					
Unit Size	$64.10	$43.29	$31.65	$23.36	$18.73
Units Needed	156	231	316	428	534
Hourly Profit	$23.08	$29.87	$36.08	$37.38	$37.65
Penetration: 5.5/6 (92%)					
Unit Size	$81.30	$52.08	$37.17	$27.17	$21.51
Units Needed	123	192	269	368	465
Hourly Profit	$39.02	$47.39	$58.73	$61.40	$61.95

Table 10.4
continued

	S17, DAS, LS				
	1–1 unit	1–2 units	1–4 units	1–6 units	1–8 units
Penetration: 4/6 (67%)					
Unit Size	$66.23	$45.25	$35.21	$25.39	$21.69
Units Needed	151	221	284	379	461
Hourly Profit	$21.86	$27.15	$33.45	$34.04	$34.27
Penetration: 4.5/6 (75%)					
Unit Size	$68.97	$46.73	$35.71	$26.67	$21.65
Units Needed	145	214	280	375	462
Hourly Profit	$24.14	$29.91	$36.07	$36.80	$36.81
Penetration: 5/6 (83%)					
Unit Size	$80.65	$52.91	$39.32	$28.99	$23.20
Units Needed	124	189	254	345	431
Hourly Profit	$34.68	$42.33	$52.36	$53.92	$54.06
Penetration: 5.5/6 (92%)					
Unit Size	$99.01	$63.69	$45.66	$33.22	$26.39
Units Needed	101	157	219	301	379
Hourly Profit	$55.45	$66.87	$83.10	$86.04	$87.09

S17, DAS	1–1 unit	1–2 units	1–4 units	1–6 units	1–8 units
Penetration: 6/8 (75%)					
Unit Size	$47.17	$32.68	$26.32	$20.12	$16.53
Units Needed	212	306	380	497	605
Hourly Profit	$10.85	$13.40	$16.58	$17.10	$17.03
Penetration: 6.5/8 (81%)					
Unit Size	$52.36	$36.50	$28.09	$21.23	$17.21
Units Needed	191	274	356	471	581
Hourly Profit	$14.14	$18.25	$22.19	$23.14	$23.06
Penetration: 7/8 (88%)					
Unit Size	$59.52	$40.32	$30.86	$22.94	$18.48
Units Needed	168	248	324	436	541
Hourly Profit	$19.05	$24.19	$31.17	32.35	$32.71

Table 10.5
Wonging Bet Spreads For Eight-Deck Games

1–1 spread. Bet 0 units at all counts below +1, 1 unit at all counts of +1 and above

1–2 spread. Bet 1 unit at +1, 2 units at +2 or higher

1–4 spread. Bet 1 unit at +1, 2 units at +2, 3 units at +3, 4 units at +4 or higher

1–6 spread. Bet 1 unit at +1, 2 units at +2, 4 units at +3, 6 units at +4 or higher

1–8 spread. Bet 1 unit at +1, 2 units at +2, 4 units at +3, 8 units at +4 or higher

S17, DAS, LS	1–1 unit	1–2 units	1–4 units	1–6 units	1–8 units
Penetration: 6/8 (75%)					
Unit Size	$58.14	$41.15	$33.11	$25.38	$20.88
Units Needed	172	243	302	394	479
Hourly Profit	$15.70	$20.16	$24.83	$25.63	$25.47
Penetration: 6.5/8 (81%)					
Unit Size	$67.11	$46.08	$35.46	$26.53	$21.65
Units Needed	149	217	282	377	462
Hourly Profit	$22.15	$27.65	$33.33	$33.96	$34.21
Penetration: 7/8 (88%)					
Unit Size	$76.34	$51.02	$38.31	$28.41	$22.88
Units Needed	131	196	261	352	437
Hourly Profit	$29.77	$36.73	$45.21	$46.59	$46.90

**Table 10.6
Semi-Wonging
Bet Spreads
for Double-Deck
Games**

1–2 spread. Bet 0 units at all
counts less than 0, 1 unit at 0,
2 units at +2 or higher

1–4 spread. Bet 1 unit at +1,
2 units at +2, 3 units at +3,
4 units at +4 or higher

1–8 spread. Bet 1 unit at +1,
2 units at +2, 4 units at +3,
8 units at +4 or higher

	H17		
	1–2 units	**1–4 units**	**1–8 units**
Penetration: 52/104 (50%)			
Unit Size	$15.65	$17.79	$13.33
Units Needed	639	562	750
Hourly Profit	$5.95	$14.23	$21.19
Penetration: 62/104 (60%)			
Unit Size	$23.92	$23.26	$15.82
Units Needed	418	430	632
Hourly Profit	$14.59	$28.14	$37.18
Penetration: 70/104 (67%)			
Unit Size	$30.77	$27.47	$17.67
Units Needed	325	364	566
Hourly Profit	$24.62	$42.58	$53.01
Penetration: 78/104 (75%)			
Unit Size	$37.45	$31.55	$19.57
Units Needed	267	317	511
Hourly Profit	$37.45	$60.89	$73.19

	H17, DAS		
	1–2 units	**1–4 units**	**1–8 units**
Penetration: 52/104 (50%)			
Unit Size	$20.79	$20.92	$14.79
Units Needed	481	478	676
Hourly Profit	$10.81	$20.29	$26.92
Penetration: 62/104 (60%)			
Unit Size	$28.57	$25.97	$17.01
Units Needed	350	385	588
Hourly Profit	$21.43	$36.10	$44.23

Penetration: 70/104 (67%)			
Unit Size	$35.21	$29.76	$18.66
Units Needed	284	336	536
Hourly Profit	$33.10	$51.48	$60.83
Penetration: 78/104 (75%)			
Unit Size	$41.49	$33.67	$20.53
Units Needed	241	297	487
Hourly Profit	$47.30	$71.38	$82.74

Table 10.6
continued

S17			
	1–2 units	1–4 units	1–8 units
Penetration: 52/104 (50%)			
Unit Size	$22.68	$22.03	$15.36
Units Needed	441	454	651
Hourly Profit	$12.47	$21.81	$28.11
Penetration: 62/104 (60%)			
Unit Size	$30.30	$26.95	$17.51
Units Needed	330	371	571
Hourly Profit	$23.33	$37.73	$45.53
Penetration: 70/104 (67%)			
Unit Size	$37.04	$31.06	$19.31
Units Needed	270	322	518
Hourly Profit	$50.44	$54.36	$63.14
Penetration: 78/104 (75%)			
Unit Size	$43.48	$34.97	$21.10
Units Needed	230	286	474
Hourly Profit	$50.44	$74.49	$84.82

Table 10.6 continued	S17, DAS		
	1–2 units	1–4 units	1–8 units
Penetration: 52/104 (50%)			
Unit Size	$27.25	$25.19	$16.81
Units Needed	367	397	595
Hourly Profit	$18.53	$29.22	$34.46
Penetration: 62/104 (60%)			
Unit Size	$34.84	$29.76	$18.80
Units Needed	287	336	532
Hourly Profit	$31.70	$47.02	$53.58
Penetration: 70/104 (67%)			
Unit Size	$40.98	$33.44	$20.37
Units Needed	244	299	491
Hourly Profit	$44.67	$64.54	$71.91
Penetration: 78/104 (75%)			
Unit Size	$47.62	$37.17	$22.12
Units Needed	210	269	452
Hourly Profit	$61.91	$86.23	$95.34

H17, DAS		
	1–4 units	1–8 units
Penetration: 2.5/4 (63%)		
Unit Size	$11.70	$11.75
Units Needed	855	851
Hourly Profit	$9.36	$15.86
Penetration: 3/4 (75%)		
Unit Size	$16.21	$14.12
Units Needed	617	708
Hourly Profit	$20.42	$31.49
Penetration: 3.5/4 (88%)		
Unit Size	$22.99	$18.28
Units Needed	435	547
Hourly Profit	$45.06	$65.26

Table 10.7
Semi-Wonging Bet Spreads for Four-Deck Games

1–4 spread. Bet 0 units at all counts less than 0, 1 unit at 0, 2 units at +1, 3 units at +2, 4 units at +3 or higher

1–8 spread. Bet 1 unit at 0, 1 unit at +1, 2 units at +2, 4 units at +3, 8 units at +4 or higher

S17, DAS		
	1–4 units	1–8 units
Penetration: 2.5/4 (63%)		
Unit Size	$14.77	$13.23
Units Needed	677	756
Hourly Profit	$14.92	$20.11
Penetration: 3/4 (75%)		
Unit Size	$18.90	$13.81
Units Needed	529	724
Hourly Profit	$27.78	$33.56
Penetration: 3.5/4 (88%)		
Unit Size	$25.77	$19.69
Units Needed	388	508
Hourly Profit	$56.69	$75.61

**Table 10.8
Semi-Wonging
Bet Spreads for
Six-Deck Games**

1–4 spread. Bet 0 units
at all counts less than 0,
1 unit at 0, 2 units at +1,
4 units at +3 or higher

1–8 spread. Bet 1 unit at 0,
2 units at +1, 4 units at +2,
8 units at +3 or higher

	H17, DAS	
	1–4 units	**1–8 units**
Penetration: 4/6 (67%)		
Unit Size	$7.69	$714
Units Needed	1300	1400
Hourly Profit	$2.69	$6.43
Penetration: 4.5/6 (75%)		
Unit Size	$11.61	$11.39
Units Needed	861	878
Hourly Profit	$6.85	$12.19
Penetration: 5/6 (83%)		
Unit Size	$15.90	$14.03
Units Needed	629	713
Hourly Profit	$14.31	$23.01
Penetration: 5.5/6 (92%)		
Unit Size	$21.83	$17.54
Units Needed	458	570
Hourly Profit	$29.67	$44.03

	H17, DAS, LS	
	1–4 units	**1–8 units**
Penetration: 4/6 (67%)		
Unit Size	$12.72	$12.72
Units Needed	786	786
Hourly Profit	$7.00	$11.32
Penetration: 4.5/6 (75%)		
Unit Size	$17.01	$15.50
Units Needed	588	645
Hourly Profit	$13.95	$21.24

Penetration: 5/6 (83%)		
Unit Size	$21.65	$18.21
Units Needed	462	549
Hourly Profit	$25.11	$36.42
Penetration: 5.5/6 (92%)		
Unit Size	$28.33	$22.17
Units Needed	353	451
Hourly Profit	$47.31	$65.84

Table 10.8
continued

S17, DAS		
	1–4 units	1–8 units
Penetration: 4/6 (67%)		
Unit Size	$17.51	$14.75
Units Needed	571	678
Hourly Profit	$14.01	$18.14
Penetration: 4.5/6 (75%)		
Unit Size	$15.87	$13.77
Units Needed	630	726
Hourly Profit	$12.70	$17.63
Penetration: 5/6 (83%)		
Unit Size	$19.76	$16.05
Units Needed	506	623
Hourly Profit	$21.93	$29.85
Penetration: 5.5/6 (92%)		
Unit Size	$25.38	$19.42
Units Needed	394	515
Hourly Profit	$39.85	$53.41

Table 10.8 continued	S17, DAS, LS	
	1–4 units	1–8 units
Penetration: 4/6 (67%)		
Unit Size	$22.88	$19.01
Units Needed	437	526
Hourly Profit	$22.65	$28.32
Penetration: 4.5/6 (75%)		
Unit Size	$21.10	$17.86
Units Needed	474	560
Hourly Profit	$21.31	$27.86
Penetration: 5/6 (83%)		
Unit Size	$25.38	$20.24
Units Needed	394	494
Hourly Profit	$34.26	$44.53
Penetration: 5.5/6 (92%)		
Unit Size	$31.85	$24.04
Units Needed	314	416
Hourly Profit	$59.24	$76.69

S17, DAS		
	1–4 units	1–8 units
Penetration: 6/8 (75%)		
Unit Size	$10.31	$9.34
Units Needed	970	1071
Hourly Profit	$6.39	$10.65
Penetration: 6.5/8 (81%)		
Unit Size	$12.42	$10.64
Units Needed	805	940
Hourly Profit	$9.94	$15.75
Penetration: 7/8 (88%)		
Unit Size	$14.88	$12.18
Units Needed	672	821
Hourly Profit	$15.18	$23.39

Table 10.9
Semi-Wonging Bet Spreads for Eight-Deck Games

1–4 spread. Bet 0 units at all counts less than 0, 1 unit at 0, 2 at +1, 4 at +2 or higher

1–8 spread. Bet 1 unit at 0, 2 units at +1, 4 units at +2, 8 units at +3 or higher

S17, DAS, LS		
	1–4 units	1–8 units
Penetration: 6/8 (75%)		
Unit Size	$14.31	$12.38
Units Needed	699	808
Hourly Profit	$11.73	$17.70
Penetration: 6.5/8 (81%)		
Unit Size	$16.81	$13.83
Units Needed	595	723
Hourly Profit	$17.31	$25.17
Penetration: 7/8 (88%)		
Unit Size	$24.45	$15.60
Units Needed	505	641
Hourly Profit	$31.54	$36.19

CONCLUSION

The Wonging and semi-Wonging styles of play can be valuable additions to your arsenal in your battle against the casinos. Unfortunately, many of the blackjack games casinos offer these days are far from the highest caliber. This often makes the play-all approach a poor choice for generating acceptable profits with a relatively low risk of ruin. As you learned in this chapter, the use of the Wonging and semi-Wonging styles of play can increase the number of acceptable playing venues and can turn an unplayable game into a profitable one. I highly recommend using these styles when the opportunity presents itself.

HEAT, BARRINGS, AND COVERS

Wherever card counters gather, you'll hear heated discussions about the pressure casinos put on them to stop them from playing blackjack in their houses. It's unfair, but the fact is, casinos don't want to lose money and will resort to a variety of tactics to intimidate card counters. In response, counters have developed a number of their own tactics to keep playing without giving themselves away. Being able to continue to play at the casinos of a card counter's choice is part of the game. This chapter leaves behind the science of blackjack and delves into the art of playing blackjack in today's casino environment, where advantage players are not welcome.

HEAT

Heat. Card counters talk about it and they commiserate over it. They try to find ways to defuse it. Some ignore it. Others let it shake them up and affect their game. In some cases, it can be very real, and in others, it can be nothing more than a figment of a card counter's imagination. *Heat* is a term for the pressure casinos put on counters to intimidate them into not playing in their houses. It can take many forms and run the gamut from mild to nasty. It is often, but not always, the prelude to a back off or barring. (See "Back Offs and Barrings" on page 202.)

I know players who have been harassed by casino personnel not only inside but *outside* a casino. I'm also familiar with cases in which a player was handcuffed, taken into a back room, and questioned by security personnel as a suspect for some alleged wrongdoing, such as cheating. This extreme form of heat is called *backrooming*. Detaining a person in this manner should be illegal, but court cases over such incidents have produced a mixed bag of results. In a casino town like Las Vegas where a large percentage of the population depends on the casinos for its livelihood, it's difficult to find a sympathetic jury. However, the plaintiffs in a recent lawsuit against a popular Las Vegas casino were awarded $500,000 when the court concluded that they had been wrongly backroomed for cheating when all they had been doing was taking advantage of the dealer's inadvertent flashing of his cards. This case will most likely be appealed, but the fact that a Las Vegas jury was sympathetic to such a complaint is good news for counters.

How to Recognize Heat

One morning, years ago, at the Golden Nugget in Las Vegas, I had the entire pit to myself. At the time, my top bet was about $40, so it should not have drawn any attention. However, after I'd been playing for about fifteen minutes, the pit boss—who I guess had nothing better to do—grabbed a chair at my table, sat down, and glared at me. His eyes were like two drill bits boring a hole right through my head. So I stared back. We sat there, staring at each other like two dogs sizing each other

Back Offs and Barrings

What exactly does it mean to be backed off or barred from playing in a casino? Depending on who you ask or where you look, you might get slightly different answers. Generally speaking, though, a back off occurs when a casino informs a player that he is no longer permitted to play blackjack in its casino although he is still welcome to play any other game it offers. In some cases, a casino will limit a player's bet spread to 1–2 or 1–3 units or will limit him to making only flat bets. Some players refer to these limitations as back offs as well. Meanwhile, a barring is a much more serious matter, and most players agree on its meaning. In this case, a casino bars a suspected card counter from its casino and threatens him with charges for trespassing if he does not comply. In other words, the player is forbidden to enter the premises.

up, for what seemed like a pretty long time. He finally broke eye contact when the phone in the pit rang. A little while later, as I was leaving the table, he approached me and said, "You kept up with the count pretty good there, buddy." He wanted me to know that he was on to me. That was a prime example of heat. I didn't play on his shift for the remainder of my trip. But the next time I played at that casino during his shift, he didn't even remember me.

When a pit boss suspects a player of counting, she'll usually make some comment to him about card counting to see what sort of reaction he has. His response can either confirm or negate her suspicions. If he gets flustered or grabs his chips and runs, she'll believe she's confirmed her suspicions. If a pit boss makes a comment to you, don't get flustered. Prepare yourself mentally in advance for such comments and simply declare ignorance without protesting so much that you give yourself away.

Even if you are sure the pit is on to you, keep your cool. If you get flustered, you will only confirm their suspicions.

Another step a pit boss might take when she suspects a player of counting is to count down the discards—especially after the player's made a big bet. She's trying to determine if the big bet coincided with a positive count. Don't let this tactic fluster you either. Once again, she's probably just looking for your reaction. However, if the countdown was preceded by a phone call to the pit or if the pit boss makes a call after counting down the discards, this may indicate that the casino is going to, or is taking, a close look at your play. At this point, you might want to make a graceful exit after a few more minutes of play. (Don't fold up your tent immediately after the countdown occurs; otherwise, you'll confirm the casino's suspicions.) Sometimes, you can diffuse the suspicions against you by making some heavy cover plays or bets, which are discussed later in this chapter.

Another form of heat can come from a casino executive who makes no secret of standing behind you to watch you play. If this goes on for a few minutes or more, chances are your play is being evaluated. Once again, don't get excited and don't be in an obvious rush to leave, but do pack it in.

Anytime you see a pit boss looking directly at you while she's on the phone, take heed. This might be a prelude to something more serious. Check out the pit boss's body language. Watch if she and the other bosses huddle up in the pit and speak in hushed tones. See what you can pick up from their behavior and expressions. (But don't get caught

The Eye in the Sky

The most dangerous kind of heat is the kind you can't detect. It comes from the "eye in the sky"— the casino's surveillance cameras. If a casino suspects you of being a card counter, it might keep a surveillance record of your play to be viewed at a later time to determine if you are a counter. Unfortunately, this tactic is nearly impossible to get around by using cover plays and bets.

staring!) Having a partner who doesn't play can be helpful in this regard. One fellow I know takes his wife along with him to the pits. Her job is to observe the pit and let him know if heat is coming his way.

Preferential shuffles can also be a form of heat. As you may recall, a preferential shuffle is when the dealer prematurely shuffles the deck to discourage counters. While I certainly don't recommend playing at a table with a dealer who consistently shuffles up on you, a premature shuffle might simply be a test. For example, I was at a low-roller casino in Las Vegas that's infamous for its preferential shuffle. I was playing with a top bet of $100 at their single-deck game, which was enough to get me barred from that sawdust joint. I'd been playing for a while and had made a number of big bets. The pit boss came by and whispered in the dealer's ear. Sure enough, on the very next big bet I made, the dealer shuffled up. But instead of leaving, I kept the big bet out and matched it with the same bet on another hand after the shuffle. The dealer rolled her eyes at the pit boss, and he smiled, shook his head, and walked away. My cover bet had fooled them. I had no trouble for the rest of the session. What made it even sweeter was that I'd won both of my off-the-top big bets.

As technology becomes more advanced, casinos are becoming more sophisticated in their fight against card counters. In addition to using outside security firms to detect card counters, casinos are now using high-tech hardware and software, such as facial-recognition software (FRS), to root out counters. This software measures certain unchangeable points of the human face from a photograph, such as the distance between the eyes, and matches the face up with those stored in its data bank. So, even if a counter uses a disguise, this software can potentially point him out to the casino. Other software can track a player's strategy and bet spread, and thereby determine if the player is counting cards.

Casinos generally share information with one another, especially those that are part of the same corporation. If a high-stakes counter is caught in one casino, there's a good chance the casino's neighbors will be informed that he's in town. This alert may include a faxed photo or a computer image of the player. Casinos have honed this practice into what they call SIN, or the *surveillance information network*. This network is normally reserved for high-stakes bettors, and not all casinos participate. In any event, it is unlikely that a player whose max bet is $200 or less is going to be noted in the network.

What Heat Isn't

A blackjack pit can be a busy place. Pit bosses are charged with keeping track of the players for comping purposes, watching over the dealers to see that they are following policy, tracking the chips that are brought into the pit and those that go out in the player's pockets, giving special attention to high rollers, watching the cards that are in play, and a myriad of other tasks. It is their job to pay special attention to the players and to keep them happy. The phone in the blackjack pit is always ringing. The pit bosses are always looking at the computers. They are always watching the players. They confer with one another constantly.

Card counters see this activity, and, through our paranoid lens, we tend to think that it is all directed toward us. In the vast majority of cases, it is not. It's normal for the pit boss to stop by to chat with you. When a pit boss checks your bet and writes it down, you are probably being rated, just like any other player who asks to be rated. When the phone rings, it could be nothing more than a host calling the pit to check out a player's level of play or the cashier's cage calling to confirm a large cash-out of chips or another pit boss suggesting that they check out the décolletage of the buxom player at table nine. It could be a call from surveillance asking about a variety of things. While it's possible that it is a call checking out a potential card counter, that is just one of many other things that could be occurring. The lower your level of play, the less likely it is that the call is about you. For another example of what heat isn't, see "Checks Play!" on page 206.

AVOIDING BARRINGS AND BACK OFFS

If you are a medium- to high-stakes bettor and you count cards, chances are you'll be backed off or barred at some point in your card-counting career. Don't worry too much about getting backed off or barred. It's part of the game. Some card counters worry themselves sick over this, and take costly measures to avoid getting barred. This is something you'll want to avoid.

Although it's illegal to bar a card counter in New Jersey, in Nevada, the courts have found that it is legal to bar a skilled player from a casino. Other states are likely to follow Nevada's lead. In general, the legal theory is that a casino is private property and its owners and their

Checks Play!

A phrase that card counters dread hearing is *checks play*. The dealer shouts these words to alert the pit crew that a player's betting level has reached a certain point. Sometimes, the call is made based on the actual amount of the bet, and sometimes it's made based on the number of chips placed in the betting square. For example, I've heard "checks play!" for a bet as small as $25 when it consisted of five $5 chips but not for a bet made with a $25 chip at the same table.

A variation of this call is *black action*. This call notifies the pit crew that a player is betting $100 or more. If it's the casino's policy, some dealers may even call out "green action!" for a $25 bet.

Counters don't like these calls because they alert the pit crew that they've made a jump in their bets, which indicates to someone in the know that the count has improved. Also, many counters actually mistake these calls for heat. But, in most cases, the dealer is just acknowledging that a significant bet has been made, with the significance varying from one casino to another and even from one table to another. Since it's the pit crew's responsibility to track a player's bets, don't worry too much if your dealer notifies them that you have changed your bet.

representatives have the right to keep undesirable persons off their property. While they cannot openly discriminate against people in a protected class, such as a minority group, they can discriminate against card counters or other advantage players by placing them in the status of an undesirable person. So, in the eyes of the casino, card counters are right up there with drunks, cheaters, thieves, and hookers.

There are two different worlds when it comes to back offs and barrings. A high-stakes player who is playing $100 or more as his minimum bet is going to be observed very closely in most casinos. If you bet big enough, long enough, and come out a winner, you can be sure they'll be watching you. In places that are designed for low rollers, a $25 bettor can get a lot of attention. Even a low-stakes bettor can get barred or backed off if he pushes it enough (see *"Persona Non Grata"* on page 208 for an example).

Although getting recognized as a card counter is inevitable if you're good enough, there are certain things you can do to lessen your risk. The following discussions should give you something to work with.

Play to a Time Limit

Even with all of the sophisticated software and surveillance techniques, a player has to be noticed before his play is closely examined. Getting in and getting out quickly can be one way to avoid this notice. So be sure to keep your sessions short—to about an hour or less. By the time the pit might be wondering if you're a counter, you will be well on your way. Chances are, they'll be too busy with something else to bother with a player who has already left the casino.

Don't make the mistake of exceeding your time limit to make up your losses in a losing session like I used to do. In an attempt to recoup my losses, I would sometimes turn a one-hour session into a four- or five-hour session. I was finally cured of this when I played at a new casino. My first couple of sessions there were relatively short, and I don't think I received much attention from my level of play with a top bet of $200. Then, I ran into a session where I had dropped about $1,600 very quickly, losing a succession of big bets and double-down hands. I wanted to get it back, so I stayed at that table for about five hours. Finally, I had recovered just about all of my loss, and I ended that session feeling quite good. The next day, I hadn't played fifteen minutes before I received a tap on the shoulder. The casino manager very politely told me that I could play any other game in the house, but not blackjack. He said my play was "too strong" for them. My level of play wouldn't normally have phased them. I spent too much time at that table the night before. I had gotten someone's attention and my guess is that they decided to review my play. After discovering that I was indeed counting cards, they noted it on my computer record and when they brought up my name the next time I sat down to play, they were ready to nail me. If I had stayed within my original game plan, I am sure I could have continued to play at that casino. I didn't. I forgot that blackjack is really just one long session. I should have stayed with my plan to play an hour or less and moved on to another casino. I would have recovered my loss in time, and it didn't have to happen in that single session at that particular casino.

Leave After a Good Run

It is a good idea to leave after a particularly good run in a short period of time, even if you haven't yet reached your time limit. This isn't to be confused with a win limit. If you have a good run during one shoe, winning big bet after big bet, it might spur the pit to pay close attention.

Persona Non Grata

Ted lives in Las Vegas and is a red-chip bettor at blackjack. He is a very effective card counter who plays a strong game. He had grown quite used to playing in most Las Vegas casinos and flying under the radar. A new casino opened up in nearby Henderson a few years ago, and it was offering a well-penetrated single-deck game with S17 and DAS rules. Ted made the drive to Henderson every day to play in this fantastic game. His top bet was about $40, and he wasn't concerned about heat.

The demeanor of the pit seemed to support his belief that heat wasn't a problem. The pit bosses greeted him warmly whenever he came in, and they gave him comps that were probably a little more than he deserved for his level of play. He was winning at a steady pace and doing quite well. This went on for a few months, but then the bottom fell out. One day, Ted went to the casino. Instead of a warm greeting, the casino manager met him at the pit and told him that his play was no longer welcome.

Ted was quite chagrined by the whole thing. There had been no warnings and no sign that he was about to get the hook. In his case, he had finally reached some limit with the casino with his accumulated winnings, and it had decided that he was *persona non grata*—personally unwelcome. Other $5 and $25 bettors continued

to play in this good game for as long as it lasted. Ted's downfall was the fact that he hit this casino day in and day out and eventually wore out his welcome.

I don't think Ted made any mistakes here. He took advantage of an extremely good game that was being offered at a casino in which he would not normally play. He hit this game for all it was worth and made a good bit of money in the process. At best, it was a temporary situation. As it turned out, the casino abandoned this game not too long after Ted was backed off, which was inevitable. Good games like this come around every so often, but most casinos don't keep them for long. Ted got in while the getting was good and exploited this game well. If he had been playing for higher stakes, he wouldn't have lasted as long as he did.

Another card counter might take a different approach, especially if it is a casino that he likes to visit and one that offers a consistently good game. If longevity is your goal, don't wear out the game. Camping out at a casino for days or weeks at a time the way Ted did will inevitably lead to a back off or barring. When visiting locales with several casinos, spread your play around. A good rule of thumb is to limit your individual sessions to an hour per casino, then revisit those casinos at different shifts and on different days.

Disguise Your Wins

Disguise your wins (and sometimes your losses) by pocketing your chips while you're playing at the table and by not coloring them up (exchanging low-denomination chips for higher ones) when you leave. Pit bosses prefer that players color up their chips before leaving the table so they can record the wins or losses of the players they're tracking. But you are under no obligation to color up, and you are more than welcome to put chips in your pocket or purse if you wish. You don't have to hide a lot of chips. Just hide away what your normal expectation might be for the period of time you will be at the table.

The best time to pocket chips is when the pit boss is looking in the other direction and when the dealer's attention is on something else—for example, when she's paying off a blackjack to another player, turning over the hands on double-down plays, taking a buy in from a player, redistributing the chips in the chip tray, or taking cards from the card shoe. When new decks are introduced, the dealer is often preoccupied with spreading them out, counting them, and so on. During this time, it's a wise idea to move your chips away from the dealer anyway. This is a good time to palm one or two chips and slip them into your pocket or purse.

Don't pocket high-denomination chips. The high-denomination chips are closely tracked by the pit, and if you try to hide them, it is likely that the pit will figure out that you are stashing chips. Stick to pocketing red or green chips. However, if green is the highest denomination chip in the tray, stick to pocketing red ones.

If you've had a good winning session and you will be cashing out a large amount of chips, don't cash the chips you stashed at the same time. The cashier's cage may call the pit to confirm the amount of chips that came out of it.

Don't Make Excuses

Avoid making excuses every time you increase your bet or make a count-induced departure from basic strategy. Over the years, the only people I have heard making excuses for their bets or their plays have been card counters. Before making a big bet, they will say something like, "I feel lucky, so I'm going to put it out there," or "I think I'll try to get my losses back with this one bet." If they are departing from basic strategy, they might say, "Hitting this sixteen has been costing me money all night. I think I'll stand for once." It sounds inane and it is. You simply stand out from the crowd when you do this, draw way too much attention to yourself and your unusual choice, and it impresses no one.

Call It Quits Before a CTR Is Necessary

If you are playing for large enough stakes, you may be in a situation where the casino will have to file a cash transaction report (CTR) with the IRS. A byproduct of the war on drugs, these reports are required when a player cashes out for $10,000 or more in a day. Such a report requires you to provide your name and social security number. When you get close to the $10,000 limit, you may want to call it a day at that casino. Pit bosses know that players don't like to fill out these reports and will sometimes warn you if you are getting close to the limit. By the way, never use a false social security number if you must file a CTR or for any other reason.

Disguise Yourself

Win enough money and regardless of the cover you use, you will eventually get barred or backed off. That doesn't mean you can't come back and play. Most full-time players have been barred at least once at most of the casinos in which they play. They keep coming back with new identities and are able to continue to play. Usually, they will stay away from the casino after a barring for a period of a few months and then return with their new persona.

A good disguise can keep the pit boss from calling surveillance to check you out if she'd otherwise recognize you from a past visit.

Getting a new identity can be as simple as giving yourself a different look by changing your hairstyle and your clothing fashions. It might involve more detailed things, such as wearing wigs and false (or newly grown) beards and mustaches. (I have heard of some counters who have even disguised themselves as members of the opposite sex to continue playing!) Although your disguise may not fool facial-recognition software, it isn't used on every person who sits down to play. A good disguise can keep the pit boss from calling surveillance to check you out if she'd otherwise recognize you from a past visit. Getting another identity can also involve using alternative IDs. However, with the heightened security that has arisen since the 9/11 tragedy, I suggest that you consult a lawyer before acquiring and using an alternative ID.

One problem with using an alternate identity is remembering who you are. One way casinos keep track of folks is by birth date. I once used an alternate identity that went by my wife's birth date so I would not go blank on the date if asked. One night, after sitting down at the table, the pit boss asked me for my birth date. Without thinking, I blurted out my real birthday instead of my wife's, then quickly corrected it. Fortunately, there were no repercussions; the pit boss just walked away, shaking his head over this moron who couldn't even remember his own birthday.

By the way, you don't have to wait to get barred to change your identify. If you have recorded a sizable win at a particular casino, change your identity next time you play there.

Play with a Smaller Bet Spread

The best kind of cover bet might be to play with a smaller bet spread than with the large spreads required for multiple-deck games. This can be done if you are using the Wonging or semi-Wonging style of play, where smaller bet spreads can be used effectively. (See Chapter 10.)

Opt for Multiple-Deck Games

In general terms, it seems that more attention is directed toward players in single- and double-deck games than in multiple-deck games. Casinos know that many counters prefer to play hand-held games, so they watch those games more closely, especially if a big bettor is at the table. It is easier to detect a counter in hand-held games, largely because the count will be fluctuating more than it does in shoe games. If a casino offers both hand-held games and shoe games, playing the shoe games can be a way to avoid quick detection.

Make Smart Cover Plays and Cover Bets

A cover play is a seemingly erroneous play on a particular hand that a player makes to mislead the pit boss or surveillance into thinking he is a poor player. A cover bet, of which there are several styles, serves the same purpose. These methods of deflecting heat can be costly to the player, however, so be sure to use them wisely.

First of all, don't waste your cover plays and cover bets on the dealer. While it isn't advisable to let the dealer know you are counting, don't use valuable cover plays or bets for her benefit alone. Most dealers probably don't care if you are a counter, and many wouldn't even know how to identify a counter. Save occasional cover plays and cover bets for when the pit boss is paying attention. If you are a player who prefers to play with constant cover, remember that you are doing it for the eye in the sky, not for the dealer.

If you deviate from basic strategy for cover purposes, do so when you have your minimum bet on the table and when the pit boss is watching. These relatively inexpensive deviations can be quite effective in deflecting heat for a little while. There are some basic strategy changes a card counter can make that may help to disguise the quality of his play, presuming the pit knows enough about basic strategy to tell the difference.

COVER PLAYS

A *cover play* is a seemingly erroneous play on a particular hand that a player makes to mislead the pit boss or surveillance into thinking he is a poor player. A *cover bet*, of which there are several styles, serves the same purpose. These methods of deflecting heat can be costly to the player, however, so be sure to use them wisely.

Table 11.1 sets forth a typical basic strategy with cover plays for card counters. Departures from basic strategy appear in red. By using these variations, a counter is avoiding making plays that are commonly recognized by casino personnel as a play that a card counter would make. For example, one of the most common deviations from basic strategy for a counter is to stand on a 16 against a dealer's 10 in positive counts. If a player is observed hitting his 16 in some situations and standing on it at other times, this can trigger closer observation of his play. By consistently making the "wrong" basic strategy play, the counter will hopefully come across to the pit crew as an unskilled player.

Although these cover plays are recommended for multiple-deck games, you can use them in single- and double-deck games. However, in those games, proper playing strategy is most important.

COVER BETS

The most common cover bet consists of two betting deviations: 1) double only after a winning hand, and 2) do not lower the bet after a winning hand, even if the count has taken a nosedive. A counter who uses this style of play will look like a gambler who presses his bets after a win. Another version of this cover bet is to increase the size of the bet only after a loss. Players who do this are known as *steamers*. This type of cover betting carries a cost. In fact, it can cut your win rate in half. By not adhering to a strict bet spread, you sometimes miss out on the opportunity to get a big payoff when the count is favorable, or you may have too much money out when the count is unfavorable. This doesn't mean you shouldn't use this style, especially if you are playing for high stakes, but you should know that it carries a steep cost.

A common cover bet in single-deck games is to make a two-unit bet when you join a game after the shuffle. If the count becomes negative or stays neutral, the bet is dropped to one unit, and if the count becomes positive, the bet is increased to four units. Pit bosses tend to notice the first bet a player makes and will mark it down as their "regular" bet for that session. So, she'll take note of the initial two-unit bet and then the subsequent four-unit bet. To her, it will look like a 1–2 bet spread. If she later sees you making a one-unit bet, she'll probably think you reduced your bet to prevent a large loss or to preserve a win. This strategy is a little more difficult to pull off in multiple-deck games in which larger bet spreads are used. A variation of this cover bet is to make your highest bet your very first bet of the session. Be sure the pit boss takes notice. Then, the next time you make that bet, it won't stand out as unusual. This kind of play has a minimal cost in most single-deck games, where the off-the-top house advantage is usually small or nonexistent.

Using odd-sized bets and not raising and lowering bets in an exact amount is another form of cover betting. For example, if you are in a double-deck game and you use a 1–8 bet spread, at $25 per unit, don't go into a rigid betting pattern and raise or lower your bet by $25 increments. If your first bet is $50, and the count becomes negative, lower your bet to $30 or $35, rather than down to $25. If the count goes up, increase your bet to $70 or $80, rather than back to $50. A betting style like this will make you look like an inexperienced gambler. Along the same lines, make it look like you are randomly grabbing a few chips to make a bet, maybe even capping your bet with a couple of $1 chips.

A simple form of cover betting that won't cost you anything is to keep your chip stack the same height each time you bet. For example, instead of using one green chip ($25), place your bet with five red chips ($5 × 5 = $25). When you increase your bet, use one green chip and four red chips ($25 + $5 × 4 = $45). The stack of chips has not grown, just its worth has. Be sure to cap the stack with one of the red chips. If the eye in the sky isn't paying close attention, your stacks will look the same at a cursory glance.

A No-Risk Cover Bet
Keep your chip stack the same height each time you bet. For example, instead of using one $25 chip, place your bet with five $5 chips. When you increase your bet, use one $25 chip and four $5 chips.

Table 11.1
Card Counter's Basic Strategy With Cover Plays for Four-, Six-, and Eight-Deck Games

When Player's Hand Is	When Dealer's Upcard Is									
	2	3	4	5	6	7	8	9	10	Ace
Hard Hand Totals										
8	H	H	H	H	D	H	H	H	H	H
9	D	D	D	D	D	H	H	H	H	H
10	D	D	D	D	D	D	D	D	H	H
11	D	D	D	D	D	D	D	D	D	D
12	H	S	S	S	S	H	H	H	H	H
13	S	S	S	S	S	H	H	H	H	H
14	S	S	S	S	S	H	H	H	H	H
15	S	S	S	S	S	H	H	H	H	H
16	S	S	S	S	S	H	H	H	S	H
17	S	S	S	S	S	S	S	S	S	S
Soft Hand Totals										
A-2	H	H	H	D	D	H	H	H	H	H
A-3	H	H	D	D	D	H	H	H	H	H
A-4	H	H	D	D	D	H	H	H	H	H
A-5	H	H	D	D	D	H	H	H	H	H
A-6	D	D	D	D	D	H	H	H	H	H
A-7	D	D	D	D	D	S	S	H	H	H
A-8	S	S	S	S	S	S	S	S	S	S
A-9	S	S	S	S	S	S	S	S	S	S
Pairs										
2-2	SP	SP	SP	SP	SP	SP	H	H	H	H
3-3	SP	SP	SP	SP	SP	SP	H	H	H	H
4-4	H	H	H	SP	SP	H	H	H	H	H
5-5	D	D	D	D	D	D	D	D	H	H
6-6	SP	SP	SP	SP	SP	H	H	H	H	H
7-7	SP	SP	SP	SP	SP	SP	H	H	H	H
8-8	SP	SP	SP	SP	SP	SP	SP	SP	SP	SP
9-9	SP	SP	SP	SP	SP	S	SP	SP	S	S
10-10	S	S	S	S	S	S	S	S	S	S
A-A	SP	SP	SP	SP	SP	SP	SP	SP	SP	SP

H – Hit.   **S** – Stand.   **D/H** – Double down if permitted; otherwise, hit.   **SP** – Split.
D/S – Double down if permitted; otherwise, stand.   **SP/H** – Split if DAS; otherwise, hit.

CONCLUSION

Avoiding heat, back offs, and barring is more of an art than a science. The advice in this chapter can help you along, but you'll need to adapt it to the circumstances that present themselves. This is an area where you must learn as you go. What works in one place may not work in another. There are some casinos where any sort of cover isn't going to make a lot of difference, and there are others where you will find that no cover at all is needed. In the end, it is difficult to avoid back offs and barrings altogether. Your level of betting and frequency of play are the biggest factors, and the simple fact is that the more you play, especially at higher stakes, the more likely it is that you will be found out by the casinos. Don't let it stop you from playing. Use this advice and your own imagination to combat the casinos. A player who doesn't play because he is afraid of being barred has effectively barred himself. The most successful players are the ones who get barred and figure out a way to come back for more.

CONCLUSION

If you have absorbed the lessons in this book, you might be ready to go into a casino and start increasing your bankroll. You should know by now that it won't be easy. Blackjack has more ups and downs than the Rocky Mountains and more twists and turns than the Mississippi River. If you are a new player, you'll probably find your sessions difficult, and there will probably be times when you think that you can't go on. But persistence and the willingness to learn will pay off if you stick to it. This book follows a certain order, and I suggest you follow the same order in learning all you can:

1. Learn basic strategy. Know it cold before you ever step into a casino.

2. Figure out the size of your betting unit based on the size of your bankroll.

3. Find out what type of comping system is in use at the casinos you'll be visiting, and use promotions to add to your expected value.

4. Plan your trips based on tolerable betting levels, on wise game selection, and on the comps you want to earn.

5. Don't play over your head. Stick to your game plan.

6. Take your play to the next level by learning how to count cards, if you think it's for you.

You certainly don't have to become a card counter if you're not interested. There's absolutely nothing wrong with being a strong basic strategy player who gets the most out of the casinos by taking advantage of comps, other freebies, and promotions. If you pay attention to the advice in this book, you can do this and virtually break even. That's far more than the vast majority of players who visit casinos are able to accomplish.

If you do want to learn how to count cards, this book is a great place to start. But card counting is serious business. The point is to beat the casinos. The serious-minded businessman is always honing his skills, learning more about his profession, and keeping up with advances in his field. You, too, should read, learn, and practice all you can and put your skills to the test.

No matter what kind of player you wish to become, this book should provide you with a good starting place and a basic grounding in everything you need to know to get started. Now get out there and give them a run for their money!

GLOSSARY

Advantage play. Any strategy that increases a player's advantage over the casino.

Backcounting. *See* Wonging.

Balanced count. A card-counting system in which all of the cards assigned positive values and all of the cards assigned negative values add up to zero.

Bankroll. *See* Total bankroll; Trip bankroll.

Basic strategy. A method of play in which a player is required to make the mathematically correct play based on the cards in his hand and the dealer's upcard.

Bet sizing. Varying the size of a bet according to the advantage.

Bet spread. The range in which players make their bets.

Betting correlation. A term used to describe the accuracy of a card-counting system in predicting when it is time to raise or lower a bet based on the count and the composition of the cards remaining in play.

Betting ramp. A term used to describe the steepness of a bet spread.

Betting unit. A term used to represent the player's smallest bet on a single hand.

Blackjack. An Ace and any 10-valued card. Also called a *natural*.

Bust. To hit to a card total over 21.

Buy in. The purchase of chips from the dealer at the game table.

Card counting. A form of advantage play in which a player keeps track of the cards by using a system that assigns a positive, negative, or neutral value to each card.

Checks. Casino slang for *casino chips*.

Comps. Rewards that casinos give their patrons for time spent playing in their casino.

Couponomy. A term coined by Anthony Curtis that is used to describe the use of casino coupons that offer special deals to players.

Cut card. A plastic card the dealer inserts into the stack of cards to indicate when it is time to shuffle. Also called a *shuffle card*.

Double down. In blackjack, an option that allows a player to increase his bet on a favorable hand by placing additional chips in the betting square. He receives only one hit card from the dealer to complete his hand.

Drop box. A box attached to the table on the dealer's right in which cash is placed when players buy in.

Early surrender. An option that allows a player to surrender his hand and forfeit half of his bet before the dealer checks her hand for blackjack when her upcard is an Ace. *See also* Late surrender.

European No-Hole Card (ENHC). A version of blackjack in which the dealer does not take a hole card until all the players complete the plays on their hands. If the dealer has blackjack, she takes all bets on doubles and splits.

Even money. A payoff on a winning hand equal to the player's original bet.

Exit strategy. *See* Semi-Wonging.

Expected value. The percentage of the total amount bet that a player can expect to win or lose over the long run for a particular set of game conditions.

Fab Four. The top-four surrender plays based on the Hi-Lo System.

Flat betting. Sticking to one bet size without raising or lowering the amount.

Funbook. A book of coupons and advertisements usually offered by a casino's players club.

Hand-held game. A game in which the dealer holds the deck or pack in her hand and pitches the cards to each player as she deals.

Hard hand. A hand in which an Ace is counted as a 1.

Heat. A form of pressure casinos put on card counters to intimidate them.

Hit. In blackjack, a play in which the player chooses to receive another card.

Hole card. In blackjack, the dealer's face-down card. *See also* Upcard.

Hole-carding. A form of advantage play in which the player takes advantage of the information provided when a dealer accidentally flashes her hole card.

House advantage. A casino's advantage over a player on any given bet.

House edge. *See* House advantage.

Illustrious 18. Eighteen of the most important basic strategy variations for card counters.

Insurance. The opportunity to make a side bet that the dealer has a blackjack if her upcard is an Ace.

Late surrender. An option that allows a player to withdraw from the hand and forfeit only half of his bet after the first two cards have been dealt. If the dealer has blackjack, however, the player does not have this option. *See also* Early surrender.

Level-one count. Any card-counting system in which cards are given a single negative and a single positive value or a value of zero.

Money management. A gambling term used to describe how to handle a bankroll.

Money plays. Making bets with cash money instead of chips.

Natural. *See* Blackjack.

No midshoe entry. A casino or table rule in which a player is prohibited from entering a game before the next shuffle.

Odds. An expression of the likelihood that a certain event will occur out of all the possibilities that exist compared to the likelihood of that same event not occurring.

Off the top. A term describing the first hand dealt in the first round of play after the shuffle.

Others. In Thorp's Ten-Count System, non-10-valued cards.

Payoff. The amount of money a player collects on a winning bet or the rate at which he is paid.

Payout. *See* Payoff.

Penetration. How far into the deck, pack, or card shoe the dealer goes before shuffling.

Per-hand expectation. The percentage of the total money bet that a player can expect to win or lose in the long run on each hand.

Pit boss. A table games supervisor.

Pitch game. *See* Hand-held game.

Players club. Casino clubs that serve to entice players by offering rewards and promotions.

Playing efficiency. The accuracy of a card-counting system in providing information about the correct playing decision given the composition of the deck as predicted by the system.

Preferential shuffle. A situation in which a dealer prematurely shuffles before dealing the next round when it is suspected that the advantage has shifted from the house to the players.

Probability. The likelihood that a certain event will occur.

Progression betting. Any system of betting where the bet size is determined by whether or not the last hand or series of hands was won or lost.

Push. A tie; when both the player and the dealer have the same card total, no money changes hands.

Risk of ruin. The percent chance a player will take of losing his entire bankroll.

Rule of six. A common penetration in single-deck games in which the number of players plus the number of rounds always adds up to six.

Running count. A total of the cards seen as they are played using pre-assigned values.

Semi-Wonging. A blackjack strategy in which a card counter exits a game when the count becomes unfavorable. Also called *exit strategy*.

Sequencing. A system of play in which a player follows a certain card (usually Aces) to the next shuffle based on the cards that immediately preceded or succeeded that card in the last shoe.

Shoe. A rectangular box that holds multiple decks of cards.

Shuffle card. *See* Cut card.

Single-parameter count. A card-counting system that does not require a player to keep any side counts of cards not given a value in the basic counting system.

Slot club. *See* Players club.

Soft hand. A hand in which an Ace is counted as an 11.

Splitting pairs. A common rule allowing a player to split a pair in his original two-card hand into two separate hands.

Stand. A play in which the player chooses not to take any more hit cards from the dealer.

Standard deviation. The square root of the variance in a game, used to describe the distribution of possible outcomes around the statistical expectation.

Stiff hand. A hand that has a value of 12 through 16.

Third baseman. The player seated closest to the dealer's right at a blackjack table.

Toke. Casino slang for *tip*.

Toking. Casino slang for *tipping*.

Total bankroll. The total amount of money a player is willing to risk gambling.

Trip bankroll. The total amount of money a player brings to a casino for a single trip.

True count. The running count divided by the fraction or number of decks left in play.

Unbalanced count. Any counting system in which the assigned values of the cards do not add up to zero.

Unit. *See* Betting unit.

Upcard. The dealer's face-up card. *See also* Hole card.

Variance. A figure determined by subtracting the expected value from each possible outcome in a game or hand, squaring the differences, and multiplying each square by its probability of occurring and then summing the total of the product.

Wonging. A strategy in which a card counter enters a game only on favorable counts.

OTHER BOOKS AND RESOURCES

There is a world of valuable information about blackjack and card counting in books, magazines, and on the Internet. Unfortunately, there is also a world of misinformation. Included here is a list of the best books and periodicals on the subject as well as reliable websites. They are listed in order of usefulness.

BOOKS

Professional Blackjack by Stanford Wong (Pi Yee Press, 1994)

If you are a Hi-Lo player, this book is a must. It contains the indices for most game conditions and has a wealth of blackjack statistics that can be used to learn about and evaluate the game. It also includes instructions for Wong's Halves System, reputed as being one of the best multilevel counts.

Blackjack Attack: Playing the Pros' Way, Third Edition, by Don Schlesinger (RGE Publishing, Ltd., 2004)

This book is an important weapon in a card counter's arsenal. If you are serious about counting cards, you should have this book on your shelf, but only after reading it a dozen or so times.

The Theory of Blackjack: The Complete Card Counter's Guide to The Casino Game of 21, Sixth Edition, by Peter A. Griffin (Huntington Press, 1999)

If you want to understand the theory of the game, this book is the key. If there is something worthwhile to be known about the theory of the game, chances are that Griffin says it here.

Knock-Out Blackjack: The Easiest Card-Counting System Ever Devised **by Olaf Vancura, PhD, and Ken Fuchs (Huntington Press, 1998)**

This book sets forth the Knock-Out System, a simple but powerful counting system that does not require keeping a true count.

Blackbelt in Blackjack: Playing 21 as a Martial Art **(Revised & Updated) by Arnold Snyder (Cardoza, 2005)**

This book explains the Red Seven Counting System, a good level-one unbalanced system, and the Zen System, which is more complex but very effective.

Beyond Counting **by James Grosjean (RGE Publishing, Ltd., 2000)**

This book explores a variety of methods for gaining an advantage in the casinos in blackjack as well as in other casino games.

Blackjack for Blood: The Card-Counters' Bible and Complete Winning Guide, **Reprint Edition, by Bryce Carlson (Pi Yee Press, 2000)**

This book is a must-read for any serious blackjack student. It contains instructions for the Advanced Omega System, one of the most powerful counting systems available. It's also full of good playing advice for any type of player.

Beat the Dealer: A Winning Strategy for the Game of Twenty-One, **Revised Edition, by Edward O. Thorp (Vintage, 1966)**

This book is the all-time best-selling blackjack book ever. It's what got the whole blackjack craze started. Although it's from the early sixties and the material centers mostly on the single-deck game of blackjack, it's a fascinating read for any card counter.

Playing Blackjack as a Business: A Professional Player's Approach to the Game of 21 **by Lawrence Revere (Replica Books, 1999)**

Although some of the advice in this book is dated, it will still make a useful addition to your blackjack library. Revere's color-coded basic strategy charts are classics.

The World's Greatest Blackjack Book, **Reprint Edition, by Lance Humble, PhD, and Carl Cooper, PhD (Main Street Books, 1987)**

This book explains the Hi-Opt I System. Although the betting advice is dated and Humble's take on cheating dealers is debatable, it is a fine work on the subject of blackjack.

Million Dollar Blackjack **by Ken Uston (Carol Publishing, 1982)**

Ken Uston is a legend in blackjack circles. Revered by many and despised by some, his stories of team play in the early Atlantic City days and in Europe make this book a classic.

Blackjack Secrets **by Stanford Wong (Pi Yee Press, 1993)**

This book is a compilation of several articles and excerpts from other books by Stanford Wong. It gets into the more esoteric aspects of the game and can add to a player's set of useful tools. It includes a full strategy for double-exposure blackjack.

Basic Blackjack **by Stanford Wong (Pi Yee Press, 1992)**

This book contains a complete listing of basic strategies for most of the different sets of rules available today. It makes a good traveling companion when venturing into casino locales.

Casino Tournament Strategy **by Stanford Wong (Pi Yee Press, 1998)**

If you are interested in tournament play, this book is a must-read. It's the most informative book on how to win in table-games tournaments.

Best Blackjack **by Frank Scoblete (Bonus Books, 1996)**

Scoblete is one of the most entertaining gambling authors who ever put pen to paper, or in today's world, kilobytes on the screen. A basic treatment of card counting, this is a good book for beginners.

Get the Edge at Blackjack **by John May (Bonus Books, 2000)**

May explores the game and different approaches to winning. The book has created some controversy in the blackjack world, but the author sticks to his guns.

The Frugal Gambler **by Jean Scott (Huntington Press, 1998)**

This book provides valuable information on how to play the comp game with the casinos, especially for low-stakes players.

Comp City: A Guide to Free Casino Vacations, **Second Edition, by Max Rubin (Huntington Press, 2001)**

This is a good companion to *The Frugal Gambler*. Rubin gets into the more sophisticated methods of squeezing comps out of the casinos. He has a take-no-prisoners approach to comps and will entertain you along the way.

Blackjack and the Law **by I. Nelson Rose and Robert A. Loeb (RGE Publishing, Ltd., 1998)**

This book gives blackjack players the lowdown on where they stand with the law. A good source for card counters who may encounter problems with the casinos.

Burning the Tables in Las Vegas: Keys to Success in Blackjack and in Life, **Second Edition, by Ian Andersen (Huntington Press, 2003)**

This book is full of cover advice for card counters, particularly for high-stakes players.

You've Got Heat: The Vegas Card Counting Adventures of LV Pro **by Barfarkel (Research Services Unlimited, 2004)**

This book relates what it's like to be a low-stakes card counter trying to build a high-stakes bankroll in Las Vegas.

MAGAZINES

Casino Player

This magazine offers its subscribers a good package of coupons from casinos all around the country.

Current Blackjack News

This magazine has the best listing of rules for American casinos.

Las Vegas Advisor

This magazine has the best coupon package for Las Vegas casinos that I've come across. It usually includes good meal offers, special promotion plays, and free rooms.

SOFTWARE

Casino Vérité Blackjack (CVBJ) by QFIT

This is the best practice software for blackjack. It's an invaluable tool for beginners and experienced players alike.

CVSIM by QFIT

This is an excellent game-simulation tool for blackjack.

CVCX by QFIT

This program takes the simulations in *Blackjack Attack* a big step further. You can get results for just about any game, set of rules, playing strategy, and betting strategy.

CVData by QFIT

This program can be used to break down and analyze a strategy. It provides countless charts and sets of data.

Statistical Blackjack Analyzer by RGE Publishing, Ltd.

The simulations in *Blackjack Attack* were run using this simulation generator. It is used by many experts in the field and forms the basis for the simulations in Blackjack Risk Manager.

Blackjack Risk Manager 2002 (BJRM 2002) by RGE Publishing, Ltd.

This program is user friendly and can get you the information you want in seconds. It has a variety of interesting features, including a quick solution for lifetime risk and an analyzer that can tell you the bankroll needed for a trip of any duration.

WEBSITES

Stanford Wong's BJ21.Com

Website: www.bj21.com

Owned and operated by Stanford Wong, this is the most visited blackjack site on the Internet. It is full of valuable information and has a batch of lively and energetic posters who are knowledgeable about the game.

Blackjack Review Network

Website: www.BJRnet.com

Owned and operated by Michael Dalton, this site has a variety of pages, including Dalton's Encyclopedia of Casino 21. This site is a labor of love for Michael, and it shows.

Viktor Nacht's Advan+agePlayer.Com

Website: www.advantageplayer.com

Presented by RGE Publishing, Ltd., this site is the abode of Don Schlesinger's *Don's Domain*, where Schlesinger answers inquiries from players.

BlackjackInfo.Com

Website: www.blackjackinfo.com

Created by Ken Smith, this is a great site for finding the perfect basic strategy for the specific game you want to play.

BJMath.com

Website: www.bjmath.com

This site is owned and operated by Richard Reid. If there's anything about the math and theory of blackjack that you want to know, you are likely to find it here.

Casino Vérité Blackjack by QFIT

Website: www.qfit.com

Owned and operated by Norm Wattenberger, this site offers test versions of software by QFIT.

The Wizard of Odds

Website: www.wizardofodds.com

The Wizard, Mike Shackleford, provides an analyses of most casino games and good advice on how to play them.

REFERENCES & CREDITS

Griffin, Peter A. *The Theory of Blackjack: The Complete Card Counter's Guide to The Casino Game of 21,* Sixth Edition. Las Vegas, NV: Huntington Press, 1999.

Schlesinger, Don. *Blackjack Attack: Playing the Pros' Way,* Third Edition. Las Vegas, NV: RGE Publishing, Ltd., 2004.

Wong, Stanford. *Professional Blackjack.* Las Vegas, NV: Pi Yee Press, 1994.

Wong, Stanford. *Current Blackjack News,* February 2005, page 26.

Table 1.3 on page 25 was adapted from *The Theory of Blackjack,* Sixth Edition, by Peter A. Griffin, Huntington Press, 1999.

Table 1.4 on page 25 was adapted from *The Theory of Blackjack,* Sixth Edition, by Peter A. Griffin, Huntington Press, 1999.

Table 7.1 on page 119 was adapted from *Blackjack Attack* by Don Schlesinger, RGE Publishing, Ltd., 2004.

INDEX

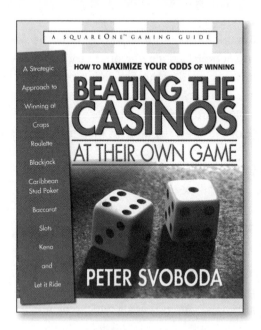

BEATING THE CASINOS AT THEIR OWN GAME

A Strategic Approach to Winning at Craps, Roulette, Black Jack, Caribbean Stud Poker, Baccarat, Slots, Keno & Let It Ride

Peter Svoboda

Beating the Casinos at Their Own Game is an easy-to-follow guide to winning at casino games. For each game, from roulette to craps and more, gambling expert Peter Svoboda first clearly explains the rules of play so that the novice gambler as well as the veteran can enter a casino with confidence. He then details the "smart" way to approach that game, including unique strategies that will increase your chance of winning. The author demonstrates which games offer the best odds, and even shows you how to manage your gambling allowance—an important key to gambling success.

With the ever-increasing popularity of Las Vegas, Atlantic City, and casinos on cruise ships and more, it's clear that the gambling industry is taking the country by storm. Now Peter Svoboda tells you not only how to get in on the action, but also how to cash in on the profits and walk away a winner.

ABOUT THE AUTHOR

Peter Svoboda is a licensed professional engineer with degrees in Mechanical and Civil Engineering from the New Jersey Institute of Technology. A veteran gambler with over twenty-five years of experience in casinos all over North America, Peter has studied the odds and probabilities of the various games to develop proven strategies of play.

$19.95 US / $29.95 • 288 pages • 7.5 x 9-inch quality paperback • ISBN 0-7570-0005-3

WINNING STRATEGIES & RULES FOR VIDEO POKER

the VIDEO POKER EDGE

How to Play Smart & Bet Right

Linda BOYD

Includes VIDEO POKER Strategy Cards

THE VIDEO POKER EDGE

How to Play Smart and Bet Right

Linda Boyd

Video poker is one of the hottest games to hit the casino floor! Flashing screens entice players to try their luck at drawing winning card combinations. Although most people believe winning is merely a matter of hit or miss, there is actually more to mastering these machines than the luck of the draw. Until now, little information has been available for those looking to maximize their winnings. Author Linda Boyd has written *The Video Poker Edge*—a detailed, user-friendly guide to help both the novice and the experienced player gain the winning edge over video poker machines.

The Video Poker Edge begins by explaining the basics of video poker. It then presents sound mathematical strategies tailored to each game's specific probability. In addition to sharing groundbreaking information on the latest technological devices—including controversial video lottery terminals—Boyd reveals which casinos have machines with the best payback percentages. Throughout the book, full-color illustrations clarify the recommended tactics for various card hands. As an added bonus, the author has included handy strategy cards with valuable tips. These cards can be removed from the book and taken along to the casino for reference during play.

So if you want the inside info on which video poker games provide the most bang for your buck . . . if you are interested in obtaining the latest strategic insight to minimize your risk and maximize your winnings, *The Video Poker Edge* is for you. It will revolutionize your video poker experience.

ABOUT THE AUTHOR

Linda Boyd spent many years as a mathematics educator—a career that proved valuable in helping her design the statistical tactics included in this book, and present them in a way that is easy to understand even for the "mathematically challenged." After years of playing blackjack and live poker, Ms. Boyd turned to the more profitable game of video poker.

$17.95 US / $26.95 CAN • 198 pages • 6 x 9-inch paperback • ISBN 0-7570-0252-8

BOOTLEGGER'S QUICK REFERENCE GUIDE TO BASIC STRATEGY PLAYS FOR BLACKJACK

This quick reference guide shows the proper basic strategy plays for 4-, 6-, and 8-deck blackjack games in which the dealer stands on hard and soft 17s. In a pinch, this strategy can be used for any set of game conditions.

A **soft hand** is any hand with an Ace that can be counted as 11 without going over 21. A **hard hand** is any hand that either does not contain an Ace or contains an Ace that can only take the value of 1.

DOUBLE/HIT: Double down if permitted; otherwise, hit.
DOUBLE/STAND: Double down if permitted; otherwise, stand.
SPLIT/HIT: Split if doubling after splits (DAS) is permitted; otherwise, hit.

PAIRS HANDS

Player's Hand	Dealer's Upcard									
	2	3	4	5	6	7	8	9	10	Ace
2-2	SPLIT/HIT	SPLIT/HIT	SPLIT	SPLIT	SPLIT	SPLIT	HIT	HIT	HIT	HIT
3-3	SPLIT/HIT	SPLIT/HIT	SPLIT	SPLIT	SPLIT	SPLIT	HIT	HIT	HIT	HIT
4-4	HIT	HIT	HIT	SPLIT/HIT	SPLIT/HIT	HIT	HIT	HIT	HIT	HIT
5-5	DOUBLE DOWN	DOUBLE DOWN	DOUBLE DOWN	DOUBLE DOWN	DOUBLE DOWN	DOUBLE DOWN	DOUBLE DOWN	DOUBLE DOWN	HIT	HIT
6-6	SPLIT/HIT	SPLIT	SPLIT	SPLIT	SPLIT	HIT	HIT	HIT	HIT	HIT
7-7	SPLIT	SPLIT	SPLIT	SPLIT	SPLIT	SPLIT	HIT	HIT	HIT	HIT
8-8	SPLIT	SPLIT	SPLIT	SPLIT	SPLIT	SPLIT	SPLIT	SPLIT	SPLIT	SPLIT
9-9	SPLIT	SPLIT	SPLIT	SPLIT	SPLIT	STAND	SPLIT	SPLIT	STAND	STAND
10-10	STAND	STAND	STAND	STAND	STAND	STAND	STAND	STAND	STAND	STAND
A-A	SPLIT	SPLIT	SPLIT	SPLIT	SPLIT	SPLIT	SPLIT	SPLIT	SPLIT	SPLIT

BOOTLEGGER'S QUICK REFERENCE GUIDE TO BASIC STRATEGY PLAYS FOR BLACKJACK

This quick reference guide shows the proper basic strategy plays for 4-, 6-, and 8-deck blackjack games in which the dealer stands on hard and soft 17s. In a pinch, this strategy can be used for any set of game conditions.

A **soft hand** is any hand with an Ace that can be counted as 11 without going over 21. A **hard hand** is any hand that either does not contain an Ace or contains an Ace that can only take the value of 1.

DOUBLE/HIT: Double down if permitted; otherwise, hit.
DOUBLE/STAND: Double down if permitted; otherwise, stand.
SPLIT/HIT: Split if doubling after splits (DAS) is permitted; otherwise, hit.

PAIRS HANDS

Player's Hand	Dealer's Upcard									
	2	3	4	5	6	7	8	9	10	Ace
2-2	SPLIT/HIT	SPLIT/HIT	SPLIT	SPLIT	SPLIT	SPLIT	HIT	HIT	HIT	HIT
3-3	SPLIT/HIT	SPLIT/HIT	SPLIT	SPLIT	SPLIT	SPLIT	HIT	HIT	HIT	HIT
4-4	HIT	HIT	HIT	SPLIT/HIT	SPLIT/HIT	HIT	HIT	HIT	HIT	HIT
5-5	DOUBLE DOWN	DOUBLE DOWN	DOUBLE DOWN	DOUBLE DOWN	DOUBLE DOWN	DOUBLE DOWN	DOUBLE DOWN	DOUBLE DOWN	HIT	HIT
6-6	SPLIT/HIT	SPLIT	SPLIT	SPLIT	SPLIT	HIT	HIT	HIT	HIT	HIT
7-7	SPLIT	SPLIT	SPLIT	SPLIT	SPLIT	SPLIT	HIT	HIT	HIT	HIT
8-8	SPLIT	SPLIT	SPLIT	SPLIT	SPLIT	SPLIT	SPLIT	SPLIT	SPLIT	SPLIT
9-9	SPLIT	SPLIT	SPLIT	SPLIT	SPLIT	STAND	SPLIT	SPLIT	STAND	STAND
10-10	STAND	STAND	STAND	STAND	STAND	STAND	STAND	STAND	STAND	STAND
A-A	SPLIT	SPLIT	SPLIT	SPLIT	SPLIT	SPLIT	SPLIT	SPLIT	SPLIT	SPLIT

HARD HAND TOTALS

Player's Hand	DEALER'S UPCARD									
	2	3	4	5	6	7	8	9	10	Ace
8	HIT	HIT	HIT	HIT	HIT	HIT	HIT	HIT	HIT	HIT
9	HIT	DOUBLE DOWN	DOUBLE DOWN	DOUBLE DOWN	DOUBLE DOWN	HIT	HIT	HIT	HIT	HIT
10	DOUBLE DOWN	DOUBLE DOWN	DOUBLE DOWN	DOUBLE DOWN	DOUBLE DOWN	DOUBLE DOWN	DOUBLE DOWN	DOUBLE DOWN	HIT	HIT
11	DOUBLE DOWN	DOUBLE DOWN	DOUBLE DOWN	DOUBLE DOWN	DOUBLE DOWN	DOUBLE DOWN	DOUBLE DOWN	DOUBLE DOWN	DOUBLE DOWN	DOUBLE DOWN
12	HIT	HIT	STAND	STAND	STAND	HIT	HIT	HIT	HIT	HIT
13	STAND	STAND	STAND	STAND	STAND	HIT	HIT	HIT	HIT	HIT
14	STAND	STAND	STAND	STAND	STAND	HIT	HIT	HIT	HIT	HIT
15	STAND	STAND	STAND	STAND	STAND	HIT	HIT	HIT	HIT	HIT
16	STAND	STAND	STAND	STAND	STAND	HIT	HIT	HIT	HIT	HIT
17	STAND	STAND	STAND	STAND	STAND	STAND	STAND	STAND	STAND	STAND

SOFT HAND TOTALS

Player's Hand	DEALER'S UPCARD									
	2	3	4	5	6	7	8	9	10	Ace
A-2	HIT	HIT	HIT	DOUBLE/HIT	DOUBLE/HIT	HIT	HIT	HIT	HIT	HIT
A-3	HIT	HIT	HIT	DOUBLE/HIT	DOUBLE/HIT	HIT	HIT	HIT	HIT	HIT
A-4	HIT	HIT	DOUBLE/HIT	DOUBLE/HIT	DOUBLE/HIT	HIT	HIT	HIT	HIT	HIT
A-5	HIT	HIT	DOUBLE/HIT	DOUBLE/HIT	DOUBLE/HIT	HIT	HIT	HIT	HIT	HIT
A-6	HIT	DOUBLE/HIT	DOUBLE/HIT	DOUBLE/HIT	DOUBLE/HIT	HIT	HIT	HIT	HIT	HIT
A-7	DOUBLE/STAND	DOUBLE/STAND	DOUBLE/STAND	DOUBLE/STAND	DOUBLE/STAND	STAND	STAND	HIT	HIT	HIT
A-8	STAND	STAND	STAND	STAND	DOUBLE/STAND	STAND	STAND	STAND	STAND	STAND
A-9	STAND	STAND	STAND	STAND	STAND	STAND	STAND	STAND	STAND	STAND

DOUBLE/HIT: Double down if permitted; otherwise, hit.

DOUBLE/STAND: Double down if permitted; otherwise, stand.

SPLIT/HIT: Split if doubling after splits (DAS) is permitted; otherwise, hit.